THE MORAL PURPOSE O

PRINCETON STUDIES IN

INTERNATIONAL HISTORY AND POLITICS

Series Editors
Jack L. Snyder and
Richard H. Ullman

———————————————

THE MORAL PURPOSE OF THE STATE

CULTURE, SOCIAL IDENTITY, AND INSTITUTIONAL RATIONALITY IN INTERNATIONAL RELATIONS

Christian Reus-Smit

PRINCETON UNIVERSITY PRESS   PRINCETON, NEW JERSEY

Library of Congress Cataloging-in-Publication Data
Reus-Smit, Christian, 1961-
The moral purpose of the state: culture, social identity, and institutional
rationality in international relations / Christian Reus-Smit
p. cm. — (Princeton studies in international history and politics)
Includes bibliographical references and index.
ISBN 0-691-02735-8 (cl : alk. paper)
1. International relations—Moral and ethical aspects.
2. International relations and culture. I. Title. II. Series.
JZ1306.R48   1999
327.1'01—dc21   98-33162 CIP

This book has been composed in Sabon

The paper used in this publication meets the minimum requirements
of ANSI/NISO Z39.48-1992 (R1997) (*Permanence of Paper*)

http://pup.princeton.edu

3   5   7   9   10   8   6   4   2
Printed in the United States of America

ISBN 13: 978-0-691-14435-1

_____ This book is dedicated to my teachers _____

JOSEPH CAMILLERI

ROBIN JEFFREY

PETER KATZENSTEIN

HENRY SHUE

Contents

Table and Figures

TABLE

FIGURES

Preface

READING a good book inspires awe, even deference. One gets a sense of intellectual mastery, a sense that the work was forged in a single act of creation, a sense that the ideas flowed with ease. Writing a book strips away this aura. One learns that intellectual frustration lies behind each chapter, that books grow out of years of trial and error, that most ideas dry up instead of flow. Behind the story on the page lies another story, and it is invariably one of labored intellectual growth, not divine inspiration.

This book has had a long gestation. It was sparked by an interest in the development of critical international theory, a theory that treats the prevailing international order as historically contingent, a theory that explores the origins of the present system of sovereign states and asks how it might change in the future. This was paralleled by an interest in Hedley Bull's idea that sovereign states can not only form international systems but also international societies. It made sense to me that modern states share certain elementary interests and values and have constructed rules and institutions to express and further those goals.

Over time these two interests converged around a desire to understand the origins, development, and transformation of the modern society of states. I had become increasingly frustrated with Bull's account of modern international society. His description of the basic institutional framework that facilitates coexistence between states is instructive, but he fails to explain why this particular framework emerged. Why isn't modern international society organized differently? Other members of the "English School"—particularly Martin Wight, Adda Bozeman, and Adam Watson—provide clues, but nothing in the way of systematic explanation.

When first conceived, this was to be a study of modern international society alone. Two things changed that. The first was Peter Katzenstein's exhortation to "study it comparatively," a recommendation that both excited and terrified me. Studying small states in world markets is one thing; studying big systems in world history is another. The second was a rereading of Bozeman's classic work, *Politics and Culture in International History*. Her tour de force taught me that different systems of states have developed different institutional practices—ancient Greek, Renaissance Italian, absolutist European, and modern sovereign states have chosen very different institutional solutions to solve their cooperation problems and achieve coexistence. This not only gave me a reason to "study it comparatively," it gave me a mystery to unravel. Why have four systems of sovereign states—all subject to the insecurities and uncertainties of anarchy—evolved markedly different fundamental institutions?

It has taken five years of research and writing to complete this book. Fortunately, I have not traveled this road alone. The journey has taught me much, and I am especially grateful for the support and intellectual guidance provided by Peter Katzenstein and Henry Shue. My project was to study the ethical foundations of international institutions, or put differently, the institutionalization of ethics. Nowhere could I have found a better pair to guide me. Both have the rare ability to nurture new ideas while offering challenging intellectual supervision, and I have been greatly influenced by the examples and standards they set. Amy Gurowitz and Richard Price have also been there for the journey, providing friendship and intellectual comradery. They have taught me the value of challenging, hard-fought debate, the type of debate where mutual respect and rapport give you the confidence to chance even the boldest and most tenuous of ideas.

I have also benefited greatly from insightful comments provided by Robyn Eckersley, James Goldgeier, Richard Falk, Paul James, Michael Janover, Audie Klotz, Marc Lynch, Albert Paolini, Margaret Nash, Judith Reppy, Gillian Robinson, Katherine Smits, Pasquale Stella, David Strang, Natalie Tomas, and Alexander Wendt, each of whom read various draft chapters and in some cases versions of the entire manuscript. Helpful comments were provided by other SSRC-MacArthur Fellows at conferences in Malaysia and Argentina, and I thank members of the Melbourne International Relations Theory Group and seminar participants at the Australian National University, Cornell University, Harvard University, the University of Minnesota, Monash University, and Yale University.

The research and writing of this book would have been more difficult and more protracted had it not been for the generous financial support provided by graduate fellowships from the Peace Studies Program at Cornell University and the Mellon Foundation, and from an SSRC-MacArthur Foundation Fellowship on Peace and Security in a Changing World. I subsequently received generous assistance from an Australian Research Council Small Grant and from the Faculty of Arts at Monash University. While writing the first draft of the manuscript I held visiting positions in the Woodrow Wilson School at Princeton University and in the Ashworth Center for Social Theory at the University of Melbourne. I thank both institutions for their support and for the use of their facilities, especially their bountiful libraries. The book was revised after I joined the Department of Politics at Monash University, and I am grateful to David Goldsworthy and Ray Nichols who, as heads of the department, made me welcome and provided constant support and encouragement.

An earlier version of the book's central argument, illustrated by condensed versions of the ancient Greek and modern cases, was published as "The Constitutional Structure of International Society and the Nature of Fundamental Institutions" in *International Organization* 51 (autumn 1997).

Special thanks go to my research assistant, Margaret Nash. To her fell the boring tasks of library searching, photocopying, and compiling the bibliography, tasks she fulfilled with great skill and good humor. Without her assistance many hours of revising would still lie ahead of me. I am also indebted to my editor at Princeton University Press, Ann Himmelberger Wald. At a time when horror stories abound about the traumas of publishing, she has been a patient source of insight, guidance, and support.

Finally, I thank my partner, Heather Rae, who helped me work through and tease out my ideas, who painstakingly read the entire manuscript, and who shares with me the joys of life in our "House in the Woods."

Christian Reus-Smit
Sherbrooke Forest
October 1997

THE MORAL PURPOSE OF THE STATE

Introduction

WHEN the representatives of states signed the General Agreement on Tariffs and Trade in 1947, they enacted two basic institutional practices. In signing the accord, they created contractual international law, adding a further raft of rules to the growing corpus of codified legal doctrine that regulates relations between states. And by accepting generalized, reciprocally binding constraints on their trading policies and practices, they engaged in multilateral diplomacy. By the middle of the twentieth century states had been enacting these paired institutional practices for the best part of a century, and they have since repeated them many times over, in areas ranging from nuclear nonproliferation and air traffic control to human rights and environmental protection. For almost 150 years the fundamental institutions of contractual international law and multilateralism have provided the basic institutional framework for interstate cooperation and have become the favored institutional solutions to the myriad of coordination and collaboration problems facing states in an increasingly complex world. Without these basic institutional practices the plethora of international regimes that structure international relations in diverse issue-areas would simply not exist, and modern international society would function very differently.

International relations scholars of diverse intellectual orientations have long acknowledged the importance of fundamental institutions. Hans Morgenthau attributes such institutions to "the permanent interests of states to put their normal relations upon a stable basis by providing for predictable and enforceable conduct with respect to these relations."[1] Hedley Bull claims that fundamental institutions exist to facilitate ordered relations between states, allowing the pursuit of "elementary goals of social life."[2] Robert Keohane likens basic institutional practices to the rules of chess or baseball, arguing that a change in these practices would alter the very nature of international relations.[3] And Oran Young observes that international "actors face a rather limited menu of available practices among which to choose. A 'new' state, for example, has little choice but to join the basic institutional arrangements of the states system."[4]

If we survey the institutional histories of modern international society and its major historical analogues, two observations can be made about

[1] Morgenthau, "Positivism, Functionalism, and International Law," 279.
[2] Bull, *Anarchical Society.*
[3] Keohane, *International Institutions*, 162–166.
[4] Young, "International Regimes," 120.

fundamental institutions. To begin with, fundamental institutions are "generic" structural elements of international societies.[5] That is, they provide the basic framework for cooperative interaction between states, and institutional practices transcend shifts in the balance of power and the configuration of interests, even if these practices' density and efficacy vary. For instance, the modern institutions of contractual international law and multilateralism intensified after 1945, but postwar developments built on institutional principles first endorsed by states during the nineteenth century, and which first structured interstate cooperation long before the advent of American hegemony. Second, fundamental institutions vary from one society of sovereign states to another. The governance of modern international society rests on the institutions of contractual international law and multilateralism, but no such institutions evolved in other historical societies of states. Instead, the ancient Greek city-states developed a system of third-party arbitration, the renaissance Italian city-states practiced oratorical diplomacy, and the states of absolutist Europe created institutions of dynastic diplomacy and naturalist international law.

Since the early 1980s, the study of international institutions has experienced a renaissance, with distinctive neorealist, neoliberal, and constructivist perspectives emerging. Yet as chapter 1 explains, none of these perspectives adequately accounts for either the generic nature of fundamental institutions or institutional variations between societies of sovereign states. According to neorealists, institutions reflect the prevailing distribution of power and the interests of dominant states. But as we shall see, these are ambiguous predictors of basic institutional forms. Fundamental institutions tend to transcend shifts in the balance of power, and under the same structural conditions, states in different historical contexts have engaged in different institutional practices.[6] Neoliberals claim that states create institutions to reduce the contractual uncertainty that inhibits cooperation under anarchy and they claim that the nature and scope of institutional cooperation reflect the strategic incentives and constraints posed by different cooperation problems.[7] Because states can choose from a wide range of equally efficient institutional solutions, however, neoliberals are forced to introduce structural conditions, such as hegemony and bipolarity, to explain the institutional practices of particular historical periods.[8] Like neorealism, this approach fails to explain institutional

---

[5] On the generic nature of fundamental institutions, see Ruggie, *Multilateralism Matters,* 10; Bull, *Anarchical Society,* 68–73; and Wight, *Systems of States.*

[6] See Kindleberger, *World in Depression;* Gilpin, *War and Change;* and Waltz, *Theory of International Politics,* 194–210.

[7] See Axelrod and Keohane, "Achieving Cooperation"; Keohane, *After Hegemony;* Keohane, *International Institutions;* and Stein, *Why Nations Cooperate.*

[8] Martin, "Rational State Choice."

forms that endure despite shifts in the balance of power and is contradicted by the emergence of different fundamental institutions under similar structural conditions. Constructivists argue that the foundational principle of sovereignty defines the social identity of the state, which in turn shapes basic institutional practices. Sovereign states are said to face certain practical imperatives, of which the stabilization of territorial property rights is paramount. The institution of multilateralism, they argue, evolved to serve this purpose.[9] While this line of reasoning is suggestive, it fails to explain institutional differences between societies of *sovereign* states. The states of ancient Greece, Renaissance Italy, and absolutist Europe also faced the problem of stabilizing territorial property rights, yet they each constructed different fundamental institutions to serve this task.

This general failure to explain the nature of fundamental institutions represents a significant lacuna in our understanding of international relations. All but the most diehard neorealists recognize the importance of basic institutional practices, yet we presently lack a satisfactory explanation for why different societies of sovereign states create different fundamental institutions. Explanations that stress material structural conditions, the strategic imperatives of particular cooperation problems, and the stabilization of territorial property rights all fail to account for such variation. The social textures of different international societies—their elementary forms of social interaction—thus remain enigmatic, undermining our understanding of institutional rationality and obscuring the parameters of institutional innovation and adaptation in particular social and historical contexts.

This book sets out to explain the form that fundamental institutions take and why they vary from one society of states to another. It explores the factors that shape institutional design and action—the reasons why institutional architects consider some practices mandatory while others are rejected or never enter their thoughts. My approach is influenced by two distinct, yet complementary, perspectives on the politics and sociology of international societies. I draw on the insights of constructivist international theory, linking basic institutional practices to intersubjective beliefs about legitimate statehood and rightful state action, though in a new and novel fashion. And I explicate the relationship between state identity and fundamental institutions through a macrohistorical comparison of different societies of states, building on the work of leading members of the "English School," particularly Martin Wight and Adda Bozeman.[10] My aim is to develop a historically informed constructivist theory of fundamental institutional construction.

[9] Ruggie, *Multilateralism Matters*, 21.

[10] See Bozeman, *Politics and Culture*; Bull, *Anarchical Society*; Bull and Watson, *Expansion of International Society*; Watson, *Evolution of International Society*; and Wight, *Systems of States*.

Like other constructivists, I explain fundamental institutions with reference to the deep constitutive metavalues that comprise the normative foundations of international society. In chapter 2, however, I argue that constructivists have so far failed to recognize the full complexity of those foundations, attaching too much explanatory weight to the organizing principle of sovereignty. If we cast our eyes beyond the standard recitations of our textbooks, and the canonical assumptions of our theories, to reflect on the actual practices of states in different historical contexts, we find that sovereignty has never been an independent, self-referential value. It has always been encased within larger complexes of metavalues, encoded within broader constitutive frameworks. To allow systematic comparisons across historical societies of states, I conceptualize these ideological complexes as *constitutional structures*. I argue that these structures can be disassembled into three normative components: a hegemonic belief about the moral purpose of the state, an organizing principle of sovereignty, and a systemic norm of procedural justice. Hegemonic beliefs about the moral purpose of the state represent the core of this normative complex, providing the justificatory foundations for the organizing principle of sovereignty and informing the norm of procedural justice. Together they form a coherent ensemble of metavalues, an ensemble that defines the terms of legitimate statehood and the broad parameters of rightful state action. Most importantly for our purposes, the prevailing norm of procedural justice shapes institutional design and action, defining institutional rationality in a distinctive way, leading states to adopt certain institutional practices and not others. Moulded by different cultural and historical circumstances, societies of sovereign states develop different constitutional structures, and it is this variation that explains their distinctive institutional practices.

Chapters 3 to 6 illustrate this argument through a comparative analysis of institutional development in four societies of sovereign states: the ancient Greek, the Renaissance Italian, the absolutist European, and the modern. All four of these systems exhibit a basic similarity—they have all been organized according to the principle of sovereignty. That is, their constituent units have claimed supreme authority within certain territorial limits, and these claims have been recognized as legitimate by their respective communities of states.[11] Although this organizing principle has received formal legal expression only in the modern era, the sovereignty of the state has been institutionally grounded in each of the four cases. Beyond simply declaring their independence, states have exercised socially

---

[11] Wight argues that for states to form an international society, "not only must each claim independence of any political superior for itself, but each must recognize the validity of the same claim by all the others." Wight, *Systems of States*, 23.

TABLE 1
Constitutional Structures and the Fundamental Institutions of International Societies

Societies of States	Ancient Greece	Renaissance Italy	Absolutist Europe	Modern Society of States
Constitutional Structures				
1. Moral Purpose of State	Cultivation of *Bios Politikos*	Pursuit of Civic Glory	Maintenance of Divinely Ordained Social Order	Augmentation of Individuals' Purposes and Potentialities
2. Organizing Principle of Sovereignty	Democratic Sovereignty	Patronal Sovereignty	Dynastic Sovereignty	Liberal Sovereignty
3. Systemic Norm of Procedural Justice	Discursive Justice	Ritual Justice	Authoritative Justice	Legislative Justice
Fundamental Institutions	Interstate Arbitration	Oratorical Diplomacy	1. Natural International Law	1. Contractual International Law
			2. "Old Diplomacy"	2. Multilateralism

sanctioned "rights" to sovereignty. Because of the anarchical structures of these interstate systems—their lack of central authorities to impose order—realists have woven them into a single narrative of historical continuity, a narrative designed to prove the ubiquity of the struggle for power and the eternal rhythms of international relations. As argued above, though, significant differences distinguish these societies of states, differences illustrated in table 1. In each case, sovereignty has been justified with reference to a unique conception of the moral purpose of the state, giving it a distinctive cultural and historical meaning. What is more, these conceptions of the moral purpose of the state have generated distinctive norms of procedural justice, which have in turn produced particular sets of fundamental institutions.

For the ancient Greeks, chapter 3 explains, city-states existed for the primary purpose of cultivating a particular form of communal life—which Aristotle calls *bios politikos*, the political life. The polis was the site in which citizens, freed from material labors, could participate—through action and speech, not force and violence—in the decisions affecting their common life. This moral purpose informed a discursive norm of procedural justice, whereby cooperation problems between individuals were resolved through a process of public political discourse, centered on the adjudication of particular disputes before large public assemblies and jury courts. In this procedure, codified law played little role in the decisions of adjudicating bodies, nor was their role to inscribe generalized rules of conduct. Assemblies and courts exercised an Aristotelian "sense of justice," involving the highly subjective evaluation of the moral standing of the disputants, the circumstances of the case at hand, considerations of equity, and the needs of the polis. This discursive norm of procedural justice also informed the ancient Greek practice of interstate arbitration. Disputes between states—spanning the entire spectrum of cooperation problems—were adjudicated in public forums, before arbitrators charged with exercising a sense of justice and equity as well as an awareness of the particularity of each case. This system involved neither the formal codification of general, reciprocally binding laws, nor the interpretation of such laws. Norms of interstate conduct certainly evolved, but they were accretions, customs born of case-specific discourse.

The moral purpose of the Italian city-state lay in the cultivation of civic glory, or *grandezza*. As chapter 4 explains, the state existed to promote communal grandeur, to guarantee that a city "grows to greatness." It was widely believed that the major obstacle to civic glory was internal discord and factionalism; *grandezza* was dependent on *concordia*. To ensure that the city attained greatness, the state was expected to combat factionalism by enforcing a distinctive form of *substantive* justice, involving the generous reward of virtue and the ruthless punishment of vice. In the patronage society of Renaissance Italy, the exercise of such reward and retribution was structured by a unique ritual norm of procedural justice, whereby the ritual enactment of virtue, through ceremonial rhetoric and gesture, determined individual worth and entitlement and, in turn, the distribution of social goods (and evils). It was this norm of procedural justice that informed the institutional practices that evolved between the Italian city-states, leading to the development of a distinctive form of oratorical diplomacy. Italian diplomacy has been decried for exhibiting "an abominable filigree of artifice," but given the cultural values of the day it was an appropriate and consistent response to the anxieties of interstate relations. The system of resident ambassadors provided the apparatus for ritual communication; it enabled states to convey carefully crafted images, cultivate and consolidate relationships of friendship and enmity, and monitor the rhetorical and gestural signals and manoeuvres of others.

The Peace of Westphalia in 1648 signaled the end of feudal heteronomy and the rise of the system of sovereign states in Europe. Yet the states that emerged out of the wreck of feudalism were absolutist, not modern. As chapter 5 explains, the legitimacy of absolutist states rested on a decidedly premodern set of Christian and dynastic constitutional values. For almost two centuries after Westphalia, the preservation of a divinely ordained, rigidly hierarchical social order constituted the moral purpose of the sovereign state. To preserve this social order, God invested European monarchs with supreme authority, and an authoritative norm of procedural justice evolved: bound only by natural and divine law, monarchs ruled without stint, their commands constituting the sole basis of legitimate law. These metavalues shaped the institutional practices that emerged between absolutist states, informing the institutions of "old diplomacy" and "naturalist international law." They also served as powerful impediments to the development of modern institutional forms, particularly contractual international law and multilateralism. Contrary to the argument recently advanced by John Ruggie, neither of these institutional practices played a significant role in defining and consolidating the territorial scope and extension of sovereign rights during the absolutist period.

Chapter 6 discusses the constitutional structure of modern international society, arguing that since the late eighteenth century the moral purpose of the modern state has become increasingly identified with the augmentation of individuals' purposes and potentialities, especially in the economic realm. Once the legitimacy of the state was defined in these terms, the absolutist principle that rule formulation was the sole preserve of the monarch lost all credence. Gradually a new "legislative" norm of procedural justice took root. Rightful law was deemed to have two characteristics: it had to be authored by those subject to the law; and it had to be equally binding on all citizens, in all like cases. The previous mode of rule determination was thus supplanted by the legislative codification of formal, reciprocally binding accords. From the 1850s onward, this legislative norm of procedural justice informed the paired evolution of the two principal institutions of contemporary international society: contractual international law, and multilateralism. The principle that social rules should be authored by those subject to them came to license multilateral forms of rule determination, while the precept that rules should be equally applicable to all subjects, in all like cases, warranted the formal codification of contractual international law, to ensure the universality and reciprocity of international regulations.

This study joins a growing number of works that seek to explain aspects of international relations through reference to the constitutive power of intersubjective ideas, beliefs, and norms. It explores what Stephen Toulmin calls "horizons of expectation,"[12] the deep-seated normative and ideological assumptions that lead states to formulate their interests within certain bounds, making some actions seem mandatory and others unimaginable. Why, for instance, did the ancient Greek city-states design and operate a successful system of interstate arbitration in the absence of a body of codified interstate law, when modern states have carefully restricted the jurisdiction of their arbitral courts to the interpretation of international legal doctrine? This line of inquiry directs my attention to the most basic of all international beliefs, to hegemonic conceptions of

[12] Toulmin, *Cosmopolis*.

the moral purpose of the state and norms of procedural justice. I consider how such beliefs constitute the state's social identity, how they shape and constrain the institutional imagination, and how they define the parameters of legitimate international political action.

The method employed in this book combines interpretation with comparative history. In adopting an interpretive approach, I explore the *justificatory frameworks* that sanction prevailing forms of political organization and repertoires of institutional action. I attempt to reconstruct the shared meanings that historical agents attach to the sovereign state—the reasons they hold for parceling power and authority into centralized, autonomous political units—and to show how these meanings structure institutional design and action between states. In sum, my aim is "to re-express the relationship between 'intersubjective meanings' which derive from self-interpretation and self-definition, and the social practices in which they are embedded and which they constitute."[13] This exercise in interpretation takes place within a "world-historical" comparison of the ancient Greek, Renaissance Italian, absolutist European, and modern societies of sovereign states.[14] As noted above, these systems have all been organized according to the principle of sovereignty; their member states have all claimed supreme authority within their territories, and these claims have been deemed legitimate by the community of states. Yet differences in how sovereignty has been justified, and differences in how actors have thought legitimate states should solve their cooperation problems, have led these societies of states to evolve very different basic institutional practices. Thus, by comparing the very systems that realists invoke with mantra-like repetition to prove the universality of the much vaunted "logic of anarchy," I can give substance to Wendt's insight that "anarchy is what states make of it."[15]

Before proceeding, three caveats are needed. First, although I engage in an ambitious reconceptualization of the normative foundations of international societies, my purpose is relatively circumscribed. My aim is to explain the nature of basic institutional practices, and this has required a new conceptual and theoretical framework. As chapter 7 concludes, this framework has implications for how we think about the nature of sovereignty, the ontology of institutional rationality, and the parameters of international systems change. But beyond explaining the nature of fundamental institutions, and helping us to think more clearly about the above issues, I make no claims, especially since I believe that the value of any

---

[13] Neufeld, "Interpretation," 49.

[14] "World-historical" comparisons, Charles Tilly argues, attempt "to fix the special properties of an era and to place it in the ebb and flow of human history." Tilly, *Big Structures*, 61.

[15] Wendt, "Anarchy Is What States Make of It."

conceptual apparatus or theoretical framework depends on the questions we ask. Second, this book is concerned with institutional *form*, not *efficacy*. The reason for this is simple: comparatively little has been written on the former subject, with the big questions of the generic nature of fundamental institutions and variations across societies of states remaining unanswered. In contrast, much has been written about institutional efficacy, with neoliberals marshaling a powerful argument that international regimes alter state behavior in a wide range of issue-areas. I begin, therefore, from the assumption that international institutions matter, and proceed on the basis that explaining the form they take in different cultural and historical contexts is necessary if we wish to develop a complete understanding of the institutional dimension of international relations. Finally, this is a book about institutional theory and comparative international history, not contemporary institutional politics. Even in the chapter on modern international society, I focus on the period between 1815 and 1945, as this was when the institutional architecture of our present system was first erected. It is also the period most deserving of further research, having attracted little attention from institutional theorists in international relations. In comparison, the post-1945 period is well-ploughed ground, with a wealth of research documenting how multilateralism and contractual international law have structured interstate cooperation across a spectrum of issues, producing an ever widening network of functional regimes.[16]

---

[16] See, for example, Krasner, *International Regimes*; Keohane, *After Hegemony*; Keohane, *International Institutions*; Stein, *Why Nations Cooperate*; Ruggie, *Multilateralism Matters*; Haas, *When Knowledge is Power*; and Haas, Keohane, and Levy, *Institutions for the Earth*.

CHAPTER ONE

The Enigma of Fundamental Institutions

> In short, as a result of the twentieth-century
> move to institutions, at least to some extent a
> multilateral political order has emerged. . . . I
> might add in conclusion that while numerous de-
> scriptions of this "move to institutions" exist, I
> know of no good explanation in the literature of
> why states should have wanted to complicate
> their lives in this manner.
> —John Gerard Ruggie, *Multilateralism Matters*

IN THE STUDY of international relations, fundamental institutions have attracted little systematic analysis. Institutionalists of all perspectives readily acknowledge the importance of basic institutional practices, yet most research focuses on the incentives and barriers to institutional cooperation in particular issue-areas, such as global trade or arms control. Theoretical and empirical studies of issue-specific regime formation and maintenance have proliferated, while the underlying practices that structure these regimes have been largely neglected. This neglect has had two unfortunate consequences. First, the definition of fundamental institutions is shrouded in ambiguity: the concept itself remains unclear, and fundamental institutions are poorly differentiated from other levels of international institutions. Second, we lack a satisfactory explanation for the nature and genesis of fundamental institutions. As noted in the introduction, existing accounts fail to explain either the generic nature of basic institutional practices or why they vary from one society of states to another. This chapter serves two tasks. It begins by defining fundamental institutions and situating them in relation to other institutional types. It then critically evaluates four prominent explanations—or proto-explanations—of fundamental institutions: those emphasizing spontaneous evolution, hegemonic construction, rational institutional selection, and state identity.

FUNDAMENTAL INSTITUTIONS DEFINED

Institutions are generally defined as stable sets of norms, rules, and principles that serve two functions in shaping social relations: they constitute actors as knowledgeable social agents, and they regulate behavior. Most definitions of international institutions recognize both functions, although one is usually emphasized over the other. Constructivists focus on the constitutive function, treating institutions as value complexes that "define the meaning and identity of the individual." But they also appreciate how institutions shape "patterns of appropriate economic, political, and cultural activity engaged in by those individuals."[1] Reversing the order of priority, neoliberals stress the way in which institutions "constrain activity" and "shape expectations." However, they acknowledge that institutions also "prescribe behavioral roles," thus defining the identities of social actors.[2]

While institutions operate at several levels of international society, research has focussed on the most immediate and tangible level of "international regimes." Contrary to neorealist expectations, international cooperation did not collapse after the decline of American hegemony in the early 1970s, in fact it expanded into new domains of international life. Cooperation has persisted, neoliberals argue, because under conditions of high interdependence states cannot fulfil many of their interests unless they engage in collective action. To facilitate such action, states have constructed a multitude of international regimes. Regimes are commonly defined as "sets of implicit and explicit principles, norms, rules, and decision-making procedures around which actors' expectations converge in a given area of international relations."[3] By lowering transaction costs, increasing information, and raising the costs of defection, regimes have enabled states to cooperate in many realms of common concern, even in the absence of a hegemon. Empirical studies have documented regime formation, and testified to the importance of such institutions, in areas ranging from security relations to environmental protection.

Fundamental institutions operate at a deeper level of international society than regimes. In fact, in the modern society of states they comprise the basic rules of practice that structure regime cooperation. When defining fundamental institutions, the challenge of achieving and sustaining international order represents an appropriate starting point. Following Hedley Bull, I define international order as "a pattern of activity that sustains the elementary or primary goals of the society of states, or international society."[4] Bull identifies these goals as security, the sanctity of agreements, and the protection of territorial property rights. In the pursuit of international order, states face two basic sorts of cooperation problems: problems of collaboration, where they have to cooperate to achieve common

---

[1] Meyer, Boli, and Thomas, "Ontology and Rationalization," 12.
[2] Keohane, *Institutions and State Power*, 3.
[3] Krasner, *International Regimes*, 2.
[4] Bull, *Anarchical Society*, 8.

interests; and problems of coordination, where collective action is needed to avoid particular outcomes.[5] To overcome these problems, societies of states develop fundamental institutions. *Fundamental institutions are the elementary rules of practice that states formulate to solve the coordination and collaboration problems associated with coexistence under anarchy.* These institutions are produced and reproduced by basic institutional practices, and the meanings actors attach to such practices are defined by the fundamental institutional rules they embody.[6] Given this mutually constitutive relationship, the terms "fundamental institution" and "basic institutional practice" are frequently used interchangeably, a convention maintained in this book.

Societies of states usually exhibit a variety of basic institutional practices. In modern international society scholars have variously, and inconsistently, identified bilateralism, multilateralism, international law, diplomacy, management by the great powers, and even war. Similarly diverse lists could be made of basic institutions in other historical societies of states. This having been said, societies of states tend to privilege certain fundamental institutions over others, albeit different ones. For instance, Athens briefly experimented with multilateralism in the fourth century B.C., yet arbitration endured for centuries as the dominant fundamental institution of ancient Greece. And although cases of arbitration occurred in the nineteenth century, contractual international law and multilateralism have become the dominant institutional practices governing modern international society. This book is concerned with these dominant fundamental institutions, and the theoretical framework advanced in the following chapter is designed to explain why different societies of states privilege different basic institutional practices.

As we shall see, the nature of basic institutional practices is conditioned by an even deeper level of international institutions, which I term "constitutional structures." The following chapter discusses these in detail. For now it is sufficient to observe that institutions exist at three levels of modern international society, with fundamental institutions occupying the middle strata. As figure 1 illustrates, constitutional structures are the foundational institutions, comprising the constitutive values that define legitimate statehood and rightful state action; fundamental institutions encapsulate the basic rules of practice that structure how states solve cooperation problems; and issue-specific regimes enact basic institutional practices in particular realms of interstate relations. These three tiers of institutions are "hierarchically ordered," with constitutional structures

---

[5] Stein, *Why Nations Cooperate*, 39–44.

[6] For a detailed discussion of the relationship between rules and practices, see Rawls, "Two Concepts of Rules."

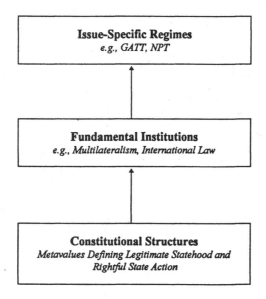

Figure 1. The Constitutive Hierarchy of Modern International Institutions

shaping fundamental institutions, and basic institutional practices conditioning issue-specific regimes. The institutions of modern international society thus form a "generative structure," in which "the deeper structural levels have causal priority, and the structural levels closer to the surface of visible phenomena take effect only within a context that is already 'prestructured' by the deeper levels."[7]

EXISTING ACCOUNTS OF FUNDAMENTAL INSTITUTIONS

The literature on international institutions presents four different accounts of basic institutional practices. They emphasize, respectively, spontaneous evolution, hegemonic construction, rational institutional selection, and state identity. All but the first of these are identified with the major schools of international relations theory: neorealism, neoliberalism, and constructivism. The remainder of this chapter critically evaluates each of these accounts, asking whether they satisfactorily account for—or have the potential to account for—the generic nature of fundamental institutions and institutional differences between societies of states.

[7] Ruggie, "Continuity and Transformation," 283.

Spontaneous Evolution

The first, and least satisfactory, account treats fundamental institutions as inevitable, quasi-natural characteristics of international societies, spontaneously constructed by sovereign states without conscious design. In a discipline preoccupied with rational choice, this explanation is proffered with surprising regularity, by scholars of diverse theoretical orientations.

Curiously, one of the clearest statements of this perspective is presented by Hans Morgenthau, the doyen of classical realism. Because states have an interest in stable relations, Morgenthau argues, they create a network of basic international institutions, notably elementary systems of international law and diplomacy. International law, which includes rules of diplomatic exchange, territorial jurisdiction, extradition, and maritime law, stems from "the permanent interests of states to put their normal relations upon a stable basis by providing for predictable and enforceable conduct with respect to these relations."[8] Likewise, "old diplomacy," based on secret negotiations between diplomatic agents, is considered an inevitable enterprise between sovereign states. "Whenever two autonomous social entities, anxious to maintain their autonomy, engage in political relations with each other, they cannot but help to resort to what we call the traditional methods of diplomacy."[9] This proposition, that societies of sovereign states necessarily produce a system of fundamental institutions, is echoed by a wide range of scholars. For instance, Keohane explicitly defers to Morgenthau on the matter, and Robert Jackson argues that fundamental institutions "are a response to the unavoidable and undeniable reality of a world of states: plurality."[10]

According to this account, fundamental institutions are not only inevitable, they are unconscious constructions. This is implied in Morgenthau's supportive attitude toward "old" fundamental institutions—which "have grown ineluctably from the objective nature of things political"—and in his savage criticism of deliberate institutional engineering, which he identified with Wilsonian internationalism. It receives theoretical expression, however, in the writings of contemporary institutionalists. Keohane, for example, argues that basic institutional practices constitute "spontaneous orders," a concept borrowed from Oran Young.[11] "Such institutions," Young writes, "are distinguished by the facts that they do not involve conscious coordination among participants, do not require explicit consent on the part of subjects or prospective subjects, and are

---

[8] Morgenthau, "Positivism, Functionalism, and International Law," 279.

[9] Morgenthau, "Permanent Values in Old Diplomacy," 11.

[10] See Keohane, *Institutions and State Power*; and Jackson, *Quasi-States*, 35.

[11] Young in turn borrowed the concept from Friedrich Hayek. Keohane, *Institutions and State Power*, 175.

highly resistant to efforts at social engineering."[12] He goes on to contrast fundamental institutions with international regimes, which are "negotiated orders," involving conscious construction and consent.[13]

Given the generic nature of fundamental institutions, it is understandable that they are considered inevitable, quasi-natural features of societies of states. And since, once firmly established, they are partly reproduced through habitual use and compliance, not explicit consent, it is tempting to treat them as unconscious constructions. For anyone seriously interested in the nature and origin of basic institutional practices, however, this perspective is less than satisfying. In particular, it begs two crucial questions: Why do sovereign states "spontaneously" create one set of fundamental institutions and not another? And why have different societies of states established different basic institutional practices to facilitate coexistence under anarchy? Unless we attribute such variation to accident, or random patterns of institutional evolution, we must give more recognition to historical processes of institutional design and construction than the notion of spontaneity allows.

Hegemonic Construction

The second account, presented by neorealists, attributes the nature and extent of international institutional cooperation to the power and interests of hegemonic states.

Neorealists believe that international anarchy severely constrains cooperation between states. The absence of a global authority to impose order means that little prevents one state from destroying or enslaving another.[14] Driven by fears of destruction and servitude, states are concerned first and foremost with their own survival, and they can only guarantee this by maximizing their own power.[15] Because survival ultimately depends on the resources states can muster in their own defense, they are preoccupied with their relative power, and a world consisting of such actors is not conducive to extensive cooperation.[16] Even if cooperation promises to deliver substantial absolute gains, states will forego participation if they expect to gain less than their partners, thus lowering their relative power position.[17]

[12] Young, "Regime Dynamics," 98.
[13] Ibid., 99.
[14] Waltz, *Theory of International Politics*, 113.
[15] Ibid., 111.
[16] See Grieco, "Anarchy and the Limits of Cooperation"; Grieco, *Cooperation Among Nations*; and Grieco, "Understanding International Cooperation."
[17] Grieco, *Cooperation Among Nations*, 44.

Despite this skepticism, neorealists do not deny the possibility of international institutional cooperation altogether. Institutional cooperation is considered feasible if there is a hegemonic distribution of power and if the dominant state is willing to define and enforce the rules of international society. Since hegemons, like all states, are self-interested power maximizers, they tend to create and maintain international institutions that further their interests and increase their power. As John Mearsheimer observes, the "most powerful states in the system create and shape institutions so that they can maintain their share of world power, or even increase it."[18] Hegemonic stability theorists employ this line of reasoning to explain why Great Britain and the United States, at the peaks of their respective power, sponsored and upheld the institutions of a liberal international economic order.[19] Neorealists claim that this perspective "offers a more complete and compelling understanding of the problem of cooperation than does neoliberal institutionalism," their principal target.[20]

As an explanation for the nature of fundamental institutions, this perspective on institutional development is problematic in three respects. First, even if hegemonic powers do help to establish and police the rules of international society, neorealists have great difficulty explaining the institutional practices that dominant states have historically employed to achieve this goal. The logic of neorealist theory suggests that hegemons will prefer bilateral forms of interstate cooperation, which better enable them to exploit their relative power over other states, in order to maximize the flexibility and minimize the transparency of their actions and to prevent weaker states from increasing their power through collective action. Yet this expectation is contradicted by the enthusiastic promotion of multilateralism by the United States after 1945.[21] Washington constructed an international security order explicitly based on multilateral principles of reciprocity and indivisibility. Steve Weber observes, however, that if "functional or utilitarian logic points in any direction at all, it points *away* from multilateralism as an institutional form for managing the West's security problem at the end of World War II."[22] The United States also built a multilateral trading order around the General Agreement on Tariffs and Trade, but Judith Goldstein argues that power alone cannot explain Washington's institutional preferences: "In the case of GATT, the asymmetry in capabilities suggests that the United States could have imposed the policy of its choosing. Still, the observation

---

[18] Mearsheimer, "False Promise," 13.

[19] See Kindleberger, *World in Depression*; and Gilpin, *War and Change*, 145.

[20] Grieco, *Cooperation Among Nations*, 227.

[21] For a detailed discussion of American policy in this regard, see Ruggie, *Winning the Peace*; and Ruggie, "False Promise of Realism."

[22] Weber, "Postwar Balance of Power," 267.

derived from this metaphor—that the United States was powerful and could thus choose the rules of the game—merely begs the key question of why one set of rules for the new trade regime was preferred by the American policy makers over others."[23]

Second, even if neorealists could establish a clear relationship between the distribution of power, the institutional preferences of hegemons, and the nature of fundamental institutions, they would still have difficulty accounting for the generic nature of basic institutional practices. As chapter 6 explains, the principle of multilateralism was first endorsed by states during the nineteenth century, and the density and efficacy of multilateral institutions increased steadily thereafter. American hegemony certainly intensified and accelerated this process, but institutional developments after the Second World War built on normative principles laid down well before *Pax Americana*, notably at the two Hague Conferences and at Versailles. The development of multilateralism has thus exhibited an evolutionary dynamic and an enduring quality that even sophisticated neorealist arguments, which invoke "institutional lags" and "punctuated equilibria" to explain institutional persistence, have difficulty accommodating.[24]

Finally, neorealist attempts to link the balance of power to institutional preferences and outcomes are further frustrated by the fact that dominant states have engaged in different institutional practices under the same structural conditions. As neorealists have frequently observed, Athens was a hegemon operating in a bipolar system, yet unlike the United States it never championed multilateral institutions to manage interstate relations.[25] For centuries the Greek city-states practiced third-party arbitration as the principal institutional mechanism for solving cooperation problems and facilitating coexistence, and it remained the key fundamental institution throughout, and long after, the period of Athenian hegemony.

Rational Institutional Selection

The third account, advanced by neoliberal institutionalists, assumes that institutions are created by rational, self-interested states, and that the nature and scope of institutional cooperation is determined by the array of state interests and the strategic dilemmas posed by different cooperation problems.

[23] Goldstein, "Creating the GATT Rules," 202.
[24] See Krasner, "State Power;" and Krasner, "Sovereignty."
[25] See Fliess, *Thucydides*; Gilpin, "Hegemonic War"; and Gilpin, "Peloponnesian War."

Neoliberals disagree with neorealists about the meaning of anarchy and its implications for cooperation between states. While neorealists stress the physical insecurity that states experience under anarchy, they emphasize the contractual uncertainty that prevails when there is no worldwide authority to enforce agreements. International cooperation is frustrated, they argue, by ineffective legal sanctions, limited and incomplete information, and high transaction costs.[26] The net result is that "cheating and deception are endemic."[27] In contrast to neorealists, neoliberals believe that states can overcome the obstacles to international cooperation by constructing issue-specific regimes: "Regimes facilitate agreements by raising anticipated costs of violating others' property rights, by altering transaction costs through the clustering of issues, and by providing reliable information to members."[28] The nature of particular institutions, they contend, is determined by the configuration of state interests and the incentives and constraints associated with cooperation in different issue-areas. While neoliberals concentrate on issue-specific institutions, or regimes, several scholars have recently used rationalist insights to explain the nature and development of fundamental institutions, with Lisa Martin's work on multilateralism being emblematic.[29]

Martin assumes "that states are self-interested and turn to multilateralism only if it serves their purposes, whatever these might be."[30] After identifying four types of cooperation problems encountered by states—collaboration, coordination, suasion, and assurance—she examines when it is rational for states to choose multilateral solutions to each problem, claiming that this approach "illuminates the functional considerations behind alternative institutional solutions for different types of games."[31] Her inquiry reveals, however, that "at this abstract level of analysis the outcomes remain indeterminate. Multiple feasible solutions exist for each problem."[32] In short, rational choice theory alone cannot predict when states will construct multilateral institutions to solve cooperation problems. To overcome this limitation, Martin invokes two structural features of the post-1945 international system—American hegemony and bipolarity—to explain why multilateral institutions proliferated. She argues that it is rational for far-sighted hegemons to promote multilateral forms of governance, and that "[o]ne of the most important impacts of bipolarity

---

[26] Keohane, *After Hegemony*, 87.
[27] Axelrod and Keohane, "Achieving Cooperation," 226.
[28] Keohane, *After Hegemony*, 97.
[29] Martin, "Rational State Choice." Also see Morrow, "Modeling International Cooperation"; and Weingast, "Rational Choice Perspective."
[30] Martin, "Rational State Choice," 92.
[31] Ibid.
[32] Ibid.

is to encourage far-sighted behavior on the hegemon's part."[33] By combining the neoliberal emphasis on rational institutional selection with the neorealist stress on structural determinants, Martin claims to overcome the indeterminance of abstract rationalism and, in turn, explain post-1945 multilateralism.

This perspective on fundamental institutions is problematic in several respects. As Martin successfully demonstrates, abstract rationalist theory cannot explain why states adopt one institutional form over another. Basic institutional practices, Keohane candidly admits, are "not entirely explicable through rationalistic analysis."[34] And appeals to structural determinants are no solution, as they expose neoliberals like Martin to the same criticisms as neorealists. To begin with, American policy makers advanced multilateral principles for structuring the post-1945 international order *before* the emergence of bipolarity. As Ruggie observes, it is "more than a little awkward to retroject as incentives for actor behavior structural conditions that had not yet clearly emerged, and were not yet fully understood, and that in some measure only the subsequent behavior of actors helped to produce."[35] Second, modern international society has experienced only one period of hegemony under conditions of bipolarity, and although multilateralism received a major boost during that period, it significantly predates *Pax Americana*, in both principle and practice. Finally, as noted earlier, attempts to deduce institutional preferences and outcomes from structural conditions such as hegemony and bipolarity are confounded by the fact that under these conditions modern and ancient Greek states engaged in different practices.

The Constitutive Role of State Identity

The final account is presented by constructivists, who argue that the foundational institution of sovereignty defines the social identity of the state, which in turn constitutes the basic institutional practices of international society.

Constructivists argue that social institutions exert a deep constitutive influence on the identities and interests of actors. "Cultural-institutional contexts," Peter Katzenstein writes, "do not merely constrain actors by changing the incentives that shape behavior. They do not simply regulate behavior. They also help to constitute the very actors whose conduct they seek to regulate."[36] International institutions, it follows, define the

---

[33] Ibid., 112.
[34] Keohane, *Institutions and State Power*, 174.
[35] Ruggie, "Multilateralism," 29.
[36] Katzenstein, *Culture of National Security*, 22.

identities of sovereign states. As Wendt and Duvall observe, "International institutions have a *structural* dimension, that generates socially empowered and interested state agents as a function of their respective occupancy of the positions defined by those principles."[37] Understanding how international institutions shape state identity is crucial, constructivists argue, because social identities inform the interests that motivate state action. "Actors do not have a 'portfolio' of interests that they carry around independent of social context; instead they define interests in the process of defining situations. . . . Sometimes situations are unprecedented in our experience. . . . More often they have routine qualities in which we assign meanings on the basis of institutionally defined roles."[38] Employing these insights, constructivists have sought to explain a wide range of international phenomena, including the practice of self-help, the international movement against apartheid, the end of the Cold War, and, importantly for our purposes, the nature of basic institutional practices.[39]

When they turn their attention to fundamental institutions, constructivists posit a tight constitutive relationship between the organizing principle of sovereignty, the social identity of the state, and basic institutional practices. Sovereignty is considered the primary institution of international society, its normative foundation.[40] The meanings that define sovereignty "not only constitute a particular kind of state—the "sovereign" state—but also a particular form of community, since identities are relational."[41] Constructivists argue that "sovereign" states have "certain practical dispositions" that shape the fundamental institutions they construct to facilitate coexistence. "The practices that instantiate these institutions," claim Wendt and Duvall, "are concerned with and structured by the constitutive principle of sovereignty."[42] In more concrete terms, Jackson argues that "[t]he classical game of sovereignty exists to order the relations of states, prevent damaging collisions between them, and—when they occur—regulate the conflicts and restore peace."[43] This game generates certain funda-

---

[37] Wendt and Duvall, "Institutions and International Order," 60.

[38] Wendt, "Anarchy Is What States Make of It," 398.

[39] See Ibid.; Finnemore, *National Interests*; Katzenstein, *Culture of National Security*; Klotz, *Norms in International Relations*; Klotz, "Norms Reconstituting Interests"; Koslowski and Kratochwil, "Understanding Change;" Ruggie, *Multilateralism Matters*.

[40] See Ashley, "Untying the Sovereign State"; Bartelson, *Genealogy of Sovereignty*; Biersteker and Weber, *Sovereignty as Social Construct*; Jackson, *Quasi-States*; Ruggie "Continuity and Transformation"; Ruggie, "Territoriality and Beyond"; Walker, *Inside/Outside*; Walker and Mendlovitz, *Contending Sovereignties*; Weber, *Simulating Sovereignty*; Wendt, "Anarchy Is What States Make of It"; and Wendt and Duvall, "Institutions and International Order."

[41] Wendt, "Anarchy Is What States Make of It," 412.

[42] Ibid.

[43] Jackson, *Quasi-States*, 36.

mental institutions. "For example, traditional public international law belongs to the constitutive part of the game in that it is significantly concerned with moderating and civilizing the relations of independent governments," says Jackson. Likewise, diplomacy "also belongs insofar as it aims at reconciling and harmonizing divergent national interests through international dialogue."[44]

Until recently this constitutive relationship between the foundational institution of sovereignty and fundamental institutions was merely asserted by constructivists, not explained or demonstrated. It has been clarified, however, by Ruggie's recent work on multilateralism. Ruggie emphasizes the connection between sovereignty and territoriality, arguing that the "distinctive feature of the modern system of rule is that it has differentiated its subject collectivity into territorially defined, fixed, and mutually exclusive enclaves of legitimate dominion."[45] The state's claim to exclusive jurisdiction within a given territory, he goes on to argue, is essentially a claim to private property.[46] When the system of sovereign states first emerged, some ongoing means had to be found to stabilize territorial property rights, as conflicting jurisdictional claims promised perpetual conflict and instability. Ruggie argues that multilateralism, with its principles of indivisibility, generalized rules of conduct, and diffuse reciprocity, was the inevitable solution to this problem. "Defining and delimiting the property rights of states," he writes, "is as fundamental a collective task as any in the international system. The performance of this task on a multilateral basis seems inevitable in the long run, although in fact states appear to try every conceivable alternative first."[47]

To explain the increased density of multilateral institutions after 1945, a number of constructivists have advanced a "second image" argument about the institutional impact of American hegemony.[48] The United States' identity as a liberal-democracy, they argue, directly influenced the policies Washington employed to structure the postwar international order. According to Anne-Marie Burley, American policy makers believed

---

[44] Ibid., 35.

[45] Ruggie, "Territoriality and Beyond," 151.

[46] Ruggie, "Continuity and Transformation," 275.

[47] Ruggie, Multilateralism Matters, 21.

[48] In particular, see Burley, "Regulating the World." Burley's argument is echoed by Ruggie in "Multilateralism" and Winning the Peace. It is important to note that not all constructivists follow Ruggie and Burley in integrating domestic sources of state identity into their explanatory frameworks. For instance, in his commitment to systemic theorizing, Wendt explicitly brackets domestic , or "corporate," sources of state identity, focusing entirely on the constitutive role of international social interaction. See Wendt, "Collective Identity." Elsewhere I have characterized these two varieties of constructivist theory as "fourth image constructivism" and "third image constructivism" respectively. See Reus-Smit, "Beyond Foreign Policy," 186–194.

that the domestic reforms of the New Deal would only succeed if compatible regulatory institutions existed at the international level. Consequently, they set about constructing multilateral institutions that embodied the same architectural principles as those of the New Deal regulatory state.[49] The identity of the world's most powerful state is thus considered a crucial factor in the proliferation of multilateral institutions after 1945. In Ruggie's words, it was "*American* hegemony that was decisive after World War II, not American *hegemony.*"[50]

The constructivist account of fundamental institutions has two principal weaknesses. First, the connection Ruggie draws between territoriality, property rights, and multilateralism sits uncomfortably with the institutional histories of the four societies of states examined in the following chapters. Each of these international societies developed different institutions to stabilize territorial property rights, with multilateralism developing only in the modern era. Second, although Burley provides a compelling explanation for why American policy makers were "ideologically" inclined toward multilateral forms of international governance, and why the United States played such a catalytic role in the proliferation of such institutions after 1945, her argument implies that the architectural principles advanced by the United States were new to the community of states. But, as noted above, American policy makers elaborated institutional principles that were first embraced and implemented by the Great Powers almost a century earlier.

SUMMARY

This chapter has advanced a definition of fundamental institutions, and argued that none of the existing perspectives satisfactorily accounts for the generic nature of basic institutional practices or institutional differences between societies of states. The proposition that fundamental institutions arise spontaneously fails to explain why certain forms emerge and not others, and why societies states evolve different practices. Neorealists have not established a clear link between hegemonic power and institutional outcomes, and their argument is confounded by institutional practices that transcend shifts in the balance of power and by states engaging in different practices under similar structural conditions. Neoliberals have themselves shown that rationalist logic alone cannot explain why states adopt certain institutional forms to solve cooperation problems, and appeals to structural variables simply expose them to the same criti-

---

[49] Burley, "Regulating the World," 125.
[50] Ruggie, "Multilateralism," 31.

cisms as neorealists. And, finally, the constitutive link constructivists draw between the foundational institution of sovereignty, the identities of states, and basic institutional practices is contradicted by the contrasting institutional records of the ancient, Renaissance, absolutist, and modern societies of states. In an effort to overcome the limitations of these perspectives, the following chapter outlines an alternative constructivist theory of fundamental institutional development.

CHAPTER TWO

The Constitutional Structure
of International Society

> In every society of moral beings, and conse-
> quently, therefore, in every society or union of
> states, certain general ideas, from which the lead-
> ing motives of conduct originate, will of necessity
> prevail. . . . To have a correct apprehension,
> therefore, of the ruling ideas of each age, and to
> exhibit the particular maxims arising from them,
> will be the first requisite of the historian.
> —A. H. L. Heeren, *History of the Political
> System of Europe*, 1846.

CONSTRUCTIVISTS rightly direct our attention to how primary social institutions shape state identity and in turn affect basic institutional practices.
As we shall see, the socially constituted identity of the state indeed exerts
a profound influence on institutional design and action. The existing constructivist account of fundamental institutions is undermined, however,
by several analytical oversimplifications. First, constructivists have failed
to appreciate the full complexity of the deep constitutive values that define
the social identity of the state, placing too much emphasis on the organizing principle of sovereignty. And, second, they have paid insufficient
attention to the discursive mechanisms that link intersubjective ideas of
legitimate statehood and rightful state action to the constitution of fundamental institutions. Together, these omissions have left constructivists unable to explain the nature of basic institutional practices or institutional
variations between societies of sovereign states.

This chapter advances an alternative constructivist explanation of fundamental institutional development. I argue that international societies
are bound together by constitutional structures, which define the social
identity of the state and the basic parameters of rightful state action.
These structures incorporate three deep constitutive values: a hegemonic
belief about the moral purpose of centralized, autonomous political organization; an organizing principle of sovereignty; and a norm of pure procedural justice. Constitutional structures exert a profound influence on

the nature of institutional cooperation, with prevailing norms of pure procedural justice shaping institutional design and action. They not only frame the organizational imaginations of institutional architects, they also structure the wider moral discourses surrounding institutional production and reproduction. Because societies of states emerge in different historical and cultural contexts and thus develop different constitutional structures, they establish different fundamental institutions.

This explanation is grounded in both theory and practice. Theoretically, it builds on existing constructivist propositions by drawing on the insights of communicative action theory, particularly the work of Jürgen Habermas. These insights inform my argument that the principle of sovereignty is necessarily embedded within a wider complex of metavalues, and also my claims about the discursive mechanisms that link constitutional structures, state identity, and fundamental institutions. Practically, the argument draws on the institutional experiences of the ancient, Renaissance, absolutist, and modern societies of states. The justificatory actions sustaining sovereign statehood in these systems, and the discursive practices surrounding their patterns of fundamental institutional construction, have pushed and shoved my conceptual and theoretical assumptions, leading me to cast aside some ideas and propose new ones. The result, I hope, is a theoretically more sophisticated, analytically more powerful, historically more accurate constructivist account of fundamental institutions.

COMMUNICATIVE ACTION AND INSTITUTIONAL CONSTRUCTION

In the following pages I adopt what James Caporaso calls "a social-communicative approach" to understanding fundamental institutions, one that treats human intentions and actions as "embedded in social relations in which communication, shared beliefs, norms, and identity commitments are present."[1] When states formulate, maintain, and redefine the fundamental institutional rules that facilitate international cooperation, they engage in a process of communicative action. That is, they debate how legitimate states should, or should not, act. Such debate does not occur in a vacuum; it takes place within the context of preexisting values that define legitimate agency and action. These values structure the debate, licensing some institutional propositions and proscribing others.

Theorists of communicative action offer three insights that are relevant to understanding the practical discourse that surrounds fundamental institutional construction. These insights, Habermas insists, are "not

---

[1] Caporaso, "International Relations Theory," 66–73.

concerned with what rational, reasonable or correct argumentation is, but with how people, dumb as they are, actually argue."[2] First, "a communicatively achieved agreement must be based *in the end* on reasons."[3] Parties have to justify the particular principles they advocate, debate revolves around the merits of particular reasons, and stable agreements, resulting in legitimate rules of conduct, ultimately rest on those reasons deemed to carry the most weight. Second, not all reasons have equal standing; only those that resonate with preexisting, mutually recognized higher order values are considered valid.[4] "In the context of communicative action," Habermas argues, "only those persons count as responsible who, as members of a communicative community, can orient their actions to intersubjectively recognized validity claims."[5] Third, the reasons that carry the greatest weight in practical discourse are those that appeal to deep-rooted, collectively shared ideas that define what constitutes a legitimate social agent.[6] *Identity values* represent the core of the "life world," the "storehouse of unquestioned cultural givens from which those participating in communication draw agreed-upon patterns of interpretation for use in their interpretive efforts."[7]

These insights inform the discussion that follows. They refer to the conditions of *successful* communicative action, to practical discourse that results in agreement about appropriate norms, rules, and principles of human conduct. If actors are not willing to provide reasons to support their claims, or if they refuse to argue within the bounds of preexisting normative precepts, then strategic action and even outright conflict, replace communicative action, and the possibility of reaching agreement about new standards of social conduct wanes. If, in a worst-case situation, actors disagree about what constitutes a legitimate social agent, then society itself is threatened.[8]

---

[2] Habermas, *Theory of Communicative Action*, 27.

[3] Ibid., 17.

[4] As Friedrich Kratochwil observes, "The 'logic' of arguing requires that our claims satisfy certain criteria, and that means that they cannot be based purely on idiosyncratic grounds." Kratochwil, *Rules, Norms, and Decisions*, 12.

[5] Ibid., 14.

[6] William Connolly argues that "[w]hen the notion at issue is conceptually connected to shared ideas about persons and responsibility, the shared, more fundamental ideas provide a common court of appeal to which the conflict can be brought and within the confines of which the disagreement can be subjected to a measure of rational control." Connolly, *The Terms of Political Discourse*, 191.

[7] Habermas, *Moral Consciousness and Communicative Action*, 54.

[8] Habermas, *Communication and the Evolution of Society*, 3–4.

SOVEREIGNTY, STATE IDENTITY, AND POLITICAL ACTION

As we saw in the previous chapter, constructivists assume that the foundational principle of sovereignty defines the social identity of the state. In David Strang's words, sovereignty is understood "as a social status that enables states as participants within a community of mutual recognition."[9] Sovereignty is thus considered the primary identity value of the international life world, the constitutive principle that empowers centralized, autonomous political units as legitimate social agents. A clearer understanding of the nature of social identities, and of the communicative practices surrounding their production and reproduction, reveals, however, that this assumption is logically problematic.

All human actors—both individual and collective—have social identities that enable them to operate in a world of complex social processes and practices. Like other constructivists, I define social identities as "sets of meanings that an actor attributes to itself while taking into account the perspective of others, that is, as a social object."[10] Social identities, as opposed to other "corporate" identities, are defined by intersubjective, socially sanctioned, and institutionalized meanings that define the nature and purpose of agents and agency in a given social context.[11] Such identities fulfil a variety of social-psychological purposes. Most importantly, they provide actors with *primary reasons for action*. This is true in two senses. In a purposive sense, McCall and Simmons argue, social identities provide "the primary source of plans for action," informing an actor's goals as well as the strategies they formulate to achieve them.[12] In a justificatory sense, social identities provide the basis on which action can be rationalized, providing actors with a reason for being and acting, a raison d'être. For instance, a doctor's social identity implies certain forms of action, such as prescribing drugs and doing surgery, but also gives reason and meaning to those actions: "I am a doctor, that's why I do such things."

Unless embedded within a wider complex of higher-order values, the principle of sovereignty cannot alone provide the state with a coherent social identity, nor has it done so historically. Sovereignty, like individual liberty, is not a self-referential value capable of independently providing

---

[9] Strang, "Contested Sovereignty," 22.

[10] Wendt, "Collective Identity Formation," 385.

[11] "Corporate identity," Wendt argues, "refers to the intrinsic, self-organizing qualities that constitute actor individuality. For human beings, this means the body and experience of consciousness; for organizations, it means their constituent individuals, physical resources, and the shared beliefs and institutions in virtue of which individuals function as 'we'." Ibid.

[12] McCall and Simmons, *Identities and Interactions*, 69.

actors with substantive reasons for action. To begin with, sovereignty has no purposive content. Without reference to some other higher-order values it cannot independently inform plans of action or strategies to achieve them. Furthermore, the principle of sovereignty provides an inadequate justificatory basis for action. If I behave in a way that annoys, frustrates, or merely affects those around me, they are entitled to ask why I acted in such a fashion. Asserting my independence or liberty cannot provide an adequate response, as they can immediately ask why I am entitled to such freedoms. At this point I must ground my claims to independence in some other deep, socially recognized identity values. Taken to an extreme, this would involve appealing to intersubjective values that define what it means to be a fully realized human being. Similarly, when states are forced internationally to justify their actions, there comes a point when they must reach beyond mere assertions of sovereignty to more primary and substantive values that warrant their status as centralized, autonomous political organizations. This is a necessary feature of international communicative action, and historically it has entailed a common moral discourse that grounds sovereign rights in deeper values that define the social identity of the state: "We are entitled to possess and exercise sovereign rights because we are ancient polises, Renaissance city-states, absolutist monarchies, or modern liberal polities."

Recognizing that the identity of the state is grounded in a larger complex of values than simply the organizing principle of sovereignty is the first step in formulating a more satisfactory constructivist account of basic institutional practices. For these values not only define the terms of legitimate statehood, they also provide states with substantive reasons for action, which in turn exert a profound influence on institutional design and action. What is more, the values that ground sovereignty have varied from one society of states to another, generating contrasting rationales for state action, and different basic institutional practices.

CONSTITUTIONAL STRUCTURES

To enable systematic comparison across historical societies of states, I conceptualize the complexes of values that define state identity as "constitutional structures." *Constitutional structures are coherent ensembles of intersubjective beliefs, principles, and norms that perform two functions in ordering international societies: they define what constitutes a legitimate actor, entitled to all the rights and privileges of statehood; and they define the basic parameters of rightful state action.* They are "constitutional" because they incorporate the basic principles that define and shape international polities, and they are "structures" because they "limit and mold agents and agencies and point them in ways that tend toward a

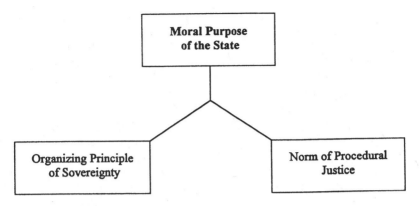

Figure 2. The Constitutional Structure of International Society

common quality of outcomes even though the efforts and aims of agents and agencies vary."[13] Reflecting on the normative practices that have sustained the interstate societies of ancient Greece, Renaissance Italy, absolutist Europe, and the modern era, constitutional structures can be said to incorporate three primary normative elements. These are, as figure 2 illustrates, a hegemonic belief about the moral purpose of centralized, autonomous political organization, an organizing principle of sovereignty, and a norm of pure procedural justice.

Hegemonic beliefs about *the moral purpose of the state* represent the core of this normative complex, providing the justificatory foundations for the principle of sovereignty and the prevailing norm of pure procedural justice. The term "purpose" refers here to the reasons that historical agents hold for organizing their political life into centralized, autonomous political units. As Aristotle writes, "Observation tells us that every state is an association, and that every association is formed with a view to some good purpose."[14] Such purposes are "moral" because they always entail a conception of the individual or social "good" served by autonomous political organization. I refer to the moral purpose of the "state" because such rationales are of a different category to the moral purposes of suzerain or heteronomous forms of political organization, and exploring these latter forms is beyond the analytical reach, and explanatory scope, of this book. Finally, the beliefs about moral purpose of the state that shape constitutional structures are "hegemonic," not because they are the only conceptions of the moral purpose of the state propagated in a given historical context, but because they constitute the prevailing, socially sanctioned justification for sovereign rights. Against these hegemonic beliefs,

[13] Waltz, *Theory of International Politics*, 74.
[14] Aristotle, *The Politics*, I.1.

alternative conceptions of the moral purpose of the state have historically assumed an oppositional quality, their proponents frequently decrying the way in which prevailing beliefs condition admission to international society and shape its basic institutional practices.[15]

Societies of sovereign states, suzerain systems, and heteronomous systems are all structured by organizing principles. These principles, Ruggie argues, establish the basis on "which the constituent units are separated from one another."[16] In other words, they define the mode of differentiation. In societies of states, the *organizing principle of sovereignty* differentiates political units on the basis of particularity and exclusivity, creating a system of territorially demarcated, autonomous centers of political authority. In contrast to traditional perspectives, constructivists treat the principle of sovereignty as a variable, arguing that its precise meaning and behavioral implications vary from one historical context to another. As Janice Thomson observes, "While sovereignty differs from heteronomy in theoretical and empirical ways, there can be much variation in the authority claims within sovereignty."[17] The actors that are deemed worthy of sovereign rights, the nature of the rights they gain and the obligations they assume, the conditions under which those rights can be legitimately exercised, and the situations where the wide community of states is licensed to intervene to compromise or remove those rights have varied greatly. The historical analysis presented in this book suggests that the greatest variations have occurred across societies of states. Historically contingent beliefs about the moral purpose of the state have provided the justificatory foundations of sovereign rights, and as these beliefs have changed from one society of states to another, so too have meanings attached to sovereignty.

In addition to a conception of the moral purpose of the state and an organizing principle of sovereignty, constitutional structures incorporate a third element: a *norm of pure procedural justice*. Norms of pure procedural justice specify the correct procedures that "legitimate" or "good" states employ, internally and externally, to formulate basic rules of internal and external conduct. These norms *do not* prescribe substantive principles of interstate justice, they simply dictate "a correct or fair procedure

---

[15] For example, note how the revolutionary states of France and the United States challenged the dynastic principles of absolutist international society in the eighteenth century; how Asian states challenged the liberal-constitutionalist "standard of civilization" that structured modern international society in the late nineteenth century; and how the Soviet Union and South Africa bucked against the same standards during the Cold War, subsequently embracing the same principles in order to gain entry to contemporary international society. See Gilbert, "The New 'Diplomacy' "; Gong, *The Standard of Civilization*; Klotz, *Norms in International Relations*; and Koslowski and Kratochwil, "Understanding Change."

[16] Ruggie, "Continuity and Transformation," 274.

[17] Thomson, *Mercenaries, Pirates, and Sovereigns*, 151.

such that the outcome is likewise correct or fair, whatever it is, providing the procedure has been properly followed."[18] The existence of a generally accepted norm of pure procedural justice is a prerequisite for ordered social relations, domestically and internationally. Unless there is a minimal, baseline agreement among society's members about how rules of coexistence and cooperation should be formulated, no basis exists for collective action or the resolution of conflict, let alone the formulation of substantive principles of justice. This is true of international societies as well as domestic societies, but as following chapters demonstrate, different conceptions of the moral purpose of the state have generated different systemic norms of pure procedural justice. Prevailing norms of pure procedural justice dictate the basic parameters of rightful state action, exerting a profound influence on the nature of fundamental institutions.

These three normative elements are mutually interconnected and dependent, forming a single, coherent normative system. One cannot argue in defense of the principle of sovereignty without, in the end, appealing to the "good" served by a system of rule based on centralized, territorially demarcated centers of political authority. What is more, it is difficult to define such a "good" without referring to some conception of procedural justice, as "justice is the first virtue of social institutions."[19] Constitutional structures are institutional attributes of societies of states, existing outside particular states, conditioning the identity and behavior of strong and weak states alike. They are not the only factors shaping relations between states; geopolitical and economic structures also affect state behavior, as neorealists and Marxists have shown. They do, however, serve to define the membership of international society, the boundaries of legitimate state action, and the nature of basic institutional practices. Constitutional structures are hegemonic, though, not totalizing. While the values they embody are dominant, this does not mean that they go uncontested. The historical record suggests, however, that in stable societies of states such contestation occurs at the margins, and assumes a counterhegemonic tone.

FUNDAMENTAL INSTITUTIONAL PRODUCTION AND REPRODUCTION

The constitutional structure of a society of states determines the nature of its basic institutional practices. Informed by prevailing beliefs about the moral purpose of the state, the systemic norm of pure procedural

[18] Rawls, *Theory of Justice*, 86.
[19] Ibid., 3.

justice shapes institutional choice, licensing some institutional solutions over others. This occurs through two principal constitutive mechanisms.

To start with, norms of pure procedural justice define the cognitive horizons of institutional architects. That is to say, they shape the institutional imaginations of those political actors engaged in producing and reproducing fundamental institutions, making some practices appear mandatory and others unthinkable. Animated by a discursive conception of procedural justice, the city-states of ancient Greece imagined and constructed the institution of interstate arbitration. Imbued with a rhetorical conception, the city-states of Renaissance Italy developed the practice of oratorical diplomacy. Upholding an authoritative view of procedural justice, absolutist states constructed institutions of dynastic diplomacy and naturalist international law. And embracing a legislative conception, modern institutional architects conceived and established contractual-legal and multilateral forms of international governance. In each of these cases, fundamental institutions were produced and reproduced partly because, in Paul DiMaggio and Walter Powell's words, "individuals often cannot even conceive of appropriate alternatives (or because they regard as unrealistic the alternatives they can imagine)."[20]

In the second constitutive mechanism, norms of pure procedural justice provide the metanorms that structure the process of communicative action that surrounds the production and reproduction of fundamental institutions. Fundamental institutions are sets of prescriptive norms, rules, and principles that specify how legitimate states "ought" to resolve their conflicts, coordinate their relations, and facilitate coexistence. The construction and maintenance of such institutions necessarily entails an ongoing moral dialogue between states about what these norms, rules, and principles should be. As theorists of communicative action observe, such dialogues are structured by a "higher-order consensus" about the primary social values that such institutions are intended to embody. "Contestants enter the discourse with different values," Agnes Heller explains, "and they all try to justify their values (as right and true). They do this by resorting to values higher than those which they want to justify, by proving that the latter are but an interpretation of the higher values, or that they can be related to these higher values without logical contradiction."[21] Systemic norms of pure procedural justice represent the salient higher-order values in the moral dialogues that produce and reproduce the fundamental institutions of international societies. The architects of modern international institutions appealed to the norm of legislative justice when justifying multilateral institutional solutions, absolutist states

[20] DiMaggio and Powell, *New Institutionalism*, 11.
[21] Heller, *Beyond Justice*, 239.

invoked authoritative norms to warrant their institutional practices, Renaissance city-states drew upon rhetorical mores to sanction oratorical diplomacy, and the norm of discursive justice provided the justificatory foundations for the ancient Greek practice of arbitration.

These constitutive mechanisms shape basic institutional practices because a consensus exists among the majority of states about the nature and validity of the prevailing systemic norm of pure procedural justice. Again, this does not mean that they agree on substantive principles of justice, only that they recognize a set of procedural precepts that "civilized" states ought to observe in resolving cooperation problems. The existence of "outlier" states, which do not subscribe to this ideological consensus, does not compromise the argument. They may not be subject to the constitutive processes outlined above, but providing they seek cooperative relations with other states, they will be drawn into the production and reproduction of basic institutional practices through two additional mechanisms.

In the first of these, the cooperative actions of outlier states are constrained by systemic norms of pure procedural justice. When such states wish to portray their interactions with other states as legitimate, they are under a strong compulsion to justify their actions in terms of the system's primary norms of coexistence. It is a general feature of human social action, Quentin Skinner observes, that "[s]uch an agent may be said to have a strong motive for seeking to ensure that his behavior can plausibly be described in terms of a vocabulary already normative within his society, a vocabulary which is capable of legitimating at the same time as describing what he has done."[22] Contrary to common assumptions, this legitimating imperative forces states to adjust more than their language. Claiming that one's relations with other states are consistent with prevailing norms of procedural justice is a successful legitimating strategy only if there is some coincidence between rhetoric and actions, at least in the longer term. The "problem facing an agent who wishes to legitimate what he is doing at the same time as gaining what he wants," Skinner argues, "cannot simply be the instrumental problem of tailoring his normative language in order to fit his projects. It must in part be the problem of tailoring his projects in order to fit the available normative language."[23] This is not to say, of course, that all states closely observe the system's norms of pure procedural justice all of the time. Rather, it is to suggest that such norms exert a constraining influence on the *institutional* actions of even those states that do not subscribe to the ideological consensus of

[22] Skinner, *Foundations*, xii.
[23] Ibid., xii–xiii.

their system, providing they desire cooperation and are conscious of the shadow of the future.

By the final mechanism, functional imperatives compel outlier states, along with others, to reproduce basic institutional practices. In a mature society of states, exhibiting an established network of fundamental institutions, states that wish to engage in stable social interaction encounter strong incentives to employ existing practices. To begin with, as Young argues, states "face a rather limited menu of available practices among which to choose. A 'new' state, for example, has little choice but to join the basic institutional arrangements of the states system."[24] Since these institutions presumably attract widespread support, and are already embedded in the practical interactions of international society, sponsoring new practices would be a costly enterprise, politically and materially. Also, in an interdependent society of states, refusal to observe basic institutional practices is likely to undermine the pursuit of national interests significantly. Functional imperatives thus drive all but the most autarkic and recalcitrant states to participate in established fundamental institutions, and in doing so they reproduce those very institutions. With every participatory action, basic institutional practices are reaffirmed and strengthened. Moreover, the reproduction of existing fundamental institutions indirectly legitimizes the prevailing norm of procedural justice, further strengthening the constitutional structure of international society.

THE PURPOSIVE FOUNDATIONS OF INTERNATIONAL SOCIETY

By grounding basic institutional practices in constitutional structures, at the core of which lie intersubjective beliefs about the moral purpose of the state, the theoretical framework advanced above is at odds with Terry Nardin's much cited conception of international society as a "practical association." According to Nardin, a "practical association is a relationship among those engaged in the pursuit of different and possibly incompatible purposes, and who are associated with one another, if at all, only in respecting certain restrictions on how each may pursue his own purposes."[25] International society, he contends, is just such an association. States pursue diverse ends, bound together only by the "authoritative practices" that facilitate coexistence, notably the fundamental institutions of international law and diplomacy.[26] "International society, according to the practical conception, is constituted by the forms and procedures that

---

[24] Young, "International Regimes," 120.
[25] Nardin, *Law, Morality, and Relations of States*, 9.
[26] Ibid., 19.

states are obligated to observe in their transactions with one another."[27] While this conception of international society is superficially plausible, as it resonates with prevailing rationalist conceptions of society and the very real diversity of the contemporary world, it is historically misleading and heuristically limited.

Practical association, for Nardin, is more fundamental than purposive association—*gesellschaft* precedes *gemeinschaft*. At the level of abstract theory, this assumption has a certain elegance, making minimal assumptions about the bonds underlying international social interaction. Reality, however, is not so elegantly rational. All historical societies of states have begun as gemeinschaft societies; that is, as communities of states linked by common sentiment, experience, and identity. Wight, in his classic comparative analysis of international societies, concludes that "we must assume that a states-system will not come into being without a degree of cultural unity."[28] This is true of the ancient Greek, Renaissance Italian, and absolutist societies of states, and it is also true of the modern. In each case, the development of a set of historically contingent intersubjective beliefs about what constitutes a legitimate state, entitled to all the rights and privileges of sovereignty, preceded and shaped the construction of practical institutions. The constitution of the state's social identity thus provided the foundations upon which authoritative fundamental institutions were constructed.

This is not to suggest, of course, that modern international society is now a gemeinschaft community, or to deny the immense practical imperatives that sustain it. As Barry Buzan astutely observes, "Present day international society is a hybrid."[29] On the one hand, it grew out of the culturally unified system of nineteenth-century Europe, and an expanding community of liberal-constitutionalist states has remained at its core, prevailing as the winning coalition after each of this century's major conflicts and standoffs, most recently the Cold War. Contemporary fundamental institutions were spawned in that earlier system, core states have been the principal agents in the production and reproduction of these practices, and their values of legitimate statehood and rightful state action have become hegemonic, shaping the modern constitutional structure, and in turn defining the discursive terrain in which institutional construction takes place. On the other hand, modern international society is multicultural, extending beyond the liberal-constitutionalist core to encompass a wide variety of states. The practical imperatives of coexistence under

---

[27] Ibid., 15.

[28] Wight, *Systems of States*, 33. It should be noted that Wight uses the term "states-system" instead of "society of states" or "international society."

[29] Buzan, "International System to International Society," 349.

conditions of high interdependence have nevertheless encouraged these states to employ, and even further, existing "Western" institutional practices. As Bull and Watson remark in their landmark study of the expansion of modern international society, a "striking feature of the global international society of today is the extent to which the states of Asia and Africa have embraced such basic elements of European international society as the sovereign state, the rules of international law, the procedures and conventions of diplomacy and international organization."[30] In one sense, therefore, modern international society is indeed a practical association, but in an equally important sense, a deep structural sense, it is informed by the institutional and organizational values of the constitutively prior European (now Western) gemeinschaft society.

The empirical observation that the ancient, Renaissance, absolutist, and modern societies of states have all had purposive foundations is unlikely to move Nardin, for his project is a narrowly deductive one. He is concerned with the *idea* of practical international society, with defending the notion that durable social relations between states can rest on the common observance of authoritative practices, even in the absence of shared goals and purposes. The historical bases of international association are not his interest. His "philosophical" project, Nardin declares, "requires neither affirmation nor denial of any theory concerning the empirical conditions of such association."[31]

While we must respect Nardin's intent, his uninterest in the actual development of historical societies of states greatly undermines the heuristic value of his perspective. Most significantly, although he gives primacy to authoritative practices, such as international law, in his account of international society, he has no way of explaining the form these practices take, or why they vary from one society of states to another. International law is presented as the codification of customary state practices,[32] but this merely begs the question of why certain practices become the favored, routinized methods of facilitating interstate cooperation. At one point, Nardin unwittingly hints at an answer, observing that practices "always reflect an ideal conception of the activities out of which they grow and of the agents engaged in them: the virtuoso performance, the just war, the responsible parent, the 'perfect ambassador'."[33] Yet his own perspective on international society forecloses any systematic analysis of these deeper intersubjective values that define legitimate agency and action.

---

[30] Bull and Watson, *Expansion of International Society*, 433.
[31] Nardin, *Law, Morality, and Relations of States*, 313.
[32] Ibid., 305.
[33] Ibid., 6.

The constructivist account of international society advanced in this book is less elegant than Nardin's. The analytical apparatus of constitutional structures is an abstraction, in part informed by theories of identity formation and communicative action, but it builds on empirical observations about society formation and institutional construction in four interstate societies. It places the intersubjective values that define the social identity of the state and rightful state action at the fore, acknowledging the historical and cultural particularity of different societies of states. The result is a complex mixture of deductive reasoning and historical interpretation. The payoff, I hope, is a logically and empirically sustainable explanation of the divergent institutional practices that have evolved in different societies of states.

SUMMARY

Societies of states, I have argued, are ordered by constitutional structures. These complexes of metavalues define the social identity of the state, and the broad parameters of legitimate state action. Hegemonic beliefs about the moral purpose of the state provide the justificatory foundations for sovereignty and generate norms of pure procedural justice. The latter exert a profound influence on institutional design and action, defining the *mentalities* of institutional architects and shaping the moral discourse that structures institutional production and reproduction. Constitutional structures are not all the same: culture and history matter. Ideas about the moral purpose of the state vary from one society of states to another, and they inform different norms of pure procedural justice. It is this variation, I contend, that explains the divergent institutional practices of historical societies of states. States create fundamental institutions that reflect their social identity, and as that identity changes, so too do basic institutional practices.

CHAPTER THREE

Ancient Greece

As for the Athenians, I advise sending a mission
to them about Potidaea and also about the other
cases where our allies claim to have been ill
treated. Especially is this the right thing to do
since the Athenians themselves are prepared to
submit to arbitration, and when one party offers
this it is quite illegal to attack him first, as
though he was definitely in the wrong.
—Archidamus, King of Sparta, 432 B.C.

THE ANCIENT GREEK system of city-states occupies a special place in the
study of international relations. It stands as one of the great analogues of
the modern state system, a familiar world of independent states in which
the eternal verities of international politics are thought to have appeared
in their most rudimentary and essential form. Thucydides, the great
chronicler of the Peloponnesian War, is upheld as the first theorist of international relations, his work lauded for its insights into the perpetual
rhythms of international politics. Classic lines from his *History* are recited
to undergraduates, the war between Athens and Sparta is invoked with
same currency as the First World War, and many a "truth" about contemporary international politics has been defended with references to ancient
Greece.

This fascination has not, however, produced a well-rounded understanding of ancient Greek interstate relations. International relations
scholars have focussed almost exclusively on the nature and causes of
conflict between the city-states, with most energies devoted to explaining
the Peloponnesian War. While this is a worthy focus, patterns of cooperation between the city-states have received very little attention. In fact, one
could easily conclude from the existing literature that the city-states of
ancient Greece existed in a constant state of war, that cooperation was
negligible or nonexistent, or that the city-states created little in the way
of institutions to facilitate coexistence. This characterization is seriously
misleading, however. The city-states engaged in extensive cooperation,
and they participated in a range of extraterritorial institutions. The most

important of these was the fundamental institution of third-party arbitration, which regulated interstate relations for more than five centuries.

This chapter eschews the traditional emphasis on conflict and war, focusing instead on the nature of institutionalized cooperation between the city-states. It concentrates on the practice of third-party arbitration, my purpose being to explain why the city-states favored this institution in particular to regulate conflict and facilitate coexistence. As anticipated in previous chapters, I attribute the nature and centrality of this practice to the constitutional structure of the ancient Greek society of states. The practice of arbitration, I contend, was informed by a distinctive conception of the moral purpose of the state and norm of pure procedural justice. My argument unfolds in a number of stages. After discussing in greater detail the scholarly neglect of institutional cooperation between the city-states, I briefly survey the range of extraterritorial institutions that evolved in ancient Greece. The discussion then turns to the constitutional structure of the ancient Greek society of states, explaining prevailing ideas of legitimate statehood and rightful state action. This is followed by a detailed analysis of how these values shaped and sustained the practice of interstate arbitration. After discounting several alternative explanations, the chapter ends with a reinterpretation of Thucydides' *History of the Peloponnesian War.*

ANCIENT GREECE AS A STATE OF WAR

Until recently, the study of ancient Greek interstate relations was a realist preserve, and this goes some way toward explaining the prevailing emphasis on conflict between the city-states.[1] Claiming Thucydides as their own, and focusing narrowly on the Peloponnesian War, realists have used the experience of the ancient Greek city-states to support their claims about the structural constraints of anarchy, the eternal struggle for power, and the dynamics of hegemonic rivalry. In its most simplistic form, this has involved the invocation of great quotes from Thucydides' text, notably the infamous line from the Melian Dialogue that "the strong do what they have the power to do and the weak accept what they have to accept."[2] A more sophisticated line of analysis finds in Thucydides' *History* a theory of hegemonic war, one that resonates with contemporary neorealist propositions. "Thucydides' theory of hegemonic war," Robert Gilpin argues, "constitutes one of the central organizing ideas for the study of interna-

---

[1] Notable exceptions to this realist monopoly are Toynbee's *Study of History*; and Lenin's *Imperialism.*

[2] Thucydides, *History of the Peloponnesian War*, Book V.89, 401–402.

tional relations."[3] Michael Howard takes this one step further, claiming that Thucydides' explanation for the Peloponnesian War is equally applicable to the Second World War: "You can vary the names of the actors, but the model remains a valid one for the purposes of our analysis."[4] Realists have also found insights about the politics of bipolarity in Thucydides' account and drawn parallels between the Peloponnesian War and the Cold War.[5] The image of ancient Greek interstate relations that emerges is one of city-states engaged in an unmitigated struggle for power. Beyond observations about the dynamics of alliance formation, realists have largely ignored the record of cooperation between the city-states.

Realist interpretations of ancient Greece and Thucydides' *History* have attracted sustained criticism, yet critics have continued to focus on the conflictual dimensions of interstate relations. Realists are not criticized for ignoring cooperation between the city-states but for misunderstanding the sources of conflict, in particular the causes of the Peloponnesian War. As in contemporary debates, the "parsimonious" structuralism employed by many realists is considered especially problematic. Richard Ned Lebow argues, for instance, that the domestic political structures of key states, particularly Sparta, and miscalculations at decisive moments, contributed more to the war than structural imperatives.[6] Also emphasizing domestic political factors, Bruce Russett claims that "Thucydides' great book actually is a penetrating analysis of the role and weaknesses of democratic politics in formulating security policy, and of linkages between the *dēmos* in one state and the *dēmos* of others."[7] On a different tack, Daniel Garst challenges the materialist conception of structure underlying neorealist analyses: "Thucydides reminds us that power and hegemony are above all bound to the existence of political and social structures and the intersubjective conventions associated with them."[8] Each of these authors alludes to aspects of cooperation between the Greek city-states. Lebow mentions city-states appealing to arbitration during the Peloponnesian War, Russett points to the tentative development of norms that democratic states should not fight one another, and Garst notes the relevance of "intersubjective conventions." These observations have not, however, been translated into systematic analyses of institutional cooperation between the city-states.

[3] Gilpin, "Theory of Hegemonic War," 591.

[4] Howard, *The Causes of War*, 16.

[5] See Fliess, *Thucydides and the Politics of Bipolarity*; and Gilpin, "Peloponnesian War and Cold War."

[6] Lebow, "Thucydides, Power Transition Theory, and the Causes of War," 126.

[7] Russett, *Grasping the Democratic Peace*, 62.

[8] Garst, "Thucydides and Neorealism," 25.

Prominent members of the "British School" are virtually alone among international relations scholars in exploring the cooperative dimensions of ancient Greek interstate relations. In his classic work, *Systems of States*, Wight argues that the cities formed a society of states, which he terms a "states-system." In fact, he concludes that "it was the most complex and highly organized of which history seems to have record before our own."[9] In the course of his analysis, Wight surveys a range of extraterritorial institutions, from the Delphic Oracle to the balance of power. Unfortunately, however, his understanding of cooperation between the city-states is hampered by a curious preoccupation with Western institutional forms. He uses the institutions of contemporary international society as an analytical template, scanning the ancient Greek system for evidence of international law, diplomacy, the balance of power, and international public opinion. Wight's study goes a long way toward demonstrating the social dimensions of the Hellenic system, but his checklist approach obscures more than it reveals. In his search for modern institutional forms, he ignores the existence or significance of interstate arbitration, the key fundamental institution of the Greek society of states. This oversight also undermines Adam Watson's more recent analysis of the Hellenic system.[10] Only Adda Bozeman manages to abandon this modern institutional mind set, producing a culturally sensitive analysis that recognizes the institutional distinctiveness of the ancient Greek society of states. Sadly, her work offers more by way of description than explanation, only hinting at the reasons behind the institutional designs of the city-states.[11]

None of the above is intended to suggest that seeking to explain conflict between the city-states is a misguided enterprise, or that power and hegemony were irrelevant in ancient Greece. As in modern international society, war was a recurring feature of interstate relations, and the balance of power was an important, if not a sole or sufficient, condition. Furthermore, the principal, and most accessible, record of relations between the city-states—Thucydides' *History*—is an account of a lengthy and devastating war, which makes an analytical emphasis on conflict somewhat inevitable. This having been said, the ancient Greek city-states were not in a constant state of war. Like modern states, they struggled to moderate the more destructive consequences of anarchy, constructing a range of institutions to further coexistence. Often these institutions successfully facilitated interstate cooperation, and at times they failed. Overall, though, they significantly altered the temper of ancient Greek interstate relations, thus warranting their further investigation. Classicists have al-

[9] Wight, *Systems of States*, 73.
[10] Watson, *Evolution of International Society*, 47–68.
[11] Bozeman, *Politics and Culture*, 66–84.

ready done much to document and understand these practices, particularly the fundamental institution of arbitration, yet curiously international relations scholars have demonstrated a lack of interest in exploring their nature or significance.

EXTRATERRITORIAL INSTITUTIONS IN ANCIENT GREECE

The city-states of ancient Greece established an array of extraterritorial institutions, regulating everything from sacred religious sites to territorial property rights. Arbitration was the core fundamental institution, but it was nested within a web of lesser institutions. The Oracle at Delphi and the periodic Olympic festivals are the best known, yet least important politically. The latter were little more than forums for political debate, places where important treaties were inscribed on pillars for public declaration.[12] The Oracle was the paramount religious institution in ancient Greece, and it often issued political advice to city-states. It appears, however, that this did not significantly alter the course of interstate affairs, as states usually sought the Oracle's advice to authorize decisions that they had already made.[13] Delphi exerted greater political influence through another type of interstate institution—the *amphictyony*. These cult-based religious leagues, of which the one centered at Delphi was the oldest, sought to protect common religious sites, guarantee the water rights of their members, and manage intraleague conflicts. Toward these ends, league members were bound by oath, and amphictyonies were empowered to wage "sacred" war against delinquents. Amphictyonies were not, however, systemwide institutions, and their religious purposes served to divide the city-states as much as unite them.[14] Across the system, the cities did establish the institution of *proxeny*, or resident agents. But these friendly citizens of another polis, who helped and protected fellow citizens when they visited, were not ambassadors. They were accorded certain privileges and immunities, and they certainly aided peaceful interaction across city-states, but they never engaged in diplomatic negotiation, limiting their political impact.

In comparison to these lesser institutions, the practice of arbitration had greater breadth and depth.[15] The city-states maintained the institution

---

[12] Wight, *Systems of States*, 48.

[13] Ibid.

[14] Adcock and Mosley, *Diplomacy in Ancient Greece*, 186.

[15] The most important English and French works on interstate arbitration in ancient Greece are: Phillipson, *International Law and Custom of Ancient Greece and Rome*, Volumes One and Two; Raeder, *L'Arbitrage*; Ralston, *International Arbitration from Athens to Locarno*; Revon, *L'Arbitrage International*; Niebuhr Tod, *International Arbitration*; and Westermann, "Interstate Arbitration."

for over five hundred years, with documented cases stretching from the sixth to first centuries B.C. Literary and historical materials, in addition to extant inscriptions, record the details of some eighty cases, the majority of which occurred after the rise of a new civic ideology in the fifth century. Unlike most of the other extraterritorial institutions, arbitration operated across the entire system, drawing in strong and weak states, members of different religious and imperial leagues, and cities of different regions. What is more, the city-states employed arbitration to solve a wide range of cooperation problems, from the treatment of foreigners to the specification and regulation of borders. The practice was also central to other instruments of interstate cooperation. Like their modern counterparts, the city-states concluded many bilateral treaties, but in contrast to modern practice, these agreements were not supported by a body of codified international treaty law, the absence of which represents one of the principal differences between the two societies of states. Instead, the city-states inserted arbitration clauses in many of their treaties, grounding specific agreements in a common framework of adjudication and lending their provisions greater legitimacy. In sum, arbitration spanned the entire system of city-states, it was implicated in many aspects of interstate cooperation, and it undergirded other instruments of coexistence, thus making it the predominant fundamental institution of the ancient Greek society of states.

THE CONSTITUTIONAL STRUCTURE OF ANCIENT GREECE

Why did the ancient Greek city-states adopt arbitration as their principal institutional practice? In no other society of states has it assumed such centrality. In spite of the renaissance fascination for all things ancient Greek, arbitration was employed only sporadically among the Italian city-states. Modern states used arbitration in the nineteenth century, and have since on several occasions, but its role has always been marginal, and close analysis reveals ancient Greek arbitration and modern arbitration to be very different institutions, sharing little more than the name. The idea that states should submit their grievances to the decision of a third party, and accept the arbitrator's decision as binding, has been raised at many points in history, yet only the ancient Greeks embraced it with any commitment or consistency. How can we explain this? The answer lies, I believe, in the constitutional structure of the ancient Greek society of states. The prevailing conception of the moral purpose of the state, which defined legitimate statehood in ancient Greece, entailed a distinctive understanding of procedural justice, an understanding embodied in the practice of interstate arbitration.

How, then, did the ancient Greeks define the moral purpose of the state? Here Aristotle's ethical and political writings provide a useful starting point. Irrespective of whether one agrees with his moral and political philosophy, Aristotle was a self-confessed empiricist, who sought to capture the essence of the social and political world in which he lived. He was concerned that moral philosophy not only reflect logical rigor but also "the views commonly expressed about it."[16]

Aristotle argues that ideal human agents—who he believes are always male—combine reason with action. "The proper function of man," he writes, "consists in an activity of the soul in conformity with a rational principle."[17] The political implications of this become clear only if we recognize that for the ancient Greeks the greatest expression of reason was the "perception of good and evil, just and unjust." In fact, this is what they thought distinguished ideal males from women and animals.[18] The rational pursuit of justice through action was deemed possible only within a particular sort of political community—the polis. There were two reasons for this. First, justice was considered an inherently social virtue, as one cannot act justly without treating the needs and interests of others equally and fairly. Second, the pursuit of justice was inextricably linked to speech, the articulation of moral claims within a wider public political discourse.[19] The quest for justice was thus thought to be an inherently political activity, and men inherently political beings. The polis was in turn considered the preeminent form of human organization. According to Aristotle: "In every kind of knowledge and skill the end which is aimed at is a good. This good is greatest, and is a 'good' in the highest sense, when that knowledge or skill is the most sovereign one, i.e. the faculty of statecraft. In the state, the good aimed at is justice; and that means what is for the benefit of the whole community."[20] The polis was considered both the arena in which men could become truly virtuous, as well as the primary object of that virtue. Its raison d'être was not, first and foremost, to provide physical security or to facilitate economic exchange, but "to engender a certain character in the citizens and to make them good and disposed to perform noble actions."[21] The moral purpose of the ancient Greek city-state thus lay in the cultivation of *bios politikos*, a form of communal life characterized by the rational pursuit of justice through action and speech.

[16] Aristotle, *Nicomachean Ethics*, Book I.8, 19.
[17] Ibid., 17.
[18] Aristotle, *Politics*, Book I.2, 60.
[19] Ibid.
[20] Ibid., Book III.12, 207.
[21] Aristotle, *Nicomachean Ethics*, Book I.9, 23.

This conception of the moral purpose of the state entailed a discursive norm of pure procedural justice, one that licensed case-by-case determination of right and wrong conduct through a process of public moral debate and deliberation.[22] This is not to say that the ancient Greeks never promulgated codified laws—the histories of the city-states are punctuated by great moments of constitutional lawmaking. But the laws in question were largely, though not exclusively, procedural in nature. Dennis Maio has shown, for instance, that Athenian law of the fourth century B.C.—when Athenians are said to have embraced "the rule of law"[23]—"was not so much a system of commands for extra-judicial activity as it was a system of regulations for the conduct of judicial process."[24] Within this procedural framework, ancient Greek jury courts and assemblies—frequently consisting of hundreds of citizens—exercised considerable deliberative discretion, adjudicating disputes without strict reference to codified substantive laws. Instead of objectively applying the letter of the law, jurors were expected to exercise an Aristotelean "sense of justice," subjectively weighing the moral rectitude of the disputants, the peculiarities of the case, the needs of the community, and principles of equity. As Sally Humphreys observes, they were "invited to behave as if they were members of the local community, deciding on the fairest solution for each particular case, rather than specialists in applying law to cases."[25] Speechwriters strove not to interpret the law but to establish the righteousness of defendants' positions, and witnesses were called not to determine the facts of a case[26] but to testify to defendants' respectability.[27] In such a legal system, general rules of social conduct were less the product of legislation than custom, with iterated discursive practices gradually generating norms of social behavior.

While this discursive norm of pure procedural justice reached its institutional apogee in classical Athens, the belief that public moral discourse was the appropriate way for civilized polities to decide questions of right and wrong shaped political and legal practices across the city-states. By the time of Plato and Aristotle, democracy was the most common form of political organization, with Athenian principles and practices influenc-

---

[22] My argument here is informed by the recent work of several classicists who have emphasized the discursive nature of ancient Greek law and legal practice. In particular, see Humphreys, "Evolution of Legal Process in Ancient Attica"; Humphreys, "Social Relations on Stage"; Humphreys, "Discourse of Law"; Maio, "*Politeia* and Adjudication"; Garner, *Law and Society*; Ober, *Mass and Elite in Democratic Athens*; and Osborne, "Law in Action."

[23] See Ostwald, *Law, Society, and Politics*; and Sealey, *History of the Greek City-States*.

[24] Maio, "*Politeia* and Adjudication," 40.

[25] Humphreys, "Evolution of Legal Process in Ancient Attica," 248.

[26] Ibid.

[27] Humphreys, "Social Relations on Stage," 313.

ing the constitutions, if not all the institutions, of many city-states.[28] More interestingly, though, the discursive norm of procedural justice also structured the practices of oligarchic states, even Sparta. The Great Rhetra— the raft of laws supposedly bequeathed to the Spartans by Lycurgus, the legendary lawgiver—was largely procedural, and beyond this there is little evidence that the Spartans ever developed an extensive body of codified substantive law. Furthermore, while it was once believed that decision-making power was concentrated in the hands of the five ephors and the Gerousia, or Council of Elders, it now appears that the public assembly, open to all adult male Spartans, "had the ultimate decision on matters of legislation and policy."[29] As we shall see, the importance of public political discourses, and the power of the assembly, are apparent in Thucydides' account of the famous Debate at Sparta, where the congregated Spartans heard and debated the moral claims of their disgruntled allies and the defensive Athenians, ultimately deciding to launch the Peloponnesian War.[30]

The classical vision of the moral purpose of state, and its associated view of procedural justice, contrast sharply with the ideals of the Homeric Age, and reflects a major social and political transformation in the nature of the city-states. During the earlier period, merit (*arete*) was measured in terms of warriorly virtues, such as courage and strength, qualities embodied in the Homeric hero.[31] These values reflected the aristocratic pattern of governance that prevailed in that earlier period, the largely preurban condition of the Greek settlements, and the turbulent conditions of the time. As Werner Jaeger observes, it "was natural that, in the warlike age of the great migrations, men should be valued chiefly for their prowess in battle"[32] By the sixth century B.C., however, the city-states had become urban centers, and the grip of aristocratic rule was eroding. Whether it took the form of Spartan oligarchy or Athenian democracy, decision making became more decentralized. This shift is symbolized by the political and economic transformation Athens experienced under Solon, who rewrote the Athenian constitution to stave off revolution, giving greater power to the *demos*, and abolished debt-bondage, paving the way for an expansion of the slave economy. In this context, the athletic virtues of the warrior were gradually supplanted by a new ideal of the just citizen.[33] "As

---

[28] Hansen, "Tradition of Athenian Democracy," 16.

[29] Sealey, *History of the Greek City-States*, 71. See also Andrews, "Government of Classical Sparta."

[30] Thucydides, *History*, Book I.66–88, 72–87.

[31] Jaeger, *Paedeia, Volume One*, chapter 1.

[32] Ibid., 6.

[33] The extent of this ideological transformation has been challenged by Arthur Adkins in *Merit and Responsibility*. He contends that "competitive" values remained dominant

we might imagine," Jaeger argues, "such praise of justice by poets and philosophers did not precede the struggle to realize the ideal, but was plainly a repercussion of the political struggles which lasted from the eighth century to the beginning of the fifth."[34] Through these struggles, arete was redefined to celebrate the political qualities of deliberation and equity, and became a guiding principle of ancient Greek education.

THE PRACTICE OF INTERSTATE ARBITRATION

I have argued so far that the ancient Greek society of states evolved a distinctive constitutional structure. The polis existed, Greeks believed, to facilitate a particular type of political life among elite male citizens, one marked by the reasoned pursuit of justice via speech and action. The prevailing conception of procedural justice, which prescribed the determination of right and wrong by means of public moral argument, flowed directly from this raison d'être. In "good" states, practical discourse was considered the source of justice. These values, I will now argue, not only shaped practices within the city-state but also those between city-states. The same norm of discursive justice that structured and legitimized jury courts and assemblies inside the polis also informed and licensed interstate arbitration, the core fundamental institution of the ancient Greek society of states. This is not to say, of course, that domestic and interstate institutions were identical, or that they functioned with the same degree of success. My point is simply that the architectural principles that animated institutional design and action domestically operated internationally as well. This normative symmetry, I suggest, explains why the ancient Greeks chose arbitration as the basic institutional mechanism for facilitating coexistence between city-states.

The ancient Greeks had good practical reasons to apply their conception of procedural justice beyond borders, and no ethical reasons not to. Their moral community was not narrowly defined by the boundaries of their particular city-states. To be a foreigner, someone who hails from another city, did not necessarily mean that one was morally outcast. *Xenos*, the ancient Greek term for foreigner, had the double meaning of "guest-friend" and "stranger." Xeni were to be treated with kindness and esteem, and there was no blanket assumption that they were outside the moral community.[35] The degree to which Greeks felt morally obliged to

---

during the fifth century B.C., and that the "cooperative" values of the just citizen never took root. The evidentiary basis of Adkin's claims have, however, been convincingly critiqued by J. L. Creed in "Moral Values in the Age of Thucydides."

[34] Jaeger, *Paedeia*, 102.

[35] Takabatake, "Idea of *Xenos* in Classical Athens," 450.

a person was less determined by the political boundaries of their city-state than by variable considerations such as the duration of a visitor's stay (the longer they stayed, the less kindly they were looked upon), the status of a visitor's home state (whether they were currently on friendly or hostile terms), and whether the visitor was a "citizen" of a polis elsewhere (if not, they would be denied appropriate respect and hospitality). As Bozeman observes, in general the Greeks found no essential reason not to extend their sense of justice to noncompatriots.[36] This sense of an extended moral community was reinforced by the concrete interrelationships that united the ancient Greek world. Shared religious sites (of which Delphi was the most celebrated), common festivals (most notably the Olympic games), the joint settlement and governance of colonies, and economic relationships all helped to undermine the exclusivity of particular city-states.

The fundamental institution of interstate arbitration brought together two, occasionally three, disputing parties and an arbitrator, the latter being charged with adjudicating the dispute and determining reparations, if deemed appropriate. Two brief examples testify to both the historical longevity of the practice and the range of issues it encompassed. Herodotus describes an early-fifth-century-B.C. dispute between Athens and Mytilene over the colony of Sigeum, which the former had seized from the latter and recolonized. He writes that the "war between Mytilene and Athens was brought to an end by Periander, who was invited by both parties to act as arbitrator; the condition that he proposed was that each state should retain what it at the moment possessed. In this way Sigeum passed into the power of Athens."[37] The second case, dated around 220 B.C., involved the regulation of a variety of relations between Knossos and Tylissus. The decision by Argos established rules governing property, calenders, sacrifices, and even "breaches of hospitality."[38] The practice of arbitration thus bridged the traumas of the Peloponnesian War, providing the primary mechanism for the settlement of a wide spectrum of issues between strong and weak states alike.

As argued above, the practice of arbitration was structured by the same discursive norm of pure procedural justice that informed legal institutions within the city-states. Arbitrators ruled without reference to a body of codified interstate law, the absence of which has long been recognized.[39] The city-states certainly concluded a large number of treaties, but these seldom enshrined general principles of international conduct. As Adcock

---

[36] Bozeman, *Politics and Culture*, 72.

[37] Herodotus, *Histories*, Book IV.93, 378.

[38] Niebuhr Tod, *International Arbitration*, 33–34.

[39] Adcock and Mosley, *Diplomacy in Ancient Greece*, 182; and Bauslaugh, *Neutrality in Classical Greece*, 36.

and Mosley observe, "It was rare for treaties to be contracted to counter some distant threat or remote contingency or to fulfil a general need for collective security."[40] The system of arbitration thus rested on the arbitrator's sense of justice, his ability to arrive at a fair and equitable decision through the deliberative assessment of competing moral claims. This was reflected in the oath that judges were required to swear before commencing deliberations. In a characteristic case between Calymma and Cos, the arbitrator swore "by Jupiter, by Lucian Apollo, and by the earth that I will judge the case joined between the parties under oath as will appear to me most just."[41] Given the responsibilities entailed, a reputation for moral excellence was the primary criterion in the selection of individuals, tribunals, or entire city-states as arbitrators. "High principle and fellow-feeling," Niebuhr Tod claims, "were requisite in the arbitrating state even more than power or wealth as such, and we hear only twice or three times of Sparta acting as arbiter, and Athens perhaps only twice."[42] As in domestic courts, arbitrators were not solely, or even primarily, concerned with the "facts" of the case, and admitted a broad range of testimony, from the moral rectitude of the parties to the considerations of equity. A "skillful pleader," Niebuhr Tod observes, "might influence a popular court by appeals which would be regarded at the present day as wholly irrelevant."[43]

Ancient Greek arbitration is best characterized, therefore, as authoritative trilateralism. It was "authoritative" because the power of decision lay solely with the arbitrator; it was "trilateral" because the arbitrator ruled within a dynamic normative environment, actively molded by the competing moral claims of the disputing parties. While it is difficult to generalize from the available evidence, especially when the universe of arbitral cases is unknown, it appears that this form of extraterritorial governance was quite successful. First, the institution of arbitration attained "normative universality," to borrow Jack Donnelly's term.[44] This does not mean that it was used by all states to settle all disputes all of the time, as the onset of the Peloponnesian War testifies. It seems, however, that city-states felt a powerful compulsion to prove the legitimacy of their claims by submitting them to arbitration, and strong and weak states frequently employed the practice instead of other forms of conflict resolution, including war. Second, as noted above, the ancient Greeks placed no apparent limit on the types of disputes they were willing to submit to arbitration. There was no quarantining of high politics or restriction of

---

[40] Adcock and Mosley, *Diplomacy in Ancient Greece*, 203.
[41] Raeder, *L'Arbitrage*, 264.
[42] Niebuhr Tod, *International Arbitration*, 96.
[43] Ibid., 132.
[44] Donnelly, *Universal Human Rights*, 1.

the institution to the margins of interstate relations. In fact, the majority of recorded cases concern the central issue of territorial sovereignty, a point I return to below.[45] Finally, the city-states not only felt obliged to submit their disputes to arbitration, they almost always abided by the arbitrators' decisions. The overwhelming majority of cases were settled by initial arbitration, and those that defied such resolution were almost always returned for a second round, not settled on the battlefield.[46] All told, the willingness of city-states to submit all manner of disputes to arbitral decision by no means eradicated violent conflict from the Greek system, but, as Niebuhr Tod observes, "arbitration did serve a valuable purpose, alike in averting war or armed reprisals between state and state, and in bringing to a speedier end conflicts which otherwise might have ended only with the destruction of one, or the exhaustion and ruin of both, of the belligerent powers."[47]

HEGEMONIC POWER, RATIONAL CHOICE, TERRITORIAL RIGHTS?

In preceding sections, I have argued that the moral purpose of the Greek city-state, and its associated norm of pure procedural justice, shaped interstate institutional design and action. As explained in chapter 1, this emphasis on the constitutive power of ideational structures runs against the grain of established explanations of international institutional formation, which stress hegemonic construction or rational choice. It also departs from the current constructivist emphasis on the principle of sovereignty and the stabilization of territorial property rights. My perspective on institutional construction is comparatively unparsimonious, focusing on less tangible and quantifiable variables than neorealists or neoliberals and positing a more complex international normative structure than other constructivists. What these perspectives gain in parsimony, however, they lose in explanatory insight. Without discounting their contribution to understanding other aspects of interstate relations, none can satisfactorily explain why arbitration became the favored institutional mechanism for governing relations between city-states.

Hegemony, for instance, tells us little about the nature of basic institutional practices in ancient Greece. To begin with, the institution of interstate arbitration was established long before the "era of hegemonic leagues" (479–379 B.C.), with cases dating back to seventh and sixth centuries B.C. Second, although many arbitrations that occurred during the hegemonic age involved conflicts between members of the same league,

---

[45] Westermann, "Interstate Arbitration in Antiquity," 199.
[46] Ibid., 208–209.
[47] Niebuhr Tod, *International Arbitration*, 190.

the institution does not appear to have been reduced simply to an instrument of imperial power. The practice undoubtedly contributed to the
internal stability of imperial leagues, thus serving hegemonic interests.
Hegemons seldom acted as arbitrators, though, and there is little evidence
to suggest that decisions were consistently slanted in their favor. If they
had been, the willingness of other states to submit to arbitration would
surely have waned, leading to the institution's steady erosion, which did
not occur. It is also important to recognize that in the hegemonic period
city-states still practiced arbitration across leagues.[48] Attempts at cross-
league arbitration clearly failed to resolve the conflicts that sparked the
Peloponnesian War, but in general such cases were no less successful than
intraleague arbitrations, and, as we shall see, the conflicts between Sparta
and Athens posed a unique challenge for the institution of arbitration.
Finally, the distribution of recorded cases indicates that the heyday of
ancient Greek arbitration occurred after, not during, the era of hegemonic
leagues. In sum, the power and interests of hegemons cannot account for
the rise or persistence of arbitration as the core fundamental institution
of the Greek society of states, even if dominant powers benefitted from
its stabilizing effects within and across their spheres of influence.

Rationalist approaches fare no better in explaining ancient Greek practices. According to neoliberals, states adopt the most efficient institutional
solutions to the cooperation problems they confront. We saw in chapter
1, however, that at a purely abstract level rationalist theory is indeterminate; as Martin demonstrates, when confronting problems of collaboration, coordination, suasion, or assurance, states can choose from a range
of equally efficient institutions.[49] Of course, Martin did not consider arbitration as an institutional solution, concentrating on modern practices
such as multilateralism. Had she done so, however, it is unlikely that
abstract rationalist theory could explain the primacy of arbitration in ancient Greece. If game-theoretic analysis revealed that arbitration was the
most efficient institutional solution to major cooperation problems, we
would have to explain its neglect in modern international society. If it
turned out to be as efficient as other practices, we would have to ask
why the Greek city-states favored it over others. And if it proved to be
suboptimal, the same question would arise, but would be even more
perplexing. Faced with such indeterminacy, rationalists could appeal to
structural factors, as Martin did in her efforts to explain post-1945 multilateralism.[50] The problem is that the practice of arbitration transcended
shifts in the balance of power, and under the same structural conditions
the Greek city-states engaged in different practices to their modern coun-

[48] Phillipson, *International Law and Custom, Volume Two*, 90.
[49] Martin, "Rational State Choice," 109.
[50] Ibid.

terparts. When Athens was a hegemon operating under conditions of bipolarity, the institution of arbitration continued. Its only experiment with
multilateralism—the short-lived Second Athenian Sea League (378
B.C.)—occurred some time after its defeat in the Peloponnesian War, when
these structural conditions had passed.[51]

Ancient Greek practices also confound existing constructivist accounts
of fundamental institutions. In the best developed of these, Ruggie argues
that the social identity of the state is defined by the principle of sovereignty, and that sovereign states have an inherent interest in stabilizing
territorial property rights. As we saw in chapter 1, he concludes that "[i]n-
stituting those little islands of alien sovereignty in the end required a multilateral solution, though differential arrangements based on the religious
preferences and social status of rulers were tried first."[52] Unfortunately,
this posited relationship between the principle of sovereignty, the identity
of the state, territoriality, and multilateralism is belied by the Greek practice of arbitration. Like their modern counterparts, the city-states were
sovereign, not only in the sense that they claimed rights to political independence and territorial jurisdiction, but also in the sense that these claims
were recognized as legitimate by the community of states.[53] The city-states
had a basic interest, therefore, in stabilizing territorial property rights, yet
the practice of multilateralism never took root. Instead, the Greeks used
interstate arbitration to regulate their holdings, with over 50 percent of
recorded cases involving the settlement of boundary disputes.[54] Only by
developing a more sophisticated understanding of the deep constitutive
values shaping state identity, and in turn institutional rationality, can we
explain this preference for authoritative trilateralism over multilateralism, a task undertaken in this book.

REREADING THUCYDIDES

If the preceding discussion is correct, then the Peloponnesian War—fought
between Athens, Sparta and their allies from 431 to 404 B.C.—occurred
within a society of states that had evolved a complex, and apparently
successful, system of third-party arbitration, one informed by a distinctive

---

[51] Sealey, *History of the Greek City-States*, 410–414.

[52] Ruggie, *Multilateralism Matters*, 16.

[53] As Wight observes, in modern international society the principle of sovereignty "has
been formulated in the doctrine of the legal equality of states. The Ancient Greek *poleis*
and the Hellenic Kingdoms, in a similar way, both claimed sovereignty and recognized one
another's." Wight, *Systems of States*, 23.

[54] I am not referring here to 50 percent of all known cases, but to 50 percent of those
cases where the matter in dispute has been recorded. I have used the cases recorded in Niebuhr Tod's *International Arbitration* as my source.

conception of the moral purpose of the state and norm of pure procedural justice. This fact, however, has had little effect on the way in which international relations scholars interpret Thucydides' *History*, despite the ancient historian's frequent references to the institution. To date, analyses have been guided by the paired assumptions that (a) the meaning of the *History* can be extracted from the text alone, and that (b) the text is the key to understanding the broader context of ancient Greek interstate relations, not the reverse. This analytical strategy has unfortunately led scholars into two traps. First, it encourages what Skinner calls a "mythology of doctrines," in which the core assumptions of contemporary international relations thought—such as the logic of anarchy—are conveniently located in Thucydides' text.[55] Second, these readings of the text are then translated into interpretations of the historical context in which it was written. Overall, as Skinner so eloquently puts it, history "becomes a pack of tricks we play on the dead."[56]

Thucydides in Context

The central task of explaining why arbitration became the principal fundamental institution of the ancient Greek society of states is now complete. In this final section, I depart from the major themes of the book to advance an alternative interpretation of Thucydides' *History*. Instead of treating the text as a self-sufficient source of meaning, I situate it within the context in which it was written. Thucydides wrote the *History* within a distinctive society of states, one characterized by historically contingent ideas about legitimate statehood and rightful state action, one regulated by particular institutions of coexistence. This affected his understanding of the Peloponnesian War and his thoughts about its significance for the system of city-states. Only by recognizing this, and reading the *History* in the light of what we know about the constitutional structure and institutional architecture of the Greek society of states, can we fully appreciate the ideas Thucydides sought to advance. This is not to advocate a form of situational determinism, but rather to treat context "as an ultimate framework for helping to decide what conventionally recognizable meanings, in a society of *that* kind, it might in principle have been possible for someone to have intended to communicate."[57] Such an approach allows us to weight certain elements in the *History* over others, in the hope of generating an interpretation that Thucydides could "accept as a correct description of what he had done."[58]

[55] Skinner, "Meaning and Understanding," 7.
[56] Ibid., 14.
[57] Ibid., 60.
[58] Ibid., 28.

Hegemony and Moral Authority

Reading the *History* in this way lends credence to Garst's thesis that Thucydides is ultimately concerned with the moral foundations of hegemonic power.[59] Realists have long stressed the centrality of hegemony in Thucydides account, but they have misrepresented how he understood such power, imposing their own materialist conception of hegemony on his thought. Thucydides recognizes the importance of military, economic, and technological capabilities, but contrary to prevailing interpretations he does not consider them a sufficient source of hegemonic power. "In Thucydides' history," Garst observes, "whether or not a state is hegemonic depends on the moral authority it is able to wield."[60] Such authority must be grounded in preexisting social norms about legitimate statehood and international action: "Attributions of power are conditional: that is, they do not necessarily follow from possession of physical resources or observable changes in the behavior of actors but are instead tied to intersubjectively defined social conventions and the institutions associated with them that delimit the conditions under which political power is held and exercised."[61] From this perspective, the rise and decline of hegemons is only partially related to shifts in the distribution of material capabilities. Since hegemony depends on authority, changes in the moral standing of dominant states is crucial, and "the establishment and maintenance of hegemony is an essentially open-ended process that requires continual activity in the form of persuasion and negotiation."[62]

Through a complex mixture of historical narrative punctuated by speeches, debates and dialogues, Thucydides recounts the steady erosion of Athens' moral authority and in turn its hegemonic power. Athens' moral standing rested on its claim to be the ultimate embodiment of the moral purpose of the ancient Greek state and its assertion that its empire was consistent with the normative ideals of the society of states. In the period preceding the Peloponnesian War, there was no appreciable change in the military balance between Athens and Sparta. Athens' military capacity remained static, it made no new imperial acquisitions, and the Spartans were satisfied with their adversary's observance of the Thirty Years' Peace.[63] Thucydides points to three conditions, however, that together undermined the legitimacy of Athenian power and ultimately led to war. First, Athens took a number of initiatives that aggrieved Sparta's

---

[59] Garst, "Thucydides and Neorealism."

[60] Ibid., 22.

[61] Ibid., 20.

[62] Ibid., 23.

[63] Kagan, *Outbreak of the Peloponnesian War*, 345–346.

junior allies, the most important being its siege of Potidaea and the decree preventing Megarian access to the ports of its empire. In themselves, these acts were insufficient to spark a hegemonic war, but they provided focal points for attacks on the Athenians' character and motives. Second, Sparta's junior allies had access to a public forum that enabled them to air their grievances. Empowered to speak before the Spartan Assembly, they were able to cast their particular concerns as universal and to chisel away at Athens' moral standing. Finally, as Lebow observes, the lack of any clear separation between this forum and the Spartan decision-making structure gave disgruntled allies disproportionate influence and allowed a shift in opinion against Athens to be translated all too easily into a declaration of war.[64]

Debates, Speeches, Dialogues

Thucydides carefully structured the dialogues and speeches of the *History* to illustrate the gradual breakdown, first, of Athens' external moral authority and, second, of its own moral consciousness. Four of these moments are particularly important: the initial Debate at Sparta, where Athens unsuccessfully defends the morality of its empire; Pericles' Speech to the Athenians, in which he upholds the moral foundations of their rule and the need to conduct a just war; the Mytilenian Debate, where the Athenians are divided over whether coercion or justice will more securely guarantee their empire; and the infamous Melian Dialogue, where real politik finally consumes the Athenians and the voice of justice is left to the ill-fated Melians. As we shall see, Thucydides uses the final act of his *History*—the disastrous Sicilian Expedition—to hammer home the moral of his story. Throughout the text, the practice of arbitration appears as an important leitmotif, with states measuring the righteousness of their positions, and the moral bankruptcy of their opponents', according to their willingness, or reluctance, to use the institution.

The Debate at Sparta is characterized by Corinth's successful efforts to portray the siege at Potidaea and the Megarian Decree as evidence of the moral decline of Athenian rule and by the Athenian representatives' corresponding failure to resuscitate the city's flagging moral authority. The Corinthian speech opens with a savage attack on Athenian actions, followed by lengthy criticism of Sparta for its conservative reluctance to act in defence of its allies. The Athenian self-defence, however, begins the most important phase of the debate. The city-state's representatives commence by emphasizing the consensual basis of Athens' imperial rule:

[64] Lebow, "Power Transition Theory," 152–153.

"We did not gain this empire by force. It came to us at a time when you were unwilling to fight on to the end against the Persians. At this time our allies came to us of their own accord and begged us to lead them."[65] It is important to note, however, that the Athenians make no attempt to deny the degree to which the empire serves the city's interests: "We have done nothing extraordinary, nothing contrary to human nature in accepting an empire when it was offered to us and then in refusing to give it up. Three powerful motives prevented us from doing so—security, honour, and self-interest."[66] Nevertheless, the crux of the Athenian defence focuses on the justice of the empire, and thus its uniqueness and worth: "Those who really deserve praise are the people who, while human enough to enjoy power, nevertheless pay more attention to justice than they are compelled to do by their situation. Certainly we think that if anyone else was in our position it would soon be evident whether we act with moderation or not."[67]

The Athenians conclude the city-state's defence by expressing a willingness to settle the outstanding disputes through arbitration—as specified under the Thirty Years' Peace treaty—thus aligning themselves with the foundational normative principles of the society of states.[68] The receptive response by the Spartan King Archidamus indicates the moral force of the Athenian strategy: "As for the Athenians, I advise sending a mission to them about Potidaea and also about the other cases where our allies claim to have been ill treated. Especially is this the right thing to do since the Athenians themselves are prepared to submit to arbitration, and when one party offers this it is quite illegal to attack him first, as though he was definitely in the wrong."[69] Unfortunately, opinion had already turned against Athens, and Archidamus's plea falls on deaf ears. Interestingly, though, Athens' prior moral worth is not denied in the final call to war, instead it is turned against it. Sthenelaidis convinces the majority of the assembly that the Athenians deserve to be punished twofold, for "though they were once good, they have now turned bad."[70]

---

[65] Thucydides, *History of the Peloponnesian War*, Book I.75, 79–80.

[66] Ibid., Book I.76, 80.

[67] They go on to argue that "unreasonably enough, our very consideration for others has brought us more blame than praise. For example, in law-suits with our allies arising out of contracts we have put ourselves at a disadvantage, and when we arrange to have such cases tried by impartial courts in Athens, people merely say that we are overfond of going to law. No one bothers to inquire why this reproach is not made against other imperial Powers, who treat their subjects much more harshly than we do." Ibid., Book I.76–77, 80–81.

[68] Ibid., Book I.85, 82.

[69] Ibid.

[70] Ibid., Book I.86, 86.

We now turn to Pericles' speech to the Athenians on the eve of the war, just after the final Spartan ultimatum for Athens to abandon the siege at Potidaea and revoke the Megarian Decree. Most of the speech is devoted to bolstering the citizens' resolve by celebrating their superior military resources and prowess. However, two features of the speech contrast markedly with later Athenian oratory and debate. First, with Athens' external moral authority fractured, Pericles tries to maintain Athenian unity and support for his decision not to give in to the Spartan ultimatum by emphasizing the justice of the Athenian position. Once again, its continued willingness to go to arbitration, and the Spartan refusal to do so, is invoked as evidence of their moral righteousness:

> It is laid down in the treaty that differences between us should be settled by arbitration, and that, pending arbitration, each side should keep what it has. The Spartans have never once asked for arbitration, nor have they accepted our offers to submit to it. They prefer to settle their complaints by war rather than by peaceful negotiations, and now they come here not even making protests, but trying to give us orders. . . . When one's equals, before resorting to arbitration, make claims on their neighbors and put those claims in the form of commands, it would still be slavish to give in to them, however big or however small such claims may be.[71]

Second, both for strategic reasons and to ensure that Athens retained the high moral ground in the forthcoming war, Pericles cautions Athenians "not to add to the empire while the war is in progress, and not to go out of your way to involve yourselves in new perils."[72] As we shall see, these emphases on the morality of Athens' stance and on fighting only a just, defensive campaign gradually dissipate as the war proceeds.

The Mytilenian Debate represents the initial fracturing of Athenian moral consciousness. The debate concerns how to punish the Mytilenians, who in 428 B.C. revolted against Athenian rule and aligned with Sparta. The island was later subdued by the Athenians, who, under Cleon's leadership, promptly decided to murder the entire adult male population and sell the women and children into slavery. After sending a ship to carry out the massacre, the Athenians had a change of heart and called an assembly to debate the death sentence. Thucydides writes that "there was a sudden change of feeling and people began to think how cruel and how unprecedented such a decision was."[73] In the subsequent debate, Cleon implores the Athenians to go through with their severe punishment of the Mytilenians, basing his argument on the absolute incompatibility of imperial

---

[71] Ibid., Book I.140, 119.
[72] Ibid., Book I.144, 122.
[73] Ibid., Book III.36, 212.

power and justice: "What you do not realize is that your empire is a tyranny exercised over subjects who do not like it and who are always plotting against you; you will not make them obey you by injuring your own interests in order to do them a favour. . . . To feel pity, to be carried away by the pleasure of hearing a clever argument, to listen to the claims of decency are three things that are entirely against the interests of an imperial power."[74] In response to these claims, Diodotus reaffirms the link between stable hegemonic power and moral authority:

> Our business, therefore, is not to injure ourselves by acting like a judge who strictly examines a criminal; instead we should look for a method by which, employing moderation in our punishments, we can in future secure ourselves the full use of those cities which bring us important contributions. And we should recognize that the proper basis of our security is in good administration rather than the fear of legal penalties. . . . [T]he right way to deal with free people is this—not to inflict tremendous punishments on them after they have revolted, but to take tremendous care of them before this point is reached, to prevent them even contemplating the idea of revolt.[75]

The arguments raised here are significant because the Athenians no longer speak with a single voice, nor assume a necessary coincidence between imperial rule and moral standing. The previous moral consensus is gone and the eventual decision to overturn the death sentence is highly contingent. Fortunately, a second ship reached Mytilene just in time to prevent the massacre.

Twelve years later the Melians were not so lucky. In 416 B.C. Athens sent a force to invade the island of Melos, which had refused to join the empire and tried to remain neutral during the war, despite the fact that it was a Spartan colony.[76] Athens dispatched representatives to negotiate with the Melians before invading, and their speech has become one of the most infamous expressions of the principle that might makes right: "Then we on our side will use no fine phrases saying, for example, that we have a right to our empire because we defeated the Persians, or that we come against you now because of the injuries you have done us—a great mass of words that nobody would believe. . . . [T]he standard of justice depends on the equality of power to compel and that in fact the strong do what they have the power to do and the weak accept what they have to accept."[77] By this time the Athenians have lost all pretence of morality,

---

[74] Ibid., Book III.37–40, 213.
[75] Ibid., Book III.46, 221.
[76] Ibid., Book V.84, 400.
[77] Ibid., Book V.89, 401–402.

no longer even debating its merits with one another. The Melians futilely try to convince the Athenians that upholding the practice of justice and fair play is in their interests: "Then in our view . . . it is at any rate useful that you should not destroy a principle that is to the general good of all men—namely, that in the case of all who fall into danger there should be such a thing as fair play and just dealing. . . . And this is a principle which affects you as much as anybody, since your own fall would be visited by the most terrible vengeance and would be an example to the world."[78] The Athenians pay no heed and proceed to massacre the adult males and sell the women and children into slavery. This tragedy marks a crucial watershed in Thucydides' account of the war. Athenian domination is now based solely on coercion, losing sight of the fact that stable rule depends on moral authority.

Thucydides' final move is to hammer home the tragic consequences of such naked power, endowing the Melian claim that Athens "would be visited by the most terrible vengeance" with sobering prescience. Intoxicated with its own power, and ignoring Pericles' earlier caution not to turn the war into a grab for new territory, Athens embarks on an ambitious invasion of Sicily.[79] Its defeat is completely devastating: "This was the greatest Hellenic action that took place during this war, and . . . the greatest action that we know of in Hellenic history—to the victors the brilliant successes, to the vanquished the most calamitous of defeats; for they were utterly and entirely defeated; their sufferings were on an enormous scale; their losses were . . . total; army, navy, everything was destroyed, and out of many, only few returned."[80]

CONCLUSION

I have sought in this chapter to highlight and understand a neglected dimension of ancient Greek interstate relations—the dimension of institutional cooperation. The city-states were not in a constant war of all against all, even if violent conflict was a recurring problem. Like modern states, they established a network of institutions to facilitate cooperation. They did not, however, develop the institutions characteristic of modern international society: contractual international law and multilateralism never evolved. Instead, they favored the practice of third-party arbitration, using it to solve a wide range of cooperation problems, most notably the stabili-

---

[78] Ibid., Book V.90, 402.
[79] Ibid., Books VI, VII, 409–537.
[80] Ibid., Book VII.87, 536–537.

zation of territorial property rights. This institutional preference, I have argued, stemmed from the distinctive constitutional structure of the ancient Greek society of states. The Greeks believed that the city-state existed to facilitate a particular form of communal life, marked by the rational pursuit of justice through action and speech, at least among the elite male citizens liberated from toil by slave labor. This moral purpose informed a discursive norm of pure procedural justice, a norm that licensed the determination of right and wrong through a process of public debate and deliberation, a norm not only embodied in domestic assemblies and jury courts but also in the practice of interstate arbitration. The available evidence supports this explanation of ancient Greek institutional preferences, and alternative accounts fail in comparison. The final test, however, is counterfactual. If the ancient Greeks had not imagined the state as they did, and not embraced a discursive conception of procedural justice, then there is little reason to believe that arbitration would have emerged as the core fundamental institution. And if such a connection had not existed between principles of legitimate statehood and arbitration, it is unlikely that the latter would have appeared as such important leitmotif in Thucydides' *History*.

CHAPTER FOUR

Renaissance Italy

For it is in the words themselves which give an
oration its greatness and magnificence, provided
that the orator employs good judgement and
care, knows how to choose those which best
express what he means, and how to enhance
them, shaping them to his purpose like wax
and arranging them in relation to one another so
that their clarity and worth are immediately evident, as if they were paintings hung in good and
natural light.
—Baldesar Castiglione,
The Book of the Courtier, 1528

UNLIKE those of ancient Greece, the city-states of Renaissance Italy
formed a coherent society of sovereign states for a relatively short time.
Until the second half of the fourteenth century, the Italian cities were
deeply enmeshed in the political and legal structures of medieval Europe.
Despite the economic power they reaped from the thirteenth-century commercial revolution, their independence was circumscribed by the political
and military machinations of the Holy Roman Empire and the Papacy.
This was compounded by, and reflected in, their lack of legal authority.
From the time of Charlemagne, German emperors claimed jurisdiction
over the northern Italian cities—*Regnum Italicum*—and were willing and
able to use military force to assert this claim well into the fourteenth
century. The cities were also caught in the web of ecclesiastical law, which
the Church used to control many aspects of Italian social, intellectual,
and political life. Only at the beginning of the fourteenth century did
Bartolus of Saxoferrato and Marsiglio of Padua formulate coherent legal
defences of the city-states' sovereignty.[1] It was not, however, until the end
of that century, when the emperor's declining power, the continuing dis-
tractions of the Hundred Years War, and the papal schism left northern
Italy relatively isolated, that the new legal doctrines were given practical
effect. The resulting society of sovereign states reached its highpoint dur-

---

[1] For a discussion of these changes in legal thought, see Skinner, *Foundations*, 3–22.

ing the fifteenth century, evolving a distinctive constitutional structure and framework of institutional cooperation. All of this began to crumble after 1498 with the onset of the Italian Wars, when the city-states were overrun by successive invasions from the north.

Although short-lived, the Italian society of states is renowned in the history of international relations for institutional innovation. The city-states enacted a novel institutional practice, which I shall term *oratorical diplomacy*. As part of this practice, they engaged in the first regularized exchange of resident ambassadors, earning them a prominent place in conventional genealogies of diplomacy. Despite this general recognition, however, diplomatic historians have reached radically different conclusions about the nature and significance of Italian diplomacy. There are those who see it as a distinctly modern institutional form, the progenitor of contemporary diplomatic practice. Renaissance diplomacy is upheld as a rational response to anarchy, "the functional expression of a new kind of state."[2] This view is directly at odds with a second interpretation, which emphasizes the irrationality of Italian practices. Far from functional, Renaissance diplomacy is decried for its florid, ornate, and extravagant character, an institution encumbered by "an abominable filigree of artifice."[3] We are thus faced with two contradictory images of Italian diplomacy, the first treating it as modern and rational, the second as "oriental" and irrational.

This chapter presents an alternative interpretation of Renaissance diplomacy, in which I seek to move beyond the polarized characterizations that currently prevail. My approach, as elsewhere in the book, is to treat institutional rationality as culturally contingent. Historically specific beliefs about legitimate statehood and rightful state action determine the institutional solutions that states deem appropriate, with institutional choices varying from one society of states to another. The Italian society of states developed a distinctive constitutional structure, in which the moral purpose of the state was linked to the pursuit of civic glory and procedural justice was intimately connected with social ritual. It was these deep constitutive values, I contend, that informed the practice of oratorical diplomacy. In addition to explaining why this fundamental institution took root in Renaissance Italy, this approach has two strengths over existing perspectives. To begin with, it respects the agency of Renaissance leaders, recognizing that they believed oratorical diplomacy to be a fitting institutional response to the environmental challenges they encountered. It also fully acknowledges the affected and ornamental character of Renaissance diplomacy. Once we acknowledge the cultural contingency of institu-

---

[2] Mattingly, *Renaissance Diplomacy*, 55.
[3] Nicolson, *Evolution of Diplomatic Method*, 24.

tional rationality, we no longer face the invidious choice of crediting only those aspects of Renaissance diplomacy that anticipate the modern or dismissing the whole practice as dysfunctional.

My argument evolves through several stages. After briefly surveying the emergence and development of the Italian society of states, I examine the contradictory images of Renaissance diplomacy found in existing accounts, identifying their relative strengths and weaknesses. I then turn to the constitutional structure of the Italian society of states, explaining the complex connections between civic glory, unity, and ritual justice. The next two sections show how these values shaped the practice of oratorical diplomacy and how this institution affected the balance of power between the city-states in the latter half of the fifteenth century. I conclude with a reformulation of Daniel Waley's classic statement that the Italian city-states "proved a dead end rather than the direct antecedent of the nation-state."[4]

THE ITALIAN CITY-STATES

The long and turbulent development of a system of sovereign city-states in northern Italy began in the latter half of the eleventh century, when the local nobility wrested political power from bishops, viscounts, and marquises, instituting the earliest forms of communal rule.[5] The consular governments they established were soon beset, however, with growing social unrest, frequently lapsing into civil war. During the twelfth century, the populations of the Italian cities multiplied, and their commercial economies boomed. This not only spurred divisions within the nobility, leading to the formation of warring *consorteria*, it encouraged the development of merchant guilds—the first popular associations. In city after city the nobility fought with itself and with the emerging middle classes, spreading urban conflict and crisis across Italy. To contain the conflict, the nobility was forced to institute a new form of executive government, in which a nobleman from another city was elected as chief magistrate, or *podesta*, for a six-month term, charged with quelling civil disorder and dispensing justice.[6] Although adopted by virtually all of the Italian cities, podestaral rule failed to deliver social harmony, as it became a site for aristocratic competition and never satisfied the aspirations of the *popolo*. Between 1197 and 1257, the largely middle-class popolo engaged in increasingly violent agitation, eventually seizing power in all of the major

[4] Waley, *Italian City-Republics*, xi.
[5] Martines, *Power and Imagination*, 7–21.
[6] Ibid., 34–44.

Italian cities. The ensuing era of "popular communes" spawned ideas and practices that had an important impact on subsequent forms of city-state governance, but a confluence of social forces brought yet another wave of constitutional change, this time in the middle of the fourteenth century.[7] Driven by war and economic need, conflict between political parties, party alliances across cities, and the continued machinations of the aristocracy, political power became concentrated in fewer and fewer hands, with some states, like Milan, yielding to a single ruler, or *signore*, and others, such as Florence, establishing republican oligarchies.[8]

It was these signorial and republican regimes that together instituted the practice of oratorical diplomacy in the middle of the fifteenth century. Signories and republican oligarchies differed in important respects, with the latter offering elites greater participation in decision-making and wider, more formalized access to offices of state. This having been said, however, the differences were not as great as those separating contemporary authoritarian regimes from liberal democracies. In fact, the similarities between the signorial and republican systems of rule are as striking as the differences. The despots who came to power in the latter half of the fourteenth century generally maintained, and worked within, the broad framework of institutions and values established in the previous era of communal rule. In the quest for legitimacy, Martines observes, "the astute *signore* tended to leash his authority. If nothing else, he observed legal forms. . . . He had to pay lip service to practices that he probably disdained, but that lip service helped to make his situation more tolerable."[9] For their part, the republican oligarchies were far from democratic. In Venice, a small group of families, constituting only 4 percent of the population, monopolized public offices; and in Florence a similar situation prevailed, with only certain families allowed access to public positions, and an even smaller number exercising effective power.[10] In sum, Peter Burke writes, "Republics in practice were not ruled by everyone, and similarly, principalities were not ruled by one man alone."[11]

In addition to these convergent characteristics, signorial and republican states were embedded in a common set of social structures, most notably the institution of patronage. The relationship between the state and patronage is central to my argument, and I return to it in greater detail below. Here it is sufficient to note that formal government in the Italian city-states—princely and republican—operated within a complex network of extended familial relations and patron-client ties. In reference to

[7] Ibid., 45–71.
[8] Ibid., 97.
[9] Ibid., 103.
[10] Burke, *Culture and Society*, 222–223.
[11] Ibid., 223.

fifteenth-century Florence, Richard Trexler argues that government "can best be conceived as a fraternity of fathers, each man representing his clientele before those brothers, the cement of government being furnished by the trust through obligations generated below the level of formal government. Government could function only as long as it permitted the defense of these patronal and client interests."[12] This connection between politics and patronage was not unique to Florence; it was an inherent characteristic of Renaissance social life, not only evident in other republics but also structuring political practices in the leading princely states.[13] As we shall see, the patronage system had a profound influence on the identity of the Renaissance city-state and on the norms of procedural justice that informed the institution of oratorical diplomacy. This influence was both negative and positive, with patronage relations contributing to factionalism, posing a number of practical imperatives for the state, and with the values of the patronage system helping to define the moral purpose of the sovereign city-state and prevailing ideas of ritual justice.

IMAGES OF RENAISSANCE DIPLOMACY

The Italian society of states occupies a special place in conventional diplomatic history, being celebrated for instituting the first systematic exchange of resident ambassadors. "In the history of diplomacy," J. R. Hale argues, "a definite change occurs in this period."[14] The city-states of the Italian Renaissance, Adam Watson writes, "made a seminal contribution to the development of the diplomatic dialogue, one of the major integrating mechanisms of the European system."[15] And Garrett Mattingly asserts, in his classic study, that "permanent diplomacy was one of the creations of the Italian Renaissance."[16] There is general agreement, therefore, that Renaissance Italy was an important site of interstate institutional innovation. Scholars are divided, however, over the nature and significance of this innovation.

From one perspective, Renaissance diplomacy is portrayed as a rational response to anarchy, an inevitable consequence of the emergence of a system of sovereign states. This structural-functionalist logic is presented succinctly in Mattingly's *Renaissance Diplomacy*. The "immediate result of the absence of severe outside pressures," he argues, "was to set the

[12] Trexler, *Public Life in Renaissance Florence*, 30.

[13] See Gundersheimer, *Style of Renaissance Despotism*; and Jones, "Communes and Despots."

[14] Hale, "International Relations in the West," 265.

[15] Watson, *Evolution of International Society*, 159.

[16] Mattingly, *Renaissance Diplomacy*, 55.

states of Italy free for their competitive struggle with one another, and so to intensify their awareness of the structure and tensions of their own peninsular system. Mainly it was these tensions that produced the new style of diplomacy."[17] Employing the same logic, Keith Hamilton and Richard Langhorne claim that Renaissance diplomacy was "the consequence of political and structural changes which led to the gradual growth of the sovereign state in place of the medieval order, and thus greatly increased the number of entities which needed to relate to each other diplomatically."[18] Adopting a less structural, though equally functionalist, position, Hale contends that the "more swiftly armies could be mobilised, the better organized had the information services of the threatened state to be; as foreign policy became more complicated, more comprehensive, more subject to sudden change, each country, especially the weak, needed to be kept in touch with the intentions of the others. This could only be done by keeping permanent embassies at their courts."[19] For each of these authors, Renaissance diplomacy was, in Mattingly's words, "a functional expression of a new kind of state," a rational-bureaucratic institution, the precursor of modern diplomatic practice.

This perspective sits uncomfortably with a second interpretation of Renaissance diplomacy, one that stresses the irrational, highly ritualized, ornamental, and premodern character of Italian practices. According to Sir Harold Nicolson, one of the doyens of diplomatic history, Renaissance diplomacy "was an intricate and unreasonable pattern; it was a pattern that ignored the practical purpose of true negotiations, and introduced an abominable filigree of artifice into what ought to be a simple machine."[20] Contradicting his earlier remarks about the institution's rationality—its functional suitability to prevailing structural circumstances—Hale writes that in "many ways Renaissance diplomacy was obtuse and irrational. It must not be forgotten that in the world of Guicciardini and Ferdinand the Catholic *naïveté* still played its part."[21] The general tendency is to attribute such irrationality to the undesirable influence of "oriental" thought on interstate practices. For instance, Nicolson claims that it "was a misfortune that this art . . . came to Europe, neither illuminated by Athenian intelligence, nor dignified by Roman seriousness, but falsified and discredited by the practices of oriental Courts."[22] From this perspective, Renaissance diplomacy was the antithesis of modern diplomatic

---

[17] Ibid., 61.
[18] Hamilton and Langhorne, *Practice of Diplomacy*, 30.
[19] Hale, "International Relations in the West," 265.
[20] Nicolson, *Evolution of Diplomatic Method*, 24.
[21] Hale, "International Relations in the West," 275.
[22] Nicolson, *Evolution of Diplomatic Method*, 24.

practice; it was public not private, personalized not detached, affected not efficient, demonstrative not deliberative, ritualized not technocratic.

Both of these interpretations have strengths and weaknesses. The view that Renaissance diplomacy was a rational response to anarchy rightly acknowledges the agency of the Italian city-states. When they instituted the practice of oratorical diplomacy, Renaissance elites were indeed responding to the environmental challenges they encountered in a manner they deemed most appropriate. The problem, however, is that institutional rationality is understood here in distinctly modern terms, forcing diplomatic historians to downplay, or ignore, those aspects of Renaissance diplomacy inconsistent with modern practices. The fact that fifteenth-century diplomacy was highly ritualized and rhetorical features little in such accounts. This view is also undermined by the failure of other societies of sovereign states to develop interstate practices akin to those of the Renaissance. As we saw in the previous chapter, the ancient Greeks confronted the challenges of systemic anarchy as well, yet they developed altogether different institutional practices.[23] The principal virtue of the second interpretation is that it emphasizes the actual nature of Renaissance diplomacy, its ornamental and affected character. Renaissance diplomacy was not a modern institution, as we would recognize it. It exhibited characteristics that indeed seem irrationally ornate by today's standards. The problem with this view, though, is that it diminishes the agency of Italian political elites, casting them as indulgent peacocks, beguiled by oriental extravagances.

In what follows, I develop an explanation of Renaissance diplomacy that seeks to overcome the weaknesses of existing perspectives while building on their relative strengths. My approach, elaborated in previous chapters, treats institutional rationality as a culturally and historically contingent form of consciousness, the product of context-specific, intersubjective beliefs about legitimate agency and right conduct. The Italian society of states evolved a distinctive constitutional structure, characterized by unique conceptions of the moral purpose of the state and pure procedural justice. These beliefs had a profound influence on institutional practices, both within and between city-states. This approach not only provides a better explanation of the nature and genesis of Renaissance diplomacy, placing its ritualized character to the fore, it respects the agency of the Italian city-states, acknowledging their struggle to achieve survival, coexistence, and cooperation using available cultural resources, resources that rendered their institutional practices meaningful and comprehensible.

---

[23] Curiously, Hamilton and Langhorne make precisely this point, observing that the city-states of ancient Greece encountered precisely the same structural imperatives, yet they

THE CONSTITUTIONAL STRUCTURE OF RENAISSANCE ITALY

State formation in Italy took place within a distinctive social context. The creation of small islands of centralized, autonomous political authority—sovereign city-states—required not only the coercive capacities to establish and defend such rule but also legitimacy, the sense that organizing power and authority in this manner was "right." The forging of a coherent social identity, or raison d'être, for the city-state was central to such legitimacy. Without a moral purpose grounded in the belief structures of both domestic society and the society of states, the sovereignty of the city-state would remain precarious, reliant solely on available military and policing resources. In the late medieval world, the carving out of such an identity was problematic, however. Transcommunal and subcommunal loci of identification also provided powerful magnets for human loyalty. Transcommunally, the Catholic Church and the Holy Roman Empire drew devotion and fealty beyond the city-state; subcommunally, the institution of patronage drew fidelity and attachment below. By the beginning of the fifteenth century, the latter posed the greatest challenge to the legitimacy of the city-state, molding the state's social identity in distinctive ways. Not only were the papacy and the empire less capable of wielding influence on the peninsula at this time, the gradual collapse of old, guild-based corporate structures, which had provided an important focus of individual identification, and the general move to princely and oligarchic rule, reinforced the institution of patronage, leading to a proliferation of patron-client relations.[24]

Patronage and Ritual

In recent years, Renaissance historians have used the concept of patronage to illuminate many aspects of Italian social life, from republican politics to the legitimation of scientific knowledge.[25] In essence, a patronage system is a network of interconnected, unsymmetrical power relationships that bind patrons and clients in a web of mutual obligations, established and maintained through rhetorical speech and ritual gesture. Patron-

---

never ask why the Greeks should have failed to adopt the institutional practices that subsequently developed in the renaissance. Hamilton and Langhorne, *Practice of Diplomacy*, 31.

[24] Najemy, "Guild Republicanism"; and Brucker, *Renaissance Florence*, 97–98.

[25] See, for example, Kent and Simons, eds., *Patronage, Art, and Society*; Kent, *Household and Lineage*; Brucker, *Civic World*; Weissman, *Ritual Brotherhood*; Trexler, *Public Life in Renaissance Florence*; and Biagioli, *Galileo Courtier*.

client relationships, Ronald Weissman argues, have five distinguishing characteristics:

1. There exists an inequality of power or resources between patron and client.

2. Patronage is a long-term relationship, having a moral or social rather than a legal basis.

3. A patronage system is not restricted to a single kind of transaction. It is multistranded and multipurpose.

4. Patronage is a relationship in which the patron provides more than simple protection. He provides brokerage, mediation, favors, and access to networks of friends of friends.

5. Mediterranean patronage has a distinctive ethos, standing outside the officially proclaimed social morality.[26]

Italian society of the Renaissance is rightly considered a patronage society, in the sense that patronage assumed a "prominent or dominant position, to the detriment of other principles of social organisation."[27] As Mario Biagioli observes, participation in the patronage system was not optional: "Patronage was a voluntary activity only in the narrow sense that by not engaging in it one would commit social suicide."[28]

Patronage clearly had a material dimension, as well as material consequences. Patrons and clients usually had unequal material resources, and material gain was an important motive for both parties, even if honor, status, and influence constituted more transcendent objectives. In essence, however, patronage was a moral system.[29] It was a practice that rested on a set of intersubjective beliefs that permeated and structured Renaissance society, beliefs about how social relations ought to be conducted, about how relationships should be established, defined, and maintained, and about how power and authority should be distributed. To paraphrase J. Boissevain, Renaissance patronage was a "system of belief and action grounded in society's value system."[30] It was a moral system in another sense as well. The bond between patron and client was sustained not by threat and coercion but by mutual obligation, by ties of loyalty and honor. Once a patronage relationship had been established, both patrons and clients assumed obligations, and to violate these obligations was to transgress an entrenched moral code and to court dishonor. Finally, patronage relationships were cultivated and maintained through an elaborate set of

---

[26] Weissman, "Taking Patronage Seriously," 25–26.

[27] Gellner, "Patrons and Clients," 4.

[28] Biagioli, *Galileo Courtier*, 16.

[29] Kent and Simmons, "Renaissance Patronage," 11; Weissman, "Taking Patronage Seriously," 33, 43; and Gellner, "Patrons and Clients," 3.

[30] Boissevain, "Patronage in Sicily," 60.

social rituals, rituals that were grounded in beliefs about rightful social conduct and appropriate modes of cooperation and exchange.

To speak of patronage as a system is somewhat of misnomer, for it is more correctly understood as a process.[31] The institution and renewal of patron-client relations was ongoing, involving constant negotiation and renegotiation. Patrons had to be courted, clients received. The principal currency in this process was honor, the Renaissance measure of individual worth. As Weissman observes, the "basic components of honor related directly to the maintenance of good patron-client relationships. Honor's first component was the proper expression of generosity and gratitude as a client, the reciprocation of favors and the demonstration of loyalty to friends and patrons. Its second component involved the potential to be a patron, that is, the control and possession of a personal network, which was a necessary condition for extending aid and repaying favors."[32] The establishment and maintenance of patronage relationships required that prospective clients demonstrate their personal honor while extolling the renowned virtues of their intended patron, and that patrons express their honor through appropriate forms of rejection or acceptance. This entire process was highly ritualized. Each approach and response was ceremonial, consisting of conventional rhetorical tropes and gestural moves.[33] Ritual communication routinized anxiety-laden social interactions, and defined and codified power relations within Renaissance society. Language and gesture in turn became valuable power resources, with clever rhetoric and artful gesture enhancing personal reputations, increasing patronal authority and influence.

Much has been made of the gap between the values undergirding Renaissance patronage and those of civic humanism. The former were inherently hierarchical, partial, and encouraged particularistic ties among individuals; the latter were egalitarian, impartial, and celebrated civic duty, communal service, and political participation. There is general agreement that civic humanism constituted the official ideology of the political elite in fifteenth-century Italy, with noted humanists occupying high office in leading republics and serving as courtiers in major principalities. Scholars are divided, however, over how deep humanist values cut, over whether they had any real influence on Renaissance social and political practices.[34] Some have gone so far as to suggest that the high social

---

[31] Simons, "Patronage in the Tornaquinci Chapel."

[32] Weissman, *Ritual Brotherhood*, 26.

[33] For detailed analyses of the relationship between patronage and ritual communication, see Trexler, *Public Life in Renaissance Florence*, 131–158; and Biagioli, *Galileo Courtier*.

[34] The most prominent work to stress the influence of civic humanism is Baron, *Crisis of the Early Italian Renaissance*. For the alternative viewpoint, see Martines, *Lawyers and Statecraft*; and *Social World of the Florentine Humanists*.

position enjoyed by prominent humanists had more to do with their successful exploitation of the patronage system than the practical application of their own civic values.[35] This debate is both interesting and important, but for our purposes it distracts attention from a significant point of convergence between the two ethical systems. Just as patronage practices encouraged ritualized forms of communication and interaction, so too did civic humanism. The humanists of the fifteenth century championed the art of rhetoric, the capacity of the orator to mold words, "shaping them to his purpose like wax and arranging them in relation to one another so well that their clarity and worth are immediately evident, as if they were paintings hung in good and natural light."[36] The study of rhetoric became one of the three main components of the *studia humanitatas*, the civic humanist education curriculum in which most of Italy's social and political elite were schooled.[37] The centrality of rhetoric and gesture as the orientating modes of social interaction was sanctioned and reinforced, therefore, by both the "low" morality of the patronage system and the "high" morality of humanism, however divergent these ethics might have been otherwise.

The Moral Purpose of the Italian City-State

Within this ideological milieu, Italians formulated a distinctive conception of the moral purpose of the state, a uniquely Renaissance rationale for sovereignty. From the middle of the thirteenth century until the beginning of the sixteenth, the pursuit of civic glory, or *grandezza*, was celebrated as the city-state's primary raison d'être. Peace and justice were exulted as well, but always in the service of a higher good—communal greatness, a standing based as much on civic honor and cultural achievement as on military capacity and wealth. The *Oculus Pastoralis*, the earliest known Italian treatise on city government, implores chief magistrates to promise that their rule will lead "to increase and glory and honor,"

[35] Martines concludes, for example, that the social positions of leading humanists are best attributed to four factors: "honorably-acquired wealth, a substantial record of service in public office, descent from an old Florentine family, and bonds of marriage with another family of some political and economic consequence." With the exception of the second factor, these indicate the salience of traditional patronal and familial values, not the more egalitarian ideals of civic humanism. Martines, *Social World of the Florentine Humanists*, 18.

[36] Castiglione, *Book of the Courtier*, 76–77.

[37] For an excellent analysis of the studia humanitatas, see Grendler, *Schooling in Renaissance Italy*. Kohl argues that studia humanitatas was only belatedly identified with a specific curriculum, and that for a long period it was identified with general civic virtues. Kohl, "Changing Concept of *Studia Humanitatas*."

guaranteeing "that the city grows to greatness."[38] This measure was reiterated time again over the next three centuries in the genre of laudatory works on the greatness of various Italian city-states, the most notable being Leonardo Bruni's panegyric on Florence, *Laudatio Florentine Urbis*, published around 1400.[39] It was Machiavelli, however, who a century later provided one of the most poetic expressions of civic glory as the underlying moral purpose of the Italian city-state. In *The Discourses* he asks a prince to reflect on the Roman Empire at its moment of greatest achievement, and to use this as a model for his rule. The prince will see, Machiavelli writes, "a ruler secure in the midst of secure citizens, and a world of peace and justice; he will see a senate with its full authority, the magistrates with their honors, the rich citizens enjoying their wealth, the nobles and ability exulted, and he will find tranquility and well-being in everything; and on the other hand, he will see rancor, licentiousness, corruption, and ambition extinguished; he will see a golden age in which a man can hold and defend whatever opinion he wishes. *He will, in the end, see the world rejoicing: its prince endowed with respect and honor, its people with love and security* [my emphasis]."[40]

This vision of the moral purpose of the state received its most articulate expression in the writings of prehumanists, humanists, and posthumanists, from Brunetto Latini to Machiavelli. (From hereon, I will use the term "humanist" to categorize this broad group of thinkers.) These authors drew inspiration from the newly rediscovered writings of classical scholars, particularly those of Rome, such as Cicero and Sallust.[41] Defining the city-state's moral purpose as the pursuit of civic glory was driven, however, by a much deeper set of legitimation imperatives, grounded in prevailing ways of constructing authoritative identities. In late medieval and Renaissance Italy, appeals to honorific grandeur undergirded all authority claims, whether transcommunal or subcommunal. The Pope and the Holy Roman Emperor cultivated auras of honor and glory assiduously, as did local patrons. It seems inevitable, therefore, that establishing sovereign city-states—small islands of political authority in a sea of competing jurisdictional claims—would involve a link between state identity and glory, in one form or another. What is more, defining the state's raison d'être as the pursuit of "civic" glory placed state and society in classical patronage relationship. To the extent that the state, in the body of the

---

[38] The *Oculus Pastoralis* was written around 1220; its author is unknown. The passages cited here are quoted in Skinner, "Pre-humanist Origins of Republican Ideas," 126.

[39] For a detailed analysis of Bruni's *Laudatio*, see Baron, *Crisis of the Early Italian Renaissance*, 163–189.

[40] Machiavelli, *Discourses*, 205–206.

[41] On the influence of classical Roman thought on civic humanism, see Skinner, *Foundations*, 23–41; "Ambrogio Lorenzetti"; and "Pre-humanist Origins of Republican Ideas."

prince or the institutions of the republic, became identified with the glory of city, it became the supreme patron, the paramount focus of individual fealty. As a patron, the state was in turn charged with bestowing honor upon society, with enhancing the power, wealth, and standing of the city. We see this relationship represented symbolically in the magisterial figure seated on the throne in Lorenzetti's fourteenth-century Sienese fresco "The Virtues of Good Government" and in later references to Cosimo de' Medici, the leading figure in the Florentine oligarchy in the middle of the fifteenth century, as *pater patriae*.[42]

The Ritual Norm of Procedural Justice

These beliefs about the moral purpose of the state related to a distinctive norm of procedural justice between Italian city-states, a norm I term "ritual justice." Understanding this relationship between the social identity of the state and ideals of interstate practice requires a two-stage archaeology of ideas. The principles espoused by civic humanists provide a useful starting point, but we must then consider how these ideas were grounded in, and structured by, the values of patronage society in Renaissance Italy.

If a city-state was to achieve true glory, humanists insisted, internal discord and factionalism had to be avoided at all costs. This is captured in Latini's advice to magistrates of divided cities: "You must point out [to the citizens] how concord brings greatness to cities and enriches their citizens, while war destroys them; and you must recall how Rome and other great cities ruined themselves with internal strife."[43] This connection between *grandezza* and *concordia* was a recurring theme in humanist writings over the next two centuries, with only Machiavelli taking the contrary position, dismaying his contemporaries by grounding civic vitality in class divisions.[44] For Latini, and the humanists who followed, internal unity could be achieved only if individuals—especially those in positions of authority—placed the common good before self-interest or factional advantage. Cicero's view, that "those who care for the interests of a part of the citizens and neglect another part, introduce into the civil service a dangerous element—dissension and party strife," was a constant refrain.[45] The common good would prevail, they went on to argue, only if rulers observed the principles of justice. In Latini's words, "A city which is governed according to right and truth, such that everyone has what he

[42] See, Skinner, "Ambrogio Lorenzetti," 44; and Najemy, "Guild Republicanism," 69.

[43] This passage is quoted in Skinner, "Pre-humanist Origins of Republican Ideas," 129.

[44] See Machiavelli's remarks in his *Discourses*, 183–185; and *Florentine History*, 1–3. For a commentary on his ideas, see Skinner, *Foundations*, 180–186.

[45] Cicero, *De Officiis*, 1.25.85, 85.

ought to have, will certainly grow and multiply, both in people and in wealth, and will endure for ever in a good state of peace, to its honour and that of its friends."[46] In drawing such connections, Latini and his successors had in mind a specific conception of *substantive* justice—justice as desert. The just ruler or magistrate was one who gave each person his or her due, meting out wealth or honors to the worthy, while punishing or killing the wicked.[47]

Humanists believed that political practices informed by this conception of substantive justice would deliver communal unity and civic greatness, thus countering the particularistic loyalties and rife factionalism that so troubled the development of the Italian city-states. Yet in defining justice as the reward of virtue and the retribution of vice, they reaffirmed long established patronal values. At its very heart, the patronage system was about the subjective assessment of honor and dishonor, and the distribution of social goods accordingly. Intentionally or otherwise, humanists transplanted this value into the official ideology of the city-state. And just as defining the moral purpose of the state as the pursuit of civic glory placed state and society in a traditional patron-client relationship, so too did defining justice as desert. Justice simply became the official term for the state-sanctioned distribution of rewards to the "good" and punishments to the "bad." The integration of this substantive conception of justice into the "high" morality of Renaissance politics in turn allowed patronal values of *procedural* justice to permeate and structure state practices. As we have seen, in a patronage society such as Renaissance Italy an individual's worth was determined through the ritual enactment of virtue, through the ceremonial use of rhetoric and gesture. For both patrons and clients, the resulting patterns of cooperation, and distribution of social goods, were considered "just." In the fourteenth and fifteenth centuries, as the city-states moved to signorial or oligarchic rule, this ritual norm of procedural justice shaped not only relations between individuals, but increasingly those between princes and subjects, oligarches and citizens. Most importantly, for our purposes, this conception of procedural justice also came to structure relations between city-states, informing the practice of oratorical diplomacy.

The humanists had not intended this ritual norm of procedural justice to permeate state practices, despite the fact that their conception of the moral purpose of the state, emphasis on rhetorical communication, and notion of substantive justice allowed, if not fueled, such a development.

---

[46] This passage is quoted in Skinner's "Pre-humanist Origins of Republican Ideas," 131.

[47] For a discussion of this conception of substantive justice in prehumanist and humanist thought, see Skinner, "Pre-humanist Origins of Republican Ideas," 130–132; and "Ambrogio Lorenzetti," 16–17.

Following Cicero, they advocated a legal norm of procedural justice, whereby constitutional rules would "compel" individuals to behave justly. This understanding of the rule of law is captured in Machiavelli's oft-quoted remark that "hunger and poverty make men industrious and laws make them good."[48] This having been said, neither the humanist conception of law, nor the Renaissance practice of law, managed to transcend patronal values. Conceptually, the humanist account of law was as conventional as it was innovative. For Machiavelli and his predecessors, the modern idea of law as a reciprocally binding accord, legislated by those subject to the law, was entirely alien. Great systems of constitutional law were bequeathed to cities, formulated and instituted by a wise and just lawgiver. The founding of a city, and the establishment of its legal system, was thus a quintessential act of patronal beneficence. Practically, the traditional norms and practices of patronage society exerted a far greater influence on the legal institutions and processes of the city-states than did humanist ideals. Nowhere was this more apparent than in the progressive decline of the judiciary as an independent institution, a casualty of signorial rule and the patriciate's colonization of republican institutions. By the fifteenth century, Martines observes, "The executive arm of the Italian cities reached out so far that in many cases no sure division was possible between the judicial and the executive functions of government."[49] Without such divisions, patronage relations were free to permeate political life, constrained only by the ritual norm of procedural justice that traditionally structured patron-client interaction.

THE PRACTICE OF ORATORICAL DIPLOMACY

To summarize the preceding argument, between the thirteenth and fifteenth centuries a small system of sovereign city-states emerged in Northern Italy. In this process of state formation, the legitimacy of the city-state was linked to the pursuit of civic glory. Internal discord was considered the major obstacle to grandezza, and the prevention of discord was thought to lie in the exercise of a distinctive kind of substantive justice— the reward of virtue and the rectification of vice. Although humanists advocated a legal norm of procedural justice to realize this form of substantive justice, patronal values and practices prevailed, with the ritual enactment of virtue, through ceremonial rhetoric and gesture, determining patterns of social and political interaction, individual worth and entitlement, and the distribution of social goods. In the remainder of this

---

[48] Machiavelli, *Discourses*, 183.
[49] Martines, *Lawyers and Statecraft*, 130.

chapter, I explain how these ideas of legitimate statehood and procedural justice structured relations between city-states, producing the fundamental institution of oratorical diplomacy.

Anxiety and Ritual Communication Among City-States

Scholars who treat Renaissance diplomacy as an inherently modern institutional form—the antecedent of contemporary practices—highlight two features of the institution: the mutual exchange of resident ambassadors, and the bureaucratic system of routine reports written by ambassadors to their home states. While deploying ambassadors was hardly new, their permanent stationing in other states was. The city-states first sent resident ambassadors in the thirteenth century, with Venice leading the way, and the earliest mutual exchange of representatives took place between Milan and Mantua in 1373. It was not until the middle of the fifteenth century, however, that the practice took off. After 1445, dispatching resident ambassadors was the norm, and by 1458 Florence, Milan, Naples, and Venice had all exchanged envoys.[50] Gathering information and reporting to the home state were among resident ambassadors' most important tasks. They were expected to write daily, documenting and interpreting all aspects of political life in their host state. Dispatches were written to a standard format, and once received and considered by governments, they were filed in vast archives, bequeathing modern historians unrivaled documentary materials on the internal and external politics of the Italian city-states.[51]

These were indeed important innovations, but they represent the mechanics of the Italian diplomatic system, not its essence. The exchange of resident ambassadors, and their submission of regular diplomatic reports, formed the *apparatus* of communication between city-states, yet alone this tells us little about the *purpose* and *nature* of such communication. In focusing on this apparatus, scholars of Renaissance diplomacy have made an error similar to that of scholars of modern multilateralism. Until recently, multilateralism was defined as "the practice of coordinating national policies in groups of three or more states."[52] But as Ruggie points out, this "nominal definition . . . misses the *qualitative* dimension of the phenomenon that makes it distinct."[53] The crucial thing about multilateralism is that it coordinates relations between three or more states in a

---

[50] Hale, "International Relations in the West," 266–267.
[51] Mattingly, *Renaissance Diplomacy*, 108–118.
[52] Keohane, "Multilateralism: An Agenda for Research," 731.
[53] Ruggie, "Multilateralism," 6.

particular way—on the basis of mutually agreed, reciprocally binding rules of state conduct.[54] Concentrating simply on the number of cooperating states thus fails to capture the essence of multilateralism as a basic institutional practice, and focusing solely on the apparatus of communication between the Italian city-states fails in a similar way. To understand Renaissance diplomacy, we must probe beneath the machinery to ask why the city-states constructed such an apparatus and try to comprehend the form of communication it facilitated.

The first step is to understand the anxieties that animated the city-states. As we have seen, those who treat Renaissance diplomacy as a distinctly modern institution argue that it was a rational response to anarchy. In one sense this is true: the city-states certainly believed that it was the most appropriate institutional response to the environmental challenges they faced. This observation gets us nowhere, though, if we don't appreciate what political elites considered those challenges to be. In other words, we have to grasp what "anarchy" meant in fourteenth- and fifteenth-century Italy. The systemic conception of international anarchy employed by neorealists and others is of little use here, as it explicitly brackets domestic political factors. For the princes and oligarchs who ruled the Italian city-states, their political survival, and often the continuation of their states as independent political units, were determined by a complex interplay between internal and external political alignments, between domestic stability and interstate stability. Internal discord threatened to tear the state apart from the inside, and rival states frequently saw factionalism as an opportunity for internal meddling and/or territorial aggrandizement. Managing "anarchy"—understood as a potent mixture of domestic and interstate lawlessness—was in the interest of all city-states. It was a prerequisite for stable sovereign rule, as well as a precondition for coexistence among states.

As we have seen, Renaissance individuals responded to the anxieties and uncertainties generated by the erosion of guild-based corporate structures, and the retreat of papal and imperial sources of authority and identification, by embracing traditional patronage relations. In such relations, the operative norm of procedural justice entailed the ritual expression of honor and self-worth through ceremonial rhetoric and gesture. These practices established an individual's identity, legitimacy, and status as a social agent, and situated that individual within a framework of obligatory social relations. While the construction of relations between states that were as formally hierarchical and reliably binding as relations between individuals was impossible, political elites observed the same norm of procedural justice when seeking to establish the social identity, legiti-

[54] Ibid., 11.

macy, and status of their city-states within the interstate system, and when courting cooperative relations with other states. In other words, the same *mentalité* that shaped how individuals responded to the anxieties of Renaissance social life also informed how princes and oligarchs reacted to the anxieties of "anarchy," as they understood it.

It was in this context that the practice of Renaissance diplomacy took root, with the apparatus of resident ambassadors enabling political elites to engage in ritual communication between city-states. It did so in three ways. First, it allowed rulers to convey carefully orchestrated images of their city-states. The Florentines, who struggled against their ignoble mercantile identity, went to elaborate lengths to project an image of civic greatness. As Trexler observes: "Florentines recording their ambassadors' court activity reflect this fact when they proudly state, 'Never had an embassy of Florence or any other power displayed such richness or garments and jewels,' and 'One speaks of nothing else in Rome but this ornateness,' or even that their emissaries 'shamed all the other ambassadors of the other powers.'"[55] Second, it permitted the rhetorical cultivation and consolidation of relationships of friendship and enmity among city-states. In Melissa Bullard's words: "Language helped to stabilize perception by referencing it to a generally accepted structure of values, one which, for example, prized virility and placed men over women. . . . Not surprisingly sexual metaphors were frequently used to indicate dominance and disrespect. . . , whereas friendly feelings towards one's allies were couched in the vocabulary of brotherhood and love, however insincerely. Love and friendship were the hackneyed metaphors for peace, and good relations were described as being full of 'love and concord.'"[56] Third, it enabled the constant monitoring and interpretation of ritual communication. Mattingly points out correctly that "it was . . . as political intelligence officers that the residents demonstrated their usefulness most decisively," yet he misses the full import of this observation.[57] As diplomatic language became more ornate, meanings and intentions became more obscure, placing a premium on the skilled interpretation of rhetoric. As Bullard argues, "Renaissance diplomatic praxis in this context encouraged close attention to words and their possible shades of meaning."[58] With the growing ambiguity of diplomatic language, however, ambassadors also became attentive to the meanings of political actions and gestures. For instance, the "Florentines refused to give credence

[55] Trexler, *Public Life in Renaissance Florence*, 294.
[56] Bullard, *Lorenzo Il Magnifico*, 92–93.
[57] Mattingly, *Renaissance Diplomacy*, 110.
[58] Bullard, "Language of Diplomacy," 270.

to 'buone parole' unless they were accompanied by 'buoni effetti' or 'demonstrazioni.'"[59]

In performing the first and second of these roles, resident ambassadors served as the rhetorical and gestural agents of their city-states, and in fulfilling the third role they acted as ritual interpreters, communicating and deciphering the language and gestures of elites in their host states. Scholars agree that residents seldom negotiated on behalf of their city-states, that role being the domain of special envoys or rulers themselves.[60] Instead, they managed the identity of their city-state, cultivating and maintaining an image of communal honor and glory in the face of attenuated lines of interstate communication. This role is clearly expressed in the advice given to new residents by Ermolao Barbaro, the Venetian ambassador to Milan and later Rome. "Since declarations of war, and treaties of peace and alliance are but affairs of a few days," he observes, "I will speak of those ambassadors who are sent with simple, general credentials, to win or preserve friendship of princes."[61] While fulfilling this role, they also struggled to interpret the rhetorical and gestural practices of political elites in states where they were based, seeking evidence of friendship or enmity, loyalty or infidelity, allegiance or duplicity. Through this system of ritual communication, the city-states affirmed and reproduced prevailing beliefs about legitimate statehood, stabilized mutual expectations through ritual performance, and made civic identity a crucial ingredient of political power, ultimately affecting the balance of interstate power on the peninsula.

Identity Construction, Oratorical Diplomacy, and the Balance of Power

In the second half of the fifteenth century, the frequency and intensity of war between the Italian city-states declined markedly. According to Mattingly, "Wars were less destructive than they had been, absorbed less of men's energies, and consumed less of the social income. No major towns were sacked; no desperately bloody fields were fought. And for three years, almost, out of four there was no fighting anywhere in Italy worth a historian's serious attention."[62] It is tempting to attribute this decline in interstate conflict to the formation of the Italian League, a collective security agreement between the major city-states, formed with the

---

[59] Bullard, *Lorenzo Il Magnifico*, 100.
[60] Mattingly, *Renaissance Diplomacy*, 102; and Bullard, *Lorenzo Il Magnifico*, 86.
[61] This passage is quoted in Mattingly, *Renaissance Diplomacy*, 108.
[62] Ibid., 96.

signing of the Treaty of Lodi in 1454.[63] Yet, despite pledges by the city-states to protect each other against aggression, to maintain the status quo on the peninsula, and to resist intervening in one another's domestic affairs, most scholars believe that the judicious maintenance of the balance of power contributed more to the peace than the formal commitments of the League.[64] In fact, claims about the beneficial effects of the balance of power border at times on the euphoric. Mattingly argues, for instance, that "by virtue of the mutual jealousies of its balanced states, by the politics of continuous tension, and by the help of its new diplomatic machinery, Italy did enjoy a kind of uneasy peace. Those forty years [1450–1490] saw the amazing flowering of the Italian, particularly Florentine genius. It seems likely that without that mild, genial springtime some of the finest fruits of the Italian Renaissance would never have ripened at all."[65] As implied by these remarks, the practice of Renaissance diplomacy is thought to have played a crucial role in the construction and maintenance of a stable balance of power between the city-states, constituting "the chief means by which Italian statecraft observed and continually readjusted the unstable equilibrium of power within the peninsula."[66]

To fully appreciate the connection between peace and stability, the balance of power, and Renaissance diplomacy after 1450, we must return to the nature of power in Renaissance society, and consider the role of diplomacy in the cultivation and expression of such power. As explained above, an individual's power did not derive solely from his or her material resources—standing and influence were greatly determined by one's reputation, by subjective measures of honor, glory, and *virtu*. This was also true of state power. Military capabilities and wealth were important, but identity was crucial. The successful presentation and projection of an image of civic grandeur could enhance a city-state's position, as well as its capacity to shape peninsula affairs. In contemporary terminology, "soft power" could compensate for deficiencies in "hard power," making the mobilization and manipulation of cultural symbols and political imagery an important determinant of the balance of power.[67] The institution of Renaissance diplomacy provided the communicative framework for the

---

[63] On the Treaty of Lodi and the Italian League, see Fubini, "The Italian League and the Policy of the Balance of Power"; Ilardi, "The Italian League, Franceso Sforza, and Charles VII"; Laven, *Renaissance Italy*, 108–129; Mallett, "Diplomacy and War"; and Rubinstein, "Lorenzo de' Medici."

[64] Fubini argues, for instance, that the League soon gave way to a policy of equilibrium, even though the League remained in existence and was renewed for a further twenty years in 1470. Fubini, "Italian League and the Policy of Balance of Power," S198.

[65] Mattingly, *Renaissance Diplomacy*, 96.

[66] Ibid., 64.

[67] On the notion of "soft power," see Nye, *Bound to Lead*.

augmentation and expression of such power. Through resident ambassadors, and a variety of complementary ritual practices, princes and oligarchs were able to convey highly crafted images of themselves and their city-states, weaving personal mantels of honorific glory and championing their cities as the supreme embodiments of the prevailing ideal of the moral purpose of the state. The institution also enabled them to interpret and assess the identity rhetoric and gestures of other city-states, in turn allowing them to "map" the relative standing and authority of the major "powers."

There is no better way to illustrate this relationship between oratorical diplomacy and the balance of power than by considering the practices employed by Lorenzo de' Medici, the Florentine patrician widely credited with engineering and maintaining the equilibrium on the peninsula after 1469.[68] Before the Treaty of Lodi, Italy had been plagued by incessant rivalries and conflicts between Florence, Milan, Naples, Rome, and Venice, each of which struggled for territorial domination and willfully meddled in the internal affairs of the others. The reduction in these tensions in the second half of the century can be attributed to two interrelated factors: a growing consciousness among the city-states that coexistence was necessary and could only be achieved by maintaining a stable balance of power,[69] and the emergence of Florence as the "arbiter of the balance." From a conventional realist perspective, the latter development is anomalous, as Florence was materially the weakest of the major powers, wielding less military might than its rivals, occupying a precarious geostrategic position, and wracked by internal dissensions that Machiavelli described as truly "remarkable."[70] That Florence achieved such a position, and assumed such influence, was due in large measure to Lorenzo's artful diplomacy, to the skillful orchestration of his personal honor and the civic grandeur of his city-state. In Bullard's words, "Lorenzo instrumentalized *onore* making it part of a brilliant political strategy."[71]

To establish his reputation as "Italian peacemaker," and Florence's standing as the "point of the balance," Lorenzo employed two techniques,

---

[68] Francesco Guicciardini, the celebrated Florentine statesman, diplomat, and historian, penned the following reflections about Lorenzo's role in preserving a balance of power on the Italian peninsula: "Realizing that it would be most perilous to the Florentine Republic and to himself if any of the major powers should extend their area of dominion, he carefully saw to it that the Italian situation should be maintained in a state of balance, not leaning more toward one side than the other." Guicciardini, *History of Italy*, 4–7.

[69] Mattingly writes that "[i]n the 1440s there began to form in certain Italian minds a conception of Italy as a system of independent states, coexisting by virtue of an unstable equilibrium which it was the function of statesmen to preserve." Mattingly, *Renaissance Diplomacy*, 83.

[70] Machiavelli, *Florentine History*, 1.

[71] Bullard, *Lorenzo Il Magnifico*, 48.

both of which drew upon prevailing cultural mores and practices. According to Bullard, Lorenzo "mastered the art of the well-chosen gesture, and he traded upon Florence's growing reputation as the center of the new style of Renaissance art and culture and humanist learning, a reputation that he in turn bolstered considerably."[72] The system of resident ambassadors provided the framework through which Lorenzo could exercise these techniques. Not only were almost all of the Florentine ambassadors renowned humanists, well versed in rhetorical and gestural expression and skilled in ritual interpretation, but Lorenzo communicated with them directly, maintaining an "unofficial" line of diplomatic control, parallel to "official" communications between ambassadors and the Florentine state.[73] This direct line of control enabled Lorenzo to craft a tight, mutually reinforcing relationship between his personal identity and that of Florence. "Lorenzo's genius," Bullard argues, "lay in being able to weld his personal reputation and that of Florence together. His image making, therefore, went beyond personal aggrandizement as an end it itself, to draw upon the very pride and glory of Florence, using one to buttress the other. Lorenzo's image making depended on Florence, just as Florence came to depend on Lorenzo."[74] The net result of Lorenzo's energetic attention to identity construction through rhetorical and gestural diplomacy was the elevation of Florentine influence far beyond that warranted by its material power, with manifest consequences for peace and stability on the peninsula. Machiavelli writes that "Lorenzo, having by his good sense and authority secured peace in Italy, turned his attention to the aggrandizement of himself and his city,"[75] but a more reasonable conclusion, given the preceding discussion, would be that by attending to the aggrandizement of himself and his city, Lorenzo secured his authority and peace in Italy.

CONCLUSION

If the argument advanced above is correct, then Renaissance diplomacy was neither the progenitor of modern diplomatic practice nor an "oriental" absurdity. Rather, it was a fundamental institution deeply embedded within the values and practices of fifteenth-century Italian society. Informed by traditional patronal beliefs about legitimate agency and rightful social interaction, and reinforced and articulated at crucial points of

---

[72] Ibid., 28.
[73] Rubinstein, "Lorenzo de' Medici," 88.
[74] Bullard, *Lorenzo Il Magnifico*, 49.
[75] Machiavelli, *Florentine History*, 358.

convergence by civic humanism, the Renaissance society of states evolved a distinctive constitutional structure. The moral purpose of the state—which provided the justificatory foundations for the city-states' sovereignty—was defined as the pursuit of civic glory, and the prevailing norm of procedural justice licensed the ritual enactment of virtue through ceremonial rhetoric and gesture. Such a norm could only operate between states if there was an apparatus of communication to facilitate ritual dialogue. The system of resident ambassadors constituted this apparatus. Through the expressive and interpretive channels provided by residents, city-states could convey carefully crafted self-images, cultivate and consolidate relationships of friendship and enmity, and monitor the rhetoric and gestures of others.

Because alternative accounts of international institutional development ignore the cultural foundations of basic institutional practices, they struggle to explain the nature of Renaissance diplomacy. Contrary to the expectations of neorealists, Italian practices cannot be attributed to the power and interests of a dominant state. Not only was the Italian system of states multipolar, but the city-states that did most to develop the diplomatic system—Florence and Venice—wielded no more material power than their counterparts, and by some measures significantly less. The rationalist perspective, adopted by neoliberals, is no more illuminating. At a purely abstract level, there was nothing especially efficient or effective about renaissance diplomacy to warrant its development as the core fundamental institution of the Italian society of states. Only by treating institutional rationality as culturally and historically contingent can we speak meaningfully of Renaissance diplomacy as a "rational" solution to the problems of coexistence encountered by the city-states. The tight constitutive link constructivists draw between the sovereignty, territoriality, and basic institutional practices is also problematic. As in ancient Greece, the institution that Ruggie considers so essential to the stabilization of territorial property rights—multilateralism—never emerged among the Italian city-states. Instead, through the ritual communication facilitated by the mutual exchange of resident ambassadors they engineered and maintained an equilibrium on the peninsula, an equilibrium that reduced interference in each other's domestic affairs and diminished violent interstate conflict.

In his classic study of late medieval Italy, Waley claims that "the city-state proved a dead end rather than the direct antecedent of the nation-state, even though Venice, Genoa, Florence, Parma and Modena remained states or the nuclei of states, far into the 'modern' period."[76] Social and political life within the city-state, he contends, involved a level of face-to-

---

[76] Waley, *Italian City-Republics*, xi.

face interaction that has not, and cannot, be replicated in modern, territorially expansive nation-states. Justin Rosenberg has reiterated Waley's observation about the disjuncture between the Italian city-states and modern nation-states, but focuses instead on the radically different economic structures undergirding the two forms of sovereign state.[77] The argument advanced in this chapter lends further credence to the "distinctiveness" case, although from a different perspective. The constitutional structure of the Italian society of states was unique; it was informed by deeply rooted social and cultural values that were neither universal nor replicable. Moreover, this set of constitutive metavalues spawned a novel practice of oratorical diplomacy, the characteristics of which defy categorization as either modern or "oriental," throwing diplomatic historians into confusion and contradiction. All of this makes two representational strategies frequently employed in the study of international relations appear strained, to the say the least. The Italian society of states can neither be cast as the origin of modern international society, nor can it be woven into a grand narrative of historical continuity, in which all societies of sovereign states are thought to exhibit like politics.

---

[77] Rosenberg, "Secret Origins of the State," 145. For a further development of this argument, see Rosenberg, *Empire of Civil Society.*

CHAPTER FIVE

Absolutist Europe

Observance of the law of nature and of divine law,
or of the law of nations . . . is binding upon all
kings, even though they have made no promise.
—Hugo Grotius, *The Law of War and Peace*,
1646

Though these precepts [of the law of nations]
have a clear utility, they get the force of law only
upon the presuppositions that God exists and
rules all things by His providence. . . . Laws necessarily imply a superior, and such a superior as
actually has governance over another.
—Samuel Pufendorf, *On the Duty of Man and
Citizen*, 1673

SCHOLARS have long debated when the modern society of sovereign states
first emerged, exhibiting all of the essential characteristics that distinguish
it from previous systems of rule. For Wight, the Council of Constance
(1414–18) marks the crucial turning point, whereas F. H. Hinsley emphasizes changes in the eighteenth century.[1] The most frequently cited date,
however, is 1648, when the Treaties of Osnabrück and Münster—which
together formed the "Peace of Westphalia"—brought an end to the
traumas of the Thirty Years War. At that moment, we are told, territorial
sovereignty was formally enshrined as the organizing principle of European politics. "The Peace of Westphalia," Kalevi Holsti argues,
"organized Europe on the principle of particularism. It represented a new
diplomatic arrangement—an order created by states, for states—and replaced most of the legal vestiges of hierarchy, at the pinnacle of which
were the Pope and the Holy Roman Empire."[2] One of the most sophisticated expressions of this thesis is found in Ruggie's work. In a series of
insightful essays, he has clarified the nature of the seventeenth-century
transition, clearly distinguishing between international orders based on

[1] Wight, *Systems of States*, 130; Hinsley, *Power and Pursuit of Peace*, 153.
[2] Holsti, *Peace and War*, 25.

heteronomous and sovereign modes of differentiation, and has drawn a tight connection between the new sovereign order instituted at Westphalia and the development of modern fundamental institutions, in particular multilateralism.[3]

This chapter takes issue with the "Westphalian thesis" about the origins of modern international society and challenges associated claims about the genesis of contemporary fundamental institutions. The seventeenth century indeed witnessed the gradual formation of a society of sovereign states in Europe, and Ruggie is correct that a deep "generative grammar" of constitutive metavalues informed the spatial and temporal reorganization of political authority. The society of states that emerged, however, was absolutist, not modern. For almost two centuries after Westphalia a decidedly premodern set of Christian and dynastic intersubjective values defined legitimate statehood and rightful state action. Under this constitutional structure, the moral purpose of the state was linked to the preservation of a divinely ordained, rigidly hierarchical social order, and procedural justice was understood in strictly authoritative terms. These values informed the basic institutional practices of the period, generating the fundamental institutions of "old diplomacy" and "naturalist international law." Just as importantly, though, the constitutional structure of absolutist international society impeded, not encouraged, the growth of modern institutional forms, such as multilateralism and contractual international law. As we shall see, the Treaties of Westphalia (1648) and Utrecht (1713–15), which were crucial in defining the scope and geographical extension of sovereign rights, bear little imprint of either institutional practice. This is also true of the Congress of Vienna (1814–15), examined in the following chapter. It was not until the middle of the nineteenth century, when a new set of constitutional values had emerged to justify the authority of sovereign state, that the fundamental institutions of multilateralism and contractual international law took off.

The chapter is divided into five main parts. It begins with a critical, yet sympathetic, analysis of Ruggie's argument about the relationship between sovereignty, territoriality, and multilateralism. The discussion then turns to the transition from feudalism to absolutism, critiquing materialist theories of state formation for underemphasizing the links between political authority, state identity, and the legitimacy of absolutist rule. Part three outlines the constitutional structure of the absolutist society of states, explaining prevailing ideas about the moral purpose of the state and procedural justice. I then show how these values informed the

---

[3] See Ruggie, "Continuity and Transformation"; "International Regimes"; "Structure and Transformation"; "Territoriality and Beyond"; and "Multilateralism: Anatomy of an Institution."

fundamental institutions of dynastic diplomacy and naturalist international law. The final part examines the consolidation of territoriality in the absolutist society of states and the role of basic institutional practices, focusing on the Peace of Westphalia and the Treaties of Utrecht.

WESTPHALIA AND THE GENESIS OF MODERN INSTITUTIONS?

In a landmark essay first published in 1981, Robert Cox advocated a critical theory of international relations, one that "does not take institutions and social and power relations for granted but calls them into question by concerning itself with their origins and how and whether they might be in the process of changing."[4] Studying the rise and potential demise of the sovereign state was clearly central to such a project, and historically informed studies of state formation and international society have since proliferated, spurred on by contemporary processes of globalization and international institutionalization.[5] Of this work, Ruggie's essays are of singular importance for this study. His efforts to develop a historically informed constructivist perspective on modern international society have been instructive, and there is a clear affinity between his emphasis on generative grammars and my focus on constitutive metavalues. What is more, he too attempts to draw systematic, empirically grounded connections between intersubjective beliefs, the social identity of the sovereign state, and the evolution of basic institutional practices.

Ruggie begins with a critique of Waltzian neorealism. The problem, he contends, "is that it provides no means by which to account for, or even to describe, the most important contextual change in international politics in this *millennium*: the shift from the medieval to the modern international system."[6] This is because Waltz denies that the differentiation of political units—the second dimension of international political structures, as he understands them—constitutes a significant variable in international systems. Ruggie argues, in contrast, that when correctly defined, as "*the basis of which the constituent units are separated* from one another," the mode of differentiation actually "serves as an exceedingly important source of

----

[4] Cox, "Social Forces," 208.

[5] Critical theorists are not alone in exploring the historical emergence and development of the system of sovereign states. For a representative sample of these studies, see Bartelson, *Genealogy of Sovereignty*; Cox, *Production, Power, and World Order*; Der Derian, *On Diplomacy*; Hobson, *Wealth of States*; Krasner, "Westphalia and All That"; Krasner, "Compromising Westphalia"; Spruyt, *Sovereign State and Its Competitors*; Thomson, *Mercenaries, Pirates, and Sovereigns*; and Weber, *Simulating Sovereignty*.

[6] Ruggie, "Continuity and Transformation," 141.

structural variation."[7] This insight provides the foundation for his thesis about the shift from the medieval system of rule to the modern. In essence, this transformation involved the supplanting of the old "heteronomous" mode of differentiation by a new "sovereign" mode. Changing ideas of territorial property rights were central to this. The "spatial extension of the medieval system of rule," he contends, "was structured by a nonexclusive form of territoriality, in which authority was both personalized and parcelized within and across territorial formations and for which inclusive bases of legitimation prevailed." In contrast, the "chief characteristic of the modern system of territorial rule is the consolidation of all parcelized and personalized authority into one public realm."[8] While he readily acknowledges the importance of changing material environments and strategic behavior in this epochal transformation, his account places special emphasis on changes in "social epistemology," symbolized in the rediscovery of "single-point perspective" in the visual arts. "Put simply," he argues, "the mental equipment that people drew upon in imagining and symbolizing forms of political community itself underwent fundamental change."[9]

According to Ruggie, the shift from a heteronomous to a sovereign mode of differentiation, from a nonexclusive to an exclusive form of territoriality, is the principal reason why multilateralism evolved as a core fundamental institution of modern international society. In the new world of spatially demarcated sovereign states, the stabilization of territorial property rights was a paramount concern: "The newly emerged territorial states conceived their essence, their very being, by the *possession* of territory and the *exclusion* of others from it. But how does one possess something one does not own? And, still more problematical, how does one exclude others from it."[10] In struggling to resolve this problem, Ruggie contends, states eventually turned to multilateralism—the formulation, among three or more states, of generalized, reciprocally binding rules of conduct. Although the evidence he cites concerning the law of the sea and diplomatic rules of extraterritoriality is rather thin, he concludes that "[w]here the definition and stabilization of at least some international property rights is concerned, an ultimate inevitability to multilateral solutions appears to exist, although 'ultimate' may mean after all possible alternatives, including war, have been exhausted."[11] In short, by drawing a connection between sovereignty, the stabilization of territorial property rights, and multilateralism, Ruggie grounds the institutional architecture

[7] Ibid., 142.
[8] Ruggie, "Territoriality and Beyond," 150–151.
[9] Ibid., 157.
[10] Ruggie, "Multilateralism: Anatomy of an Institution," 15.
[11] Ibid., 17.

of modern international society in the epochal transformations of the seventeenth century.

Ruggie's initial proposition, that the collapse of the feudal order and the rise of a system of territorially demarcated states involved a shift in the prevailing mode of differentiation from heteronomy to sovereignty, is not in question here. This insight is both historically illuminating and conceptually fruitful. What is in question is the modernity of this transformation. The idea that "modern" international society took form in the seventeenth century, and the concomitant claim that multilateralism dates from this period, sit uncomfortably with certain characteristics of the post-Westphalian international order. To begin with, the system of sovereign states that emerged in Europe in the seventeenth century, and structured political life until the beginning of the nineteenth, lacked the principle of sovereign equality. Where a state stood in the divine order of things mattered, and states squabbled incessantly over their position in the hierarchy. Second, multilateralism and the related practice of contractual international law featured little in relations between states in this period. Ruggie posits a lag between the emergence of the system of sovereign states and the development of these practices, caused by the costly exercise of trial and error, but this is less than satisfying, especially since states only embraced these practices after a revolutionary transformation in the terms of legitimate statehood and rightful state action in the nineteenth century, suggesting that more was going on than a simple, if painful, process of learning. Finally, Ruggie's account neglects altogether the two institutional practices that did emerge in the post-Westphalian period: "old diplomacy" and "naturalist international law," both of which reached their apogees at this time. Furthermore, nothing in his theoretical framework explains the advent or nature of these institutions.

Ruggie's failure to acknowledge and account for important aspects of the post-Westphalian international system stems, in my view, from two interrelated simplifications that unnecessarily handicap his analytical framework: one theoretical, the other conceptual. With regard to the former, his specification of the normative foundations of international society is too sparse to accommodate the crucial differences between the international society that existed before 1850 and that which has emerged since. Since sovereignty alone is thought to define the identity of the state, and since the organizing principle of sovereignty has persisted throughout the post-Westphalian period, such differentiation is theoretically problematic, if not impossible. This in turn leads to a second, conceptual simplification in Ruggie's analytical framework. Despite the fact that sociologists of state formation have long drawn a conceptual distinction between the absolutist system of states and its modern successor, Ruggie's theoretical assumptions cast an unnecessary veil of homogeneity over the last four hundred years. While rightly focusing our attention on the epochal transformations of the seventeenth century, his conceptual reduction of the ensuing sovereign order into a single international society obscures the equally important transformations that straddle the late eighteenth and early nineteenth centuries.

In seeking to explain the aspects of the post-Westphalian order left anomalous by Ruggie's analytical framework, the following discussion treats the absolutist society of states as an distinct institutional interregnum between the medieval and modern systems, marked by a unique constitutional structure and set of basic institutional practices.

ABSOLUTISM, POLITICAL AUTHORITY, AND STATE IDENTITY

The most prominent accounts of absolutist state formation focus on capitalism, war-fighting, or institutional rationality. For Immanuel Wallerstein, the needs of emerging capitalist classes were crucial in the rise of absolutist states: "Local capitalist classes—cash-crop landowners (often, even usually, nobility) and merchants—turned to the state, not only to liberate them from non-market constraints . . . but to create new constraints on the new market, the market of the European world-economy."[12] This interpretation has met with sustained criticism, not the least for its inadequate explanation of the different organizational structures assumed by absolutist states. The missing factor, one prominent line of criticism holds, is the role that warfare played in the process of state formation. Charles Tilly contends that the emergence of territorial states, and the various organizational forms they took, resulted from the dialectical interplay between capital and coercion, between mutually reinforcing procrustean and mercantile interests.[13] According to the third explanation, rapidly changing patterns of ownership and exchange demanded new regimes to protect property rights, and sovereign states emerged because they met this need more efficiently than alternative political institutions. As North and Thomas observe, "Governments were able to define and enforce property rights at a lower cost than could voluntary groups, and these gains became more pronounced as markets expanded."[14] This was not a straightforward process, Hendrik Spruyt argues. Initially three institutional forms emerged: city-states, city-leagues, and absolutist states. Only later did sovereign states prevail, demonstrating over time a

---

[12] Wallerstein, *Capitalist World Economy*, 18.

[13] Tilly, *Coercion, Capital, and European States*. For an earlier discussion of the role of war-fighting in absolutist state formation, see Tilly, "State-Making as Organized Crime."

[14] North and Thomas, *Rise of the Western World*, 7.

greater capacity to rationalize their economies and mobilize resources, control external relations, and delegitimate rival institutional forms.[15]

These explanations each capture an important factor in the state formation process. Yet they have little to say about the central, defining characteristic of the shift from medievalism to absolutism—the reorganization and redistribution of political authority. As H. L. A. Hart argues in his critique of Austin's theory of jurisprudence, political authority is more than the capacity to rule, it is the right to rule.[16] In the heteronomous world of medieval Europe, a wide range of actors claimed, and successfully upheld, rights to rule, and the nature and jurisdictional scope of these rights varied greatly in their temporal, spatial, and substantive domains.[17] Political authority was thus decentralized and nonexclusive. The transition from medievalism to absolutism involved two interrelated processes: the centralization and territorial demarcation of authority, and the rationalization and consolidation of hierarchy. In the first of these processes, European monarchs claimed the right to determine the predominant religion within their territorial jurisdictions, thus depriving the Catholic Church of its transnational authority. They also freed themselves from the overarching authority of the Holy Roman Empire, asserting their rights to interpret law, impose taxes, and declare war. This process necessarily entailed a concomitant rationalization of social and political hierarchy within the emerging territorial units. The domestic order of the state assumed a pyramidal form, with the monarch claiming singular authority at the apex of an escalating system of superordinate/subordinate relations: adults over children, men over women, nobles over commoners, kings over aristocrats, God over mortals.

Legitimacy, not coercion, is the necessary prerequisite for stable political authority, and investing European monarchs with supreme political authority was, in essence, a process of legitimation. Before an agent can command political authority it must establish its status within the social context in which it seeks to act. "To have power," Richard Ashley writes, "an agent must first secure its recognition as an agent capable of having power, and, to do that, it must first demonstrate its competence in terms of the collective and coreflective structures (that is, the practical cognitive schemes and history of experience) by which the community confers meaning and organizes collective expectations."[18] In the context of abso-

---

[15] Spruyt, *Sovereign State and Its Competitors.*

[16] Hart, *Concept of Law*, 80–88.

[17] Perry Anderson writes that the "political map" of medieval Europe "was an inextricably superimposed and tangled one, in which different juridical instances were geographically interwoven and stratified, and plural allegiances, asymmetrical suzerainties and anomalous enclaves abounded." Anderson, *Lineages of the Absolutist State*, 37–38.

[18] Ashley, "Poverty of Neorealism," 291–292.

lutist state formation—and all state formation for that matter—this process of legitimation involved the construction of a coherent state identity, or raison d'être. As argued in chapter 2, social identities not only inform plans of action, they provide justificatory foundations for action. If absolutist rulers were to command authority, if they were to justify their dictates as legitimate, then their identities as social actors, rightfully ordained with decision-making power, had to be established. To instill authority and inspire fealty, the identity of the absolutist state had to be grounded in prevailing cultural values.[19] It had to resonate with existing systems of meaning, especially those defining legitimate power and rightful social action. As the following section explains, political elites of the sixteenth and seventeenth centuries drew on prevailing Christian and dynastic values when fashioning the postmedieval order. Rejecting the transnational authority of the Church did not entail a rejection of Christianity per se, rather the natural and social universe was reimagined to invest territorial monarchs with authority direct from God.

THE CONSTITUTIONAL STRUCTURE OF THE ABSOLUTIST SOCIETY OF STATES

By the end of the seventeenth century, this process of political legitimation had established in the consciousness of European elites a distinctive set of constitutional metavalues, an ensemble of intersubjective beliefs that mandated the sovereign state as the paramount political institution and licensed the supreme authority of the dynastic monarch, the very embodiment of the state. In this normative schema, the moral purpose of the state was defined as the preservation of a divinely ordained, rigidly hierarchical social order. To fulfil this purpose, monarchs were endowed with supreme authority—their commands were law. Procedural justice was thus defined in strict, authoritative terms. God's law and natural law were the ultimate arbiters of what constituted justice, and they received worldly expression in the commands of dynastic monarchs.

In explaining absolutist ideals of the moral purpose of the state and procedural justice, the following discussion focuses on French political and legal thought. This focus is warranted for several reasons. First, France was central to the development of absolutism in Europe. It was the home of the *ancien régime*, the site where absolutism achieved its greatest ideological and institutional expression. As Herbert Rowen argues, the "creation of an effective state for rule over men reached its greatest height during the early modern period in France; but it was also there

---

[19] Swidler, "Culture in Action," 280.

that the idealization of the state . . . was most advanced."[20] As such, it became a model for state-building monarchies elsewhere in Europe, an institutional reference point for those engaged in the territorial aggregation of authority. Second, French political and legal thought had a pervasive influence on political debate in other emerging European states. Even in early-seventeenth-century England, where the Civil War would soon shake the foundations of divine right absolutism and inspire Hobbes' protoliberal justification for absolutism, Bodin's ideas, and those of other French theorists, had considerable influence on political debate.[21] Finally, French statecraft played a crucial role in the institutional and geopolitical evolution of absolutist international society. France was not only implicated in all three of the major conflicts and settlements of the period, it pioneered the development of "old diplomacy," with French writers producing classic works in diplomatic theory, and the French state developing the most sophisticated diplomatic service in Europe.

The Moral Purpose of the Absolutist State

Jean Bodin's *Six Books of the Commonwealth*, completed in 1576, is the most celebrated statement of this justification for the absolutist state. At the heart of his thesis is the patriarchal family, which he upholds as the ideal social unit. For Bodin, this collectivity combines a perfect division of labor and a model authority structure: "A family may be defined as the right ordering of a group of persons owing obedience to the head of the household. . . . Authority in the family rests on the fourfold relationship between husband and wife, father and child, master and servant, owner and slave."[22] This image of the patriarchal family informs Bodin's theory of absolutism in two ways. First, the ideal state is the family writ-large: "Thus the well-ordered family is a true image of the commonwealth, and domestic comparable with sovereign authority. It follows that the household is the model of right order in the commonwealth."[23] Second, families, not individuals, are the principal constituents of the state: "A commonwealth may be defined as the rightly ordered government of a number of families, and of those which are their common concern, by a sovereign power."[24]

Bodin's vision is entirely Platonic, with individuals fully subordinated to the needs of the social and political organism. To begin with, the mean-

[20] Rowen, *King's State*, 28.
[21] Burns, "Idea of Absolutism," 27.
[22] Bodin, *Six Books of the Commonwealth*, 6, 9.
[23] Ibid., 6.
[24] Ibid., 1.

ing and trajectory of individuals' lives are determined by their functions in society. The state is likened to the human body, enjoying health only "when every particular member performs its proper function."[25] It follows, therefore, that humans are far from equal, either in status or rights: there "never was a commonwealth, real or imaginary, even if conceived in the most popular terms, where citizens were in truth equal in all rights and privileges. Some always have more, some less than the rest."[26] The irrelevance of individual purposes and potentialities for Bodin's justification of absolutism is apparent in two features of his work. First, he lists families, colleges, and corporate bodies among the constituent units of the state but makes no mention of the individual.[27] Second, unlike the modern depiction of the individual as self-reflective, aware of an inner self in need of fulfillment, Bodin's individual is conscious only of external natural, social, and heavenly realms. The development of human consciousness moves through physical, social, astrological, and divine phases, but the self never features as an object of contemplation.[28]

According to Bodin, the social and political order is merely a reflection of the natural order, and exhibits a harmony and logic ordained by God. The preservation of this order constitutes the moral purpose of the absolutist state, providing the justificatory basis for sovereign rights. Just as the father is granted authority over the family, monarchs receive their political authority directly from God: there "are none on earth, after God, greater than sovereign princes, whom God establishes as His lieutenants to command the rest of mankind."[29] Monarchical authority is thus unconditional, it is "absolute and perpetual."[30] This is reflected in Bodin's conception of citizenship. In contrast to the modern ideal of the citizen as a participant in the decision-making processes of the state, Bodin defines the citizen as one who submits to the authority of the sovereign: "It is therefore the submission and obedience of a free subject to his prince, and the tuition, protection, and jurisdiction exercised by the prince over his subjects that makes a citizen."[31]

These views were echoed a century later by Jean Domat, a leading French jurist in the reign of Louis XIV. Domat, like Bodin, begins with a holistic conception of society, in which the needs of the divinely ordained social order dictate the roles, positions, and interests of individuals. "All know," he writes, "that human society forms a body of which each person

---

[25] Ibid., 7.
[26] Ibid., 22.
[27] Ibid., 7.
[28] Ibid., 4–5.
[29] Ibid., 40.
[30] Ibid., 25.
[31] Ibid., 21.

is a member. This truth, which Scripture teaches us and the light of reason makes evident, is the foundation of all duties that determine each man's conduct toward all others and toward the whole. For these duties are nothing but the functions that are proper to the position in which each man finds himself according to his rank in the body." It is the role of the sovereign—indeed the moral purpose of the state—to maintain this social organism. It is "necessary that a head coerce and rule the body of society and maintain order among those who should give the public the benefit of the different contributions that their stations require of them." To this end, God enthrones dynastic monarchs as his lieutenants on earth. God "is the only natural sovereign over men," Domat argues, and "is it from Him that all who govern hold their power and authority, and it is God himself they represent in their functions." Monarchs thus hold supreme authority, subject only to the strictures of natural and divine law: "Since government is necessary for the common good and God himself established it, it follows that those who are its subjects must be submissive and obedient." Citizenship, we see, is again defined as subjection to the commands of a legitimate monarch.[32]

The Authoritative Norm of Procedural Justice

This rationale for the sovereignty of the dynastic state implies an authoritative conception of procedural justice. Standards of right and wrong social conduct were not to be determined by discursive engagement (as in ancient Greece), by the ritual enactment of virtue (as in Renaissance Italy), or by the democratic legislation of codified law (as in the modern era); they were to be dictated by the command of a supreme authority, God in the first instance, monarchs by deputation.

Nowhere is this more apparent than in the prevailing conception of law—law as command. Rightful action was defined by law, and law was defined by the sovereign. "The word law," Bodin argues, "signifies the right of command of that person, or those persons, who have absolute authority over all the rest without exception, saving only the law-giver himself, whether the command touches all subjects in general or only some in particular."[33] In Bodin's schema, law as command operates on two levels. There is the command of God, found in natural law and divine law, to which all are subject, including absolutist monarchs: "All princes of the earth are subject to them, and cannot contravene them without

---

[32] The passages quoted here are from translated extracts of Jean Domat's *Le Droit Public*, published in Church, *Impact of Absolutism in France*, 76–80.

[33] Bodin, *Six Books of the Commonwealth*, 43.

treason and rebellion against God."[34] And there is the command of the sovereign, in the form of civil law, to which all of the inhabitants of a given territory are bound. It "is a law both divine and natural," Bodin writes, "that we should obey the edicts and ordinances of him whom God has set in authority over us, providing his edicts are not contrary to God's law."[35] Because civil law represents the will of the sovereign, the monarch alone is unbound by its precepts: "That is why it is laid down in civil law that the prince is above the law, for the word *law* in Latin implies the command of him who is invested with sovereign power."[36]

This conception of law as command implies a vertical theory of legal obligation. Subjects are not obliged to obey the law because they consented to it but because it is the command of the sovereign—the legitimate political authority. According to Bodin, "The principal mark of sovereign majesty and absolute power is the right to impose laws generally on all subjects regardless of their consent."[37] This view is echoed by Domat: "As obedience is necessary to preserve the order and peace that unite the head and members of the body of the state, it is the universal obligation of all subjects in all cases to obey the ruler's orders without assuming the liberty of judging them."[38] This does not mean, however, that the authority of dynastic monarchs was unlimited. In fact, they were bound by the same principal of legal obligation. As Bodin's schema indicates, monarchs were obliged to rule in accordance with divine and natural law, the will of God, their superior. In Bodin's words, "Absolute power only implies freedom in relation to positive laws, and not in relation to the law of God."[39] Domat explains the logic behind this principle: "Since the power of princes comes to them from God and is placed in their hands as an instrument of his providence and his guidance of the states that He commits to their rule, it is clear that princes should use their power in proportion to the objectives that providence and divine guidance seek."[40]

This notion of law as the command of a paramount authority, and the authoritative norm of procedural justice it embodied, represented a significant departure from the ideals of medieval society. As Gianfranco Poggi observes, "The idea that the ruler could, by an act of his sovereign will, produce new law and have it enforced by his own increasingly pervasive and effective system of courts was wholly revolutionary. It

[34] Ibid., 29.
[35] Ibid., 34.
[36] Ibid., 28.
[37] Ibid., 32.
[38] Church, *Impact of Absolutism in France*, 78.
[39] Bodin, *Six Books of the Commonwealth*, 35.
[40] Church, *Impact of Absolutism in France*, 79.

transformed law from a *framework of* into an *instrument for* rule."[41] Where law had once constituted a complex set of rights, an ancient system of entitlements, claimed and upheld by diverse feudal authorities, it now became a centralized catalogue of decrees, proclaimed and enforced by a titular power.[42]

Ideological Challenges, Institutional Variations

The belief that the state existed to preserve a divinely ordained social order, and the idea that rightful social conduct should be determined by the command of a supreme authority, defined the terms of legitimate statehood and rightful state action in Europe from the end of the sixteenth century to the middle of the nineteenth. This does not mean, however, that these ideas went unchallenged, or that they received the same institutional expression in all states. One finds, though, that the principal ideological challenges to divine-right absolutism either reaffirmed the prevailing authoritative norm of procedural justice or they remained the province of radicalism. Furthermore, the institutional differences between states, significant as they were, represented distinctions *of* kind, not *in* kind.

Divine-right absolutism was challenged by relatively moderate, contractarian rationales for absolutist rule, and by more subversive, liberal accounts of sovereignty. Indicative of the former, Hobbes advanced a secular defense of absolutism, grounding the authority of the state in a hypothetical social contract. Yet despite this innovation, Hobbes ended up embracing the same authoritative conception of procedural justice as Bodin. Law was again defined as the command of a superior—natural and divine law the command of God, civil law the command of the sovereign: it "is not counsel, but command; nor command of any man to any man; but only of him, whose command is addressed to one formerly obliged to obey him."[43] Early liberals, like John Locke, offered far deeper critiques of divine right absolutism, reconceiving the moral purpose of the state, promoting the sovereignty of the "people," and advocating a legislative conception of procedural justice.[44] Yet as Richard Ashcraft observes, this was the voice of radicalism, even in the more constitutionalist climate of late-seventeenth-century England.[45] There were, of course, other political creeds that challenged the establishment radicalism of

---

[41] Gianfranco Poggi, *Development of the Modern State*, 72–73.

[42] On the medieval conception of law, see Ullmann's, *Medieval Idea of Law*, and *History of Political Thought*.

[43] Hobbes, *Leviathan*, 244.

[44] Locke, *Two Treatises of Government*, 354–375.

[45] Ashcraft, *Revolutionary Politics*.

Lockian liberalism, advocating protosocialism, universal suffrage, and participatory democracy, but in the ideological climate of absolutist Europe, these were marginal indeed. In Christopher Hill's words, the Diggers, Ranters, and Levellers of post–Civil War England constituted "a revolt within a revolution."[46]

The ideology of divine-right absolutism provided the justificatory framework for European state formation—the language and symbolism of legitimate territorial rule—but it did not produce institutionally homogenous states. Preexisting regional variations in feudal social relations, differences in the fiscal strategies monarchs employed to sustain warfighting, contrasting bargains between monarchs, nobles and cities, and the imperatives of terrain and geographical scale all encouraged institutional variation.[47] Nevertheless, this was bounded variation, in much the same way that institutional differences between modern liberal democracies represent variations on a theme. Within these bounds, France in the reign of Louis XIV was the archetype, with decision-making authority, if not effective power of implementation, concentrated in the hands of the monarchy.[48] As Michael Kimmel argues, in "France state and monarchy were nearly conterminous; kings did not need to consult any but their councillors to develop policy, and all potentially representative institutions existed only by the pleasure of the king."[49] Of the other major European states, Spain, Russia, and Sweden developed institutional structures that approached the French "ideal." The Austrian Hapsburgs strove for such heights, but were thwarted by a strong feudal nobility and by the geographical fragmentation and the religious and cultural diversity of their territories. England provided the least fertile terrain for absolutism. Imitating French experience, the Stuart Kings—James I (1603–25), Charles I (1625–49), Charles II (1660–85), and James II (1685–88)—grasped for absolute rule, bypassing parliament to legislate by decree, level taxes without consent, raise standing armies, and dictate the religion of the realm. Yet sustained resistance, peaking with the Civil War (1642–88) and the Glorious Revolution (1688), quashed these ambitions, leaving

[46] Hill, *World Turned Upside Down*.

[47] See Anderson, *Lineages of the Absolutist State*; Ashley, *Age of Absolutism*; Beloff, *Age of Absolutism*; Bonney, *European Dynastic States*; Doyle, *Old European Order*; Kimmel, *Absolutism and Its Discontents*; Miller, *Absolutism in Seventeenth-Century Europe*; Strayer, *Medieval Origins of the Modern State*; and Tilly, *Coercion, Capital, and European States*.

[48] See Briggs, *Early Modern France*; Church, *Impact of Absolutism in France*; Keohane, *Philosophy and the State in France*; Kisser, "Formation of State Policy in Western European Absolutisms"; Major, *From Renaissance Monarchy to Absolute Monarchy*; Mettam, "France"; Mousnier, *Institutions of France under the Absolute Monarchy*; Parker, "Sovereignty, Absolutism, and the Function of Law"; Poggi, *Development of the Modern State*; Rowen, *King's State*.

[49] Kimmel, *Absolutism and Its Discontents*, 19.

the monarchy at the beginning of the eighteenth century with theoretical control over government, but dependent financially upon parliamentary consent.[50] The result, in Kimmel's words, was a "clear disjunction between the English Monarchy and English state."[51]

In sum, divine-right absolutism provided the dominant discourse of legitimate sovereignty in postmedieval Europe, and although the institutional structures of emerging sovereign states never fully realized these ideals and while differences between national institutions were many, absolutist principles provided the broad architectural template for state formation, particularly on the Continent. In 1846, looking back at a "states-system" then in decline, A. H. L. Heeren wrote that the "European political system, notwithstanding its internal variety, was, till within these few years, a system of predominant monarchies; where republics . . . were merely tolerated. This predominance," he concluded, "had a considerable influence on general politics."[52]

THE FUNDAMENTAL INSTITUTIONS OF ABSOLUTIST INTERNATIONAL SOCIETY

The constitutional structure of absolutist international society had a profound effect on the nature of basic institutional practices. This effect was both negative and positive. The metavalues of the system impeded the development of institutional forms that subsequently flourished in the modern era. In a world where social hierarchy was the norm, the principle of sovereign equality never took root. What is more, the predominant authoritative norm of procedural justice, and the attendant notion of law as command, undermined the development of contractual international law, and this in turn inhibited extensive multilateralism. This is not to suggest, however, that the absolutist society of states was an institutional void, even if it was comparatively underdeveloped. The seventeenth and eighteenth centuries saw the emergence of two basic institutional forms: naturalist international law and old diplomacy. Yet the preoccupation with precedence and hierarchy among states, and the prevailing authoritative norm of procedural justice, shaped these institutions in distinctive ways. Since the principle of sovereign equality was rejected and legal obligation rested on fealty to a supreme authority, legal publicists, such as

[50] See Anderson, *Lineages of the Absolutist State*; Burgess, "Divine Right of Kings Reconsidered"; Collins, *Divine Cosmos to Sovereign State*; Corrigan and Sayer, *Great Arch*; Harris, "Tories and the Rule of Law in the Reign of Charles II"; Kimmel, *Absolutism and Its Discontents*; and Miller, "Britain."

[51] Kimmel, *Absolutism and Its Discontents*, 19.

[52] Heeren, *History of the Political System of Europe and Its Colonies*, 7.

Hugo Grotius and Samuel Pufendorf, had to appeal to the will of God, in the form of natural and divine law, to sanction a system of legal restraints on state conduct. Moreover, the concern with hierarchy, and the secondary importance attached to mutually legislated, contractual international law, encouraged the development of a particular kind of diplomatic practice, one that was essentially bilateral, secretive, and hierarchical.

Sovereign Inequality

In modern international society, the principle of sovereign equality is an unquestioned given. Irrespective of size, wealth, military capacity, or religious and cultural character, sovereign states have equal standing under international law; that is, they receive the same recognition as legal subjects and possess the same rights and obligations. As Article 2 of the United Nations Charter specifies, the "Organization is based on the principle of the sovereign equality of all of its members."[53] In absolutist Europe, however, no such principle existed. At Westphalia, Sweden tried to establish the idea that all monarchs had equal standing, only to be firmly rebuffed. François de Callières—the preeminent diplomatic theorist of the sixteenth and seventeenth centuries—records that "some crowns attempted, during the negotiation of the peace of Münster, to introduce a pretended equality among all the Kings of Europe, but, notwithstanding that innovation, which was ill grounded, and unheard of till that time, France has remained in possession of its ancient right of preeminence."[54] As Wight correctly observes, the "leveling" of international society—the general acceptance that all sovereign states are equal—was not achieved until after the Napoleonic Wars, at the beginning of the nineteenth century.[55]

The belief that sovereignty was bestowed by a Christian God, and the pyramidal conception of society that prevailed, produced an unstable, and perpetually challenged, hierachization of absolutist international society. This occurred at two levels. Among the Christian states that formed the core of the system, conflicts over precedence were endemic. Claiming that monarchs were God's lieutenants on earth was one thing, but establishing a reliable means to determine which of God's lieutenants was closer to the Divine was another. While successive French monarchs consistently claimed the status of "the most Christian King," and while these

---

[53] *Charter of the United Nations*, Article 2.1, 4.

[54] de Callières, *Art of Diplomacy*, 125–26.

[55] Wight, *Systems of States*, 136.

claims were often recognized in treaties and by the Papacy, European states never reached a stable agreement about their relative preeminence. "The result," Hamilton and Langhorne contend, "was bitter, often unedifying, sometimes comic battles over precedence."[56] The idea that Christian monarchs were the only legitimate sovereigns, and their's the only legitimate states, also sanctioned a hierarchical division between European international society and the rest of the world. Nowhere was this more apparent than in the distinction drawn between the Christian community of dynastic states and the Ottoman Empire. In Wight's words, European powers considered the Islamic world a "historical, even an eschatological, embodiment of evil."[57] Even Grotius, the "father of international law," clearly differentiated between the European society of Christian states and the Islamic world, arguing that Christian states had stronger moral and legal obligations to each other than to "the Turk."[58]

Wight argues that a society of states exists when states claim supreme authority within their territorial boundaries and when these claims are recognized as legitimate by the wider community of states. The lack of any sense of sovereign equality, and the enduring concern with social and religious hierarchy, suggest that the second of these characteristics—mutual recognition—existed in absolutist international society, but in a thin, rather contradictory form. It was increasingly accepted that monarchs were entitled to exercise supreme authority within the territorial limits of their respective states: this was, after all, the idea of divine right absolutism. The development of a deeper sense of mutual recognition was both encouraged and impeded, however, by prevailing frameworks of political identification, conceptions of society, and notions of procedural justice. It was encouraged by the religious and dynastic ties that united European monarchs, but offset by their inability to understand social relationships, even among sovereigns, in anything other than hierarchical terms, and by the vertical conception of legal obligation.

Naturalist International Law

Because monarchs denied the principle of sovereign equality, and since the authoritative norm of procedural justice, enshrined in the notion of law of command, obliged them to obey only the will of God, absolutist Europe was not fertile terrain for the growth of contractual international

---

[56] Hamilton and Langhorne, *Practice of Diplomacy*, 64.

[57] Wight, *Systems of States*, 120.

[58] For discussions of Grotius' views on this issue, see Bull, Kingsbury, and Roberts, *Grotius*, 14, 47–48; and Neumann and Welsh, "Other in European Self-Definition," 339.

law. States certainly negotiated treaties, and several basic principles of international conduct began to take shape during this period, but as a fundamental institution of international society, grounded in the practices of states, international law lacked both depth and breadth.[59] It was a marginal factor in the constitution of actors and poorly linked to other interstate activities. With reverence for the command of God providing the only moral compulsion for states to observe the law of nations, its development took place primarily in the works of celebrated legal publicists. This was, in Wight's words, "a law-aspiring period."[60] Furthermore, until the end of the eighteenth century, international legal theorists affirmed, rather than challenged, dominant rationales for sovereignty, conceptions of society, and understandings of procedural justice and law, building on these assumptions to construct a distinctive "naturalist" account of international law.

Despite important differences between their works, Hugo Grotius and Samuel Pufendorf agree that the moral purpose of the state lies in the preservation of a divinely ordained social order. According to Grotius, "Among the characteristic traits of man is an impelling desire for society, that is for social life—not of any and every sort, but peaceful, and organized according to a measure of his intelligence, with his own kind."[61] While expediency and self-interest contribute to this urge, it is the law of nature, reflecting God's will, that ultimately leads humans to form societies. "The nature of man compels men into society," Grotius writes, "and is thus the mother of the law of nature."[62] In this schema, monarchs are invested with political authority to maintain the social order, much as "guardianship was instituted for the sake of the ward."[63] Pufendorf is less enamored with the innate sociability of humans, and argues that the amalgamation of families into extensive state-based societies was driven, in large measure, by fear and insecurity.[64] Nevertheless, he too believes that this move was entirely consistent with the will of God, who "is understood to have given prior command to the human race, mediated through the dictates of reason, that when it had multiplied, states should be constituted."[65] Once again, the sovereign authority of the monarch is thought necessary to maintain this social order, to ensure its internal peace and

---

[59] The idea of institutional depth and breadth is discussed in Krasner, "Sovereignty: An Institutional Perspective," 75.

[60] Wight, *Systems of States*, 148.

[61] Grotius, *Law of War and Peace*, 11.

[62] Ibid., 15.

[63] Ibid., 110.

[64] In fact, at one point Pufendorf's account bears a striking resemblance to Hobbes's. *On the Duty of Man and Citizen*, 115–140.

[65] Ibid., 138.

external safety. It follows, Pufendorf contends, that sovereign authority has "its own particular sanctity."[66]

Reiterating the central precept of absolutist thought, both authors argue that a monarch's authority is unlimited, except by natural and divine law. "That power is called sovereign," Grotius argues, "whose actions are not subject to the legal control of another, so that they cannot be rendered void by the operation of another human will."[67] Likewise, the authority of the state, Pufendorf contends, "is not dependent on a superior; it acts by its own will and judgement; its actions may not be nullified by anyone on the ground of superiority."[68] Against such authority, the people retain little right of resistance. Grotius vehemently rejects the idea "that everywhere and without exception sovereignty resides in the people, so that it is permissible for the people to restrain and punish kings whenever they make a bad use of their power. How many evils this opinion has given rise to, and can even now give rise to if it sinks into men's minds."[69] Pufendorf concurs, arguing that when a sovereign "has threatened them with the most atrocious injuries, individuals will protect themselves by flight or endure any injury or damage rather than draw swords against one who remains the father of their country, however harsh he may be."[70]

Not surprisingly, Grotius and Pufendorf follow the lead of domestic political theorists in defining law as command. Grotius distinguishes between two types of law: law as a rule of action, and law as a body of rights. The former is divided into "rectorial law," which governs unequal social relations ("between father and children, master and slave, and king and subjects"), and "equatorial law," which coordinates relations among equals ("between brothers, or citizens, or friends, or allies"). He also subdivides bodies of rights, this time between the public rights of the state over the lives and property of its members, and the private rights of the individual. According to Grotius, the rectorial law of the superior, and the public rights of the state, always take precedence.[71] Lacking Grotius' nuance, Pufendorf merely asserts that "[l]aw is a decree by which a superior obliges one who is subject to him to conform his actions to the superior's prescript."[72]

Having defined law as the command of a superior, Grotius and Pufendorf proceed to base international law on the law of nature—the command of God. Grotius draws a distinction between the law of nature and

---

[66] Ibid., 147.
[67] Grotius, *Law of War and Peace*, 102.
[68] Pufendorf, *On the Duty of Man and Citizen*, 146.
[69] Grotius, *Law of War and Peace*, 103.
[70] Pufendorf, *On the Duty of Man and Citizen*, 147.
[71] Grotius, *Law of War and Peace*, 34–36.
[72] Pufendorf, *On the Duty of Man and Citizen*, 27.

the law of nations, the former providing an overarching moral code, the latter consisting of the customary and conventional practices of states. The law of nature is the expression of divine will and is not the product of instrumental state interests. The "first principles of nature," he contends, "ought to be more dear to us than those things through whose instrumentality we have brought to it."[73] The law of nations, on the other hand, has "its origins in the free will of man."[74] By "mutual consent it has become possible that certain laws should originate as between all states, or as great many states; and it is apparent that the laws thus originating had in view the advantage, not of particular states, but of the great society of states."[75] Although Grotius treats the law of nations as a human artifact, he is at pains to stress that the obligation to obey such law does not derive from consent: "Observance of the law of nature and of divine law, *or of the law of nations* . . . is binding upon all kings, even though they have made no promise [my emphasis]."[76] Obedience to God, the paramount authority, thus provides the primary basis of obligation to international law. Examples of treaties and conventions, drawn almost exclusively from Greek and Roman history, in turn provide a posteriori evidence of the law of nations. The circularity of the argument is hard to miss.

Because Grotius acknowledges the relevance, if not the autonomy or primacy, of voluntary international law, scholars have debated the depth of his naturalism.[77] Pufendorf's work, on the other hand, inspires no such controversy. Although he recognizes that states create treaties and conventions to regulate their relations, he denies that these constitute law, because they were not promulgated by a superior authority.[78] As the will of God, only natural law provides the basis for genuine international law: "Though these precepts have clear utility, they get the force of law only upon the presuppositions that God exists and rules all things by His providence. . . . Laws necessarily imply a superior, and such a superior as actually has governance over another."[79] In deducing the precepts of true international law—that is, international law based on the will of God—Pufendorf merely extrapolates from individuals to states. States, as hierarchical collectivities endorsed by natural law, became international persons, with rights and obligations analogous to individuals.[80]

---

[73] Grotius, *Law of War and Peace*, 52.

[74] Ibid., 24.

[75] Ibid., 15.

[76] Ibid., 121.

[77] For a good overview of this debate see the essays collected in Bull, Kingsbury, and Roberts, *Grotius*.

[78] Pufendorf, *Elements of Universal Jurisprudence*, 147.

[79] Pufendorf, *On the Duty of Man and Citizen*, 36.

[80] Ibid., chapter 16.

"Old Diplomacy"

The lack of any sense of sovereign equality, and the prevailing naturalist understanding of international law, encouraged the development of a particular form of diplomatic practice. Where neither legal principle nor material power compelled states to think of one another as diplomatic equals, and where faith, not contract, sanctified international law, the normative prerequisites for the development of extensive multilateralism did not exist. This was, however, the heyday of classical diplomacy, the era in which the most celebrated works in diplomatic theory were published, the period when European, particularly French, diplomacy reached its apogee. "Old diplomacy," as it has since been labeled, exhibited four characteristics in general: it was incidental, bilateral, secretive, and hierarchical.

Old diplomacy was incidental in the sense that absolutist states were less concerned with the negotiation of generalized, reciprocally binding rules of international conduct than with the resolution of particular conflicts and crises. For European monarchs, the idea of meeting to formulate regulatory principles that would apply to all like cases at all times held little attraction. They engaged in diplomatic interaction when particular circumstances demanded, when unilateral claims and the use of force failed to realize their objectives. In this respect, old diplomacy was reactive, not anticipatory or preventive. As we shall see, the major diplomatic encounters of the period—Westphalia, Utrecht, and Vienna—occurred after devastating conflagrations, and the complex treaties they produced were devoted, in large measure, to resolving the proximate causes of those conflicts. To be sure, the Peace of Westphalia built on the earlier Peace of Augsburg (1555) to establish principles governing the religious prerogatives of monarchs; the Treaties of Utrecht implied, through their provisions, that rights of succession could be qualified by the requirements of a stable balance of power; and the Congress of Vienna instituted the principle that Great Powers should concert to maintain an equilibrium of power and combat revolutionary nationalism. But as Holsti observes, the Westphalia and Utrecht settlements were not animated by any deep normative commitment to establishing general rules of international conduct: "they looked to the past."[81] The Congress of Vienna went beyond these

---

[81] "Westphalia," Holsti writes, "set free the dynasts to pursue whatever interests motivated them, with few guidelines as to how these interests might be moderated." He goes on to argue: "Like Westphalia, Utrecht looked to the past. It solved the particular problem posed by France and Spain, but it failed to address the more generic problems associated with a system of independent sovereignties based on dynastic ambitions." Holsti, *Peace and War*, 26, 80.

earlier settlements by instituting "peacetime" conferences of the Great Powers to maintain international order, but these meetings remained conflict and crisis specific, concerned with managing a given revolutionary upheaval or countering the expansionist ambitions of one of their number.

The incidental nature of old diplomacy privileged narrow, bilateral negotiations between conflicting parties over broader, multilateral negotiations among the general membership of international society or even a significant proportion thereof. In comparison to the modern era, multilateral negotiations and accords were the exception rather than the rule. Between 1648 and 1815, European states concluded only 127 treaties involving three or more states, amounting to less than one per year.[82] Although difficult to ascertain with any precision, the number of these treaties that were genuinely multilateral—that is, which enshrined generalized, mutually binding rules of conduct—was substantially lower than these figures suggest. Even the major peace settlements of the time, which sought to resolve systemic conflicts that were of interest to the society of states as a whole, were negotiated largely, although not exclusively, bilaterally. The general tendency was to disaggregate a systemic conflict into dyadic subconflicts, negotiate resolutions to these disputes separately, and then aggregate the resulting agreements into a complex of treaties, which together formed a "Peace." This was true of the negotiations at Westphalia, Utrecht, and Vienna, although in the last of these cases, negotiations among the five Great Powers at times approached multilateral diplomacy.

The most commonly noted feature of old diplomacy was its secrecy. In the preeminent study of diplomatic practice published during the absolutist period, de Callières describes secrecy as "the life of negotiations."[83] Although conducted by agents of the state, diplomacy was a private, not a public, affair, at least at the level of process, if not interest. Diplomacy was conducted behind closed doors, not only shielding negotiations from the people but also from other powers. States in turn went to elaborate measures to protect the confidentiality of their diplomatic communications, and encryption became a veritable art form. Although the results of secret diplomacy were usually published, often they were not, with clandestine treaties and undisclosed clauses proliferating. This preoccupation with secrecy stemmed in part from the enduring realities of negotiation, where compromising hard-felt interests is easier done away from the public eye. But secret diplomacy was also a practice that suited the age, an age when monarchs considered foreign policy their private domain

---

[82] In the following century, the number of treaties concluded between three or more states leapt to 817. Mostecky, *Index of Multilateral Treaties*.

[83] de Callières, *Art of Diplomacy*, 164.

and thought themselves accountable only to God, a mentality reinforced by the lack of effective parliamentary institutions in most European states. And since the idea that states should engage in multilateral negotiations to legislate contractual international law held little sway at this time, nothing spurred the development of more public, conference-based diplomacy. The primacy of secret diplomacy clearly differentiates the institutional practices of absolutist international society from those of other societies of states. While secret negotiations have always played a role in international affairs, ancient Greek arbitration revolved around public discourse, Renaissance diplomacy rested on public ritual, and modern multilateralism entails the public legislation of codified law.

The general assumption that sovereign states differed in status, and the preoccupation with preeminence and precedence this generated, gave old diplomacy a distinctly hierarchical character. Enhancing and protecting the state's international standing was a key objective of absolutist diplomacy, with increases in stature constituting a significant foreign policy achievement and decreases a humiliating failure. As Hamilton and Langhorne observe, "Victories and defeats on the battleground of precedence were both significant in themselves and could be signals of shifts in the balance of power between states."[84] Even when hierarchy was not the core issue animating interstate negotiations, it structured the process by which those negotiations were conducted. After declaring the notion of sovereign equality "ill-founded," de Callières devotes an entire chapter to "ceremonies and civilities," to the elaborate code of engagement that due respect for precedence demanded.[85] Unless this code was observed and the correct hierarchy established and respected, progress in negotiations could be delayed, or cease altogether. At Westphalia, for instance, the first six months of negotiations were wasted deciding how the parties would be seated and in what order they would enter the room.[86] When settlements were finally reached, the concern with preeminence and precedence was reflected in the lengthy preambles to treaties, those celebratory declarations of the parties' exalted titles, all ranked according to status. Toward the end of the absolutist period, this concern with standing was secularized, gradually transmutating into the idea that there were "Great Powers," endowed with special rights and obligations in international society.

After the American and French Revolutions, old diplomacy was increasingly maligned, decried as an archaic, corrupt, inflammatory, and antidemocratic practice. By the middle of the nineteenth century, states

---

[84] Hamilton and Langhorne, *Practice of Diplomacy*, 67.
[85] de Callières, *Art of Diplomacy*, 124–129.
[86] Wedgwood, *Thirty Years War*, 475.

began to embrace a "new" form of public diplomacy, animated by the institutional principles of multilateralism. For many diplomatic historians and classical realists, the shift from "old" to "new" diplomacy constituted a precipitous fall from rationality into idealism. As we saw in chapter 1, Morgenthau considers old diplomacy to be a natural, even inevitable, response to the imperatives of anarchy, a practice that grew "ineluctably from the objective nature of things political."[87] The development of multilateral diplomacy, he contends, "is no substitute for these procedures. On the contrary, it tends to aggravate rather than mitigate international conflicts and leaves the prospect of peace dimmed rather than brightened."[88] Critics, such as Morgenthau, have correctly attributed the rise of multilateralism to a deep-seated ideological revolution in the nineteenth century, one that transformed the terms of domestic and international governance. "It was the belief," Nicolson argues, "that it was possible to apply to the conduct of *external* affairs, the ideas and practices which, in the conduct of *internal* affairs, had for generations been regarded as the essentials of liberal democracy."[89] In emphasizing the inherent rationality of old diplomacy, however, Morgenthau, Nicolson, and others ignore, or deliberately downplay, the fact that it too was an ideological and cultural artefact. As this chapter has shown, the same ideals of legitimate statehood and procedural justice that licensed and structured rule within absolutist states also shaped the fundamental institutions of absolutist international society, namely, naturalist international law and old diplomacy.

GENERATIVE GRAMMAR, INSTITUTIONAL PRACTICES, AND TERRITORIALITY

As explained at the beginning this chapter, Ruggie draws a tight connection between the principle of sovereignty, the institutional practice of multilateralism, and the development of exclusive, territorially demarcated states. We have seen that a deep "generative grammar" of constitutive ideas about legitimate statehood and rightful state action indeed structured absolutist international society, but it was more complex than Ruggie appreciates, and its institutional impact quite different from the one he posits. A Christian, patriarchal conception of the moral purpose of the state provided the justificatory foundations for sovereignty and informed an authoritative norm of procedural justice. These constitutional values

---

[87] Morgenthau, "Permanent Values in Old Diplomacy," 11.

[88] Morgenthau, *Politics Among Nations*, 576.

[89] Nicolson, *Evolution of Diplomatic Method*, 84.

sanctioned sovereign inequality and licensed the institutional practices of naturalist international law and old diplomacy over contractual international law and multilateralism. If this is correct, then Ruggie's claim that multilateralism provided the institutional framework for the consolidation of territorial rule is untenable, as neither the necessary institutional mind-set nor the practical apparatus had taken root when territoriality was being established.

This final section takes a closer look at the relationship between generative values, institutional practices, and territoriality in absolutist Europe. In this period, the development of territorial rule moved through constitutive and configurative phases, with each phase culminating in a major peace settlement: Westphalia and Utrecht, respectively.[90] In the constitutive phase the substantive scope of sovereign rights was defined; in the configurative phase the geographical extension of sovereign rights was delineated. At no point in this process did contractual international law or multilateralism play a significant role. In the sparse institutional environment of absolutist international society, divine-right absolutism provided the language of legitimate statehood, and naturalist international law and old diplomacy constituted the basic framework for the negotiation and stabilization of territorial rule, however inefficient or redundant that might seem with hindsight.

Constitution: Westphalia

In 1618, over half a century of festering religious, dynastic, and strategic tensions erupted into civil war in the Holy Roman Empire, subsequently engulfing the entire European continent in thirty years of exhausting and utterly devastating warfare. Wars are seldom simple affairs, but the Thirty Years War was even more complex than most, prompting endless scholarly debates about its causes and the motives of the major protagonists.[91] The war was sparked by a Protestant rebellion in Bohemia. Angered by Emperor Matthias's attempts to crush Protestantism and impose a Catho-

---

[90] This periodization of the absolutist period modifies Ruggie's own characterization of the evolution of European warfare. He argues that warfare has moved through a constitutive phase, culminating in the Peace of Westphalia, a configurative phase, centered on the Wars of Succession, a positional phase, marked by the quest for universal empire, and, finally, a national phase, in which warfare became an expression of the national interests. Ruggie, "Territoriality and Beyond," 162–63.

[91] For a representative sample of this debate, see Bonney, *European Dynastic States*; Gutmann, "Origins of the Thirty Years War"; Hagen, "Seventeenth Century Crisis"; Lee, *Thirty Years War*; Limm, *Thirty Years War*; Parker, *Thirty Years' War*; Sutherland, "Origins of the Thirty Years War"; Ward, "Peace of Westphalia"; and Wedgwood, *Thirty Years War*.

lic, Ferdinand of Styria, as king of Bohemia, rebels established a provisional government, installed a Calvinist, Frederick of Palatinate, as king and sought external military support. While the rebels scored a string of early victories, the election of Ferdinand of Styria as Emperor Ferdinand II in 1619, papal subsidies, and Spanish military assistance gave the empire the advantage, enabling Catholic forces to crush the Bohemian rebellion, depose Frederick, and conquer the Palatinate in 1622. Catholic military successes in the German states threatened the Lutheran states of the Baltic, encouraging Christian IV of Denmark to strike a military alliance in 1625 with England and France (both of which feared Habsburg hegemony), and the Dutch Republic (which was once again at war with Spain). After a series of humiliating defeats, however, Denmark withdrew from the war in 1629. In the same year, Ferdinand II decreed the Edict of Restitution, returning to Catholic control all church lands that had become Protestant after 1552. These events sparked a new Protestant offensive, with Sweden and the German states of Saxony and Brandenburg joining forces to invade the Rhineland and enter Bavaria. The tide of the war turned again, however, in 1632 after Gustavus Adolphus, the Swedish king, was killed in the Battle of Lützen. In 1634, Imperial, Bavarian, and Spanish forces combined to defeat the Protestant states, prompting a succession of German states to withdraw from the war. Concerned by Sweden's flagging war effort, Cardinal Richelieu swung French forces into the war in 1635, aiming to counter the threat of Habsburg hegemony. Though seriously defeated initially, the French recovered and, with Swedish, English and Dutch assistance, inflicted devastating losses on the Austrian and Spanish Habsburgs between 1637 and 1648, ultimately forcing Emperor Ferdinand III to accede to the Treaties of Westphalia, signed at Münster and Osnabrück on 24 October 1648.

The product of seven years of diplomatic wrangling and protracted negotiation, the Peace of Westphalia is generally seen as a crucial watershed in the transition from a heteronomous system of rule to a system of territorial sovereign states. In Mark Zacher's words, it "recognized the state as the supreme or sovereign power within its boundaries and put to rest the church's transnational claims to political authority."[92] This representation of the Westphalian settlement has attained almost canonical status in the discourse of international relations, but it should not be overdrawn. Significant as they were, the Treaties of Münster and Osnabrück were but one step in the territorialization of sovereign authority. As Stephen Krasner correctly observes, Westphalia did not institute a fully formed system of territorially demarcated states; the consolidation of empirical and juridical sovereignty was in process at least until the

---

[92] Zacher, "Westphalian Temple," 59.

conclusion of the Wars of Succession, early in the eighteenth century.[93] This having been said, the Treaties of Westphalia played a crucial role in defining the *scope* of territorial rule. That is, they defined and codified an historically contingent range of substantive areas over which princes and monarchs could legitimately exercise political authority.[94] The geographical extension of these political rights, however, was left ill-defined, with the reach of dynastic ties and ancient feudal rights defying the clear territorial demarcation of sovereignty.

The Treaties of Westphalia extended the scope of princely and monarchical rule through two provisions. Under the first, the "Electors, Princes and States of the *Roman* Empire" were guaranteed "free exercise of Territorial Right, as well as Ecclesiastik."[95] With regard to "ecclesiastik" rights, the Treaty of Osnabrück reaffirmed the 1555 Peace of Augsburg, which granted Lutheran states of the empire the freedom to "enjoy their religious belief, liturgy and ceremonies as well as their estates and other rights and privileges in peace," and extended this to Calvinists. Furthermore, all Protestant lands confiscated under the Edict of Restitution were redistributed according to the holdings that prevailed in 1624, and it was declared there should be "an exact and reciprocal Equality amongst all of the Electors, Princes and States of both religions" in the empire.[96] Under the second provision, the constituent states of the empire were guaranteed "without contradiction the Right of Suffrage in all Deliberations touching the Affairs of the Empire," especially the making or interpreting of Laws, the declaring of Wars, the imposing of Taxes, levying or quartering of Soldiers, erecting new fortifications in the Territories of States" and the forming of alliances."[97] While this latter provision assumed the continued viability and operation of imperial decision-making institutions, it severely impeded the emperor's political autonomy and began to transfer powers of legislation, taxation, defense, and "external" affairs to the constituent states of the empire.

These provisions represented a significant move toward territorial sovereignty, yet other aspects of the Westphalian settlement reaffirmed the preexisting nonterritorial, heteronomous system of rule. As we have seen,

---

[93] Krasner, "Westphalia and All That."

[94] This idea of the scope of territorial rule is akin to the "second dimension" of sovereignty identified by Janice Thomson. Whereas the "first dimension" of sovereignty involves "the claim to ultimate or final authority in a particular political space," the second dimension "is the specific set of authority claims made by a state over a range of activities within its political space." My point, of course, is that a "set of authority claims" was established before the applicable "political space" was defined. See Thomson, *Mercenaries, Pirates, and Sovereigns*, 14–15.

[95] "Treaty of Münster," Article 65.

[96] "Treaty of Osnabrück," Article 55.

[97] "Treaty of Münster," Article 65.

in medieval Europe political authority was decentralized and nonexclusive; a multitude of actors held rights to rule, and the content and jurisdictional purview of these rights varied temporally, spatially, and substantively, often overlapping in complex and contradictory ways. Originally, such rights were held *en fief*, bestowed by a superior lord in return for aid and counsel. In the late medieval period, however, the possession of feudal rights hardened; the idea that they were bestowed from above and maintained by conditional bonds of mutual obligation receded into the background, and feudal rights came to be seen as patrimony, as rightful inheritance.[98] The variegated, nonexclusive character of feudal rights, and their solidification over time, had two implications for the consolidation of territorial rule at Westphalia and beyond. First, the transfers of fiefs, with all the political rights they entailed, was just as important to the Westphalian settlement as the expanded scope of princely rule in the German states. For instance, under the Treaty of Osnabrück, Sweden gained a catalogue of fiefs in the Holy Roman Empire, most notably in Pomerania, Mecklenburg, Wismar, Bremen, and Verden, which together gave Sweden a seat in the Imperial Diet.[99] Similarly, the Treaty of Münster granted France a range of feudal rights in Elsass.[100] Second, the translation of feudal rights into personal patrimony meant that dynastic ties and bonds of lineage—more than clearly demarcated territorial boundaries—defined the extension of rule. By granting imperial fiefs to France and Sweden, the Treaties of Westphalia reaffirmed this aspect of European heteronomy, and it was not displaced by territorial definitions of bounded rule until after the Wars of Succession, over half a century later.

Hinsley argues that the Treaties of Westphalia "came to be looked upon as the public law of Europe."[101] In what sense, however, did the settlement of 1648 have the status of law, international or otherwise? It is clear from the texts of the treaties, and from accounts of the negotiations, that the settlement's legality did not derive from the existence of formal "contractual" agreements between the princes and monarchs of Europe, or at least not primarily. The treaties were written and duly signed accords, but the bases of their legal sanctity lay elsewhere. The peace rested on two noncontractual legal foundations. The first was the observance of God's will. The preamble to the Treaty of Osnabrück states that "[a]t last it fell out by an Effect of Divine Bounty, that both sides turn'd their Thoughts towards the means of making peace. . . . After having invok'd the Assistance of God . . . they transacted and agreed among themselves, to the Glory of

[98] Poggi, *Development of the Modern State*, 30.
[99] "Treaty of Osnabrück," Article 10, 244–245.
[100] "Treaty of Münster," Article 75.
[101] Hinsley, *Power and the Pursuit of Peace*, 168.

God, and the Safety of the Christian World."[102] Virtually the same words prefaced the Treaty of Münster. The second, more secular legal foundation was imperial law. Indicative of the persistence of medieval institutions at that time, the treaties were enshrined in the constitutional law of the Holy Roman Empire. "For the greater Firmness of all and every one of these Articles," declares the Treaty of Münster, "this present Transaction shall serve for a perpetual Law and established Sanction of the Empire, to be inserted like other fundamental Laws and Constitutions of the Empire in the Acts of the next Diet of the Empire, and the Imperial Capitulation."[103] To the extent, therefore, that the Peace of Westphalia became "the public law of Europe," obligation to observe that law rested on a naturalist conception of international law as the will of God and the decaying legal structures of the Holy Roman Empire, the very institution that the treaties helped to erode.

The practice of old diplomacy provided the basic framework of interaction for the negotiation of the Westphalian treaties. The hierarchical nature of the conference has already been noted, the parties squabbling for months over issues of preeminence and precedence. Added to this, the conference never met as a single negotiating unit. Not only were negotiations with the Empire divided between the Protestant states in Osnabrück and the Catholic states in Münster, but within those groupings accommodations were often reached bilaterally, not multilaterally. Moreover, a veil of secrecy shrouded the negotiations, with pairs of states frequently reaching agreements without the knowledge of other parties. For instance, de Callières records that: "[t]he peace of Münster . . . was not the work alone of the many ambassadors who had a hand in it. A confident Duke Maximilian of Bavaria, who was sent privately to Paris, adjusted the prime conditions of it with Cardinal Mazarin. And when he was once convinced that this was his interest, he drew in the emperor, and the whole empire, and determined them to conclude the peace with France, Sweden, and their allies, pursuant to the project which had been settled at Paris."[104] When these diplomatic practices are combined with the relative unimportance of contractual international law in undergirding the treaties, it is not surprising that there were few, if any, genuine multilateral aspects to the Westphalian settlement. As we have seen, the treaties played an important role in defining the scope of territorial rule, yet they were pastiches of particularistic territorial and political accommodations, and one searches in vain for indivisible, generalized, and reciprocally binding rules.

---

[102] "Treaty of Osnabrück," Preamble.
[103] "Treaty of Munster," Article 120.
[104] de Callières, *Art of Diplomacy*, 178–79.

Configuration: Utrecht

The Peace of Westphalia resolved the long-standing, hard-fought issue of the rights of monarchs to determine the predominant religion in their domains, reaffirming and refining the principle of *cujus regio ejus religo*. In doing so, it removed the principal source of ideological conflict in Europe, with doctrinal differences receding from the international agenda for almost 150 years, only to erupt again, albeit in a different form, with the French Revolution and the Napoleonic wars. As noted above, however, the Westphalian settlement clarified the scope of sovereign authority, particularly in the area of religion, but it left the geographical extension of sovereign rule ill defined. This ambiguity became the principal source of contestation and war after 1648. It was manifest in a series of struggles over dynastic succession, over the rights of monarchs to inherit political rights, thus extending their authority through the reach of the family tree. Not only had feudal rights come to be seen as patrimony, as the accoutrements of birth, but it was widely, and conveniently, held that monarchs could not renounce such rights without violating their sacred obligation to God. Since a complex web of feudal rights still enmeshed Europe, the pursuit of dynastic entitlements invariably provoked conflicts on several fronts: the claims themselves were often questionable and subject to legal challenge; grasping for patrimonial rights, frequently in noncontiguous regions, clashed with the simultaneous trend toward the territorial consolidation of sovereign rule; and dynastic aggrandizement by major powers threatened the peace and stability of the entire continent.

The problem of dynastic inheritance came to a head with the War of Spanish Succession (1701–13).[105] In the latter half of the seventeenth century, Louis XIV sought to maximize his authority by asserting rights of inheritance to a plethora of provinces, estates, and fiefs across Europe. None of these were more ambitious nor more threatening to the rest of Europe than the claim he laid to the Spanish throne. This was first expressed in 1662 when Louis declared that the Spanish Low Countries rightly belonged to his wife, Marie Thérèse. Marshalling elaborate legal arguments, he claimed that under the succession laws of these regions private property passed to the eldest surviving child of a first marriage, and that his wife's renunciation of these rights upon their wedding was doubly illegal: the dowry that she was meant to receive was never paid, and at any rate renunciations were violations of God's law. Louis's

---

[105] On the War of Spanish Succession, see Elliot, *Imperial Spain*; Heeren, *History of the Political System of Europe and Its Colonies*, 173–194; Hill, *History of Diplomacy, Vol.3*; Hinsley, *Power and Pursuit of Peace*, 153–185; Holsti, *Peace and War*, 43–82; and Rowen, *King's State*, 93–122.

attempts to enforce this claim resulted in the War of Devolution (1667–68), in which he occupied the Spanish territories in Franche-Comté and the Netherlands, only to relinquish much of these in the 1668 Treaty of Aix-la-Chapelle. In the ensuing years, his attention turned to the Spanish crown itself. After Charles II, wracked by illness and unlikely to produce an heir, ascended the Spanish throne in 1665, both the French Bourbons and Austrian Habsburgs staked claims to the succession. In anticipation of Charles's early death, the English and Dutch encouraged Louis to accept the partition of Spanish territories, hoping to prevent the fusion of French and Spanish power. These attempts failed, though, when in 1700 Charles died, naming Philip of Anjou, Louis's grandson, as his rightful heir. Despite stipulations that Philip would have to relinquish the Spanish crown if he subsequently became king of France, and that the crown would then pass to his younger brother, the duke of Berry, Louis declared Philip the new king of Spain, telling his court that "[h]is birth called him to this crown, as well as the late king's testament."[106] Within a year the other major powers had formed a Grand Alliance to combat French hegemony, and in 1702 England, the emperor, and the United Provinces declared war on France. More than a decade later, with France and Spain exhausted and England fearful that a French defeat could bring a union of between Austria and Spain, the major powers sued for peace at Utrecht in 1713.

The Treaties of Utrecht were pivotal in delineating the geographical extension of sovereign rights, making a decisive contribution to the consolidation of territoriality. In contradiction to the unbounded proprietorial sovereignty previously championed by Louis and others, the treaties established the principle that the reach of dynastic entitlements could legitimately be curtailed to preserve European peace and security. While divine right remained a powerful rationale for expanding the scope of sovereign rule within a given territory, after Utrecht it was no longer a legitimate basis for the geographical aggregation of power and authority, for the transnational aggrandizement of dynasties. The treaties began by recognizing that succession claims, particularly those linking France and Spain, posed a major threat to the stability of the emergent international system. It is clear, the treaty between England and France states, "that the Security and Libertys of *Europe* could by no means bear the Union of the Kingdoms of *France* and *Spain* under one and the same King."[107] To prevent such an occurrence, the treaties determined that it was both legitimate and essential that succession rights be circumscribed to prevent hegemony and avoid the resulting "Effusion of Christian Blood." In ac-

---

[106] Quoted in Rowen, *The King's State*, 114.
[107] "Treaty of Utrecht between Great Britain and France," Article 6.

cepting this principle, the Bourbon monarchs and their immediate heirs issued a series of dynastic renunciations, forever separating the French and Spanish crowns. On the Spanish side, Philip renounced his claims to the monarchy of France; on the French side, the duke of Berry renounced his rights to the monarchy of Spain and the Indies.[108] That these moves were designed to contain sovereign rights within territorial boundaries is clearly evident in the duke of Berry's renunciation: "It has been agreed in the Conferences and Treatys of Peace . . . to establish an Equilibrium, and political Boundarys between the Kingdoms [of France and Spain]."[109]

The Peace of Utrecht was the first international accord to uphold the maintenance of a stable balance of power as one of its primary objectives.[110] "One of the principal Positions of the Treatys of Peace . . . ," Philip declared in his renunciation, was "the Maxim of securing for ever the universal Good and Quiet of Europe, by an equal Weight of Power, so that many being united in one, the Ballance of the Equality desired, might not turn to the Advantage of one, and the Danger and Hazard of the rest."[111] Beyond preventing a dynastic union between France and Spain, however, the treaties did little to advance this idea of peace through equilibrium; as the following chapter demonstrates, it was not until the Congress of Vienna a century later that it was given any detailed conceptual or practical expression. Nonetheless, the preliminary articulation of such an idea at Utrecht testifies to the consolidation of territorial sovereignty instituted by the treaties. While the constitutional doctrine of the separation of powers demonstrates that there is no necessary connection between the balancing of power and political territoriality, in international history the two have almost always been entwined: it is territorially demarcated sovereign states that are weighed in the scales of international

---

[108] Louis declared that "the King of Spain, our said Brother and Grandson, keeping the Monarchy *Spain* and of the *Indies*, should renounce for himself and his Descendants for ever, the Rights which his Birth might at any time give him and them to our Crown; that on the other hand, our most dear and beloved Grandson the Duke of *Berry*, and our most dear and most beloved Nephew the Duke of *Orleans*, should likewise renounce for themselves, and for their decedents, Male and Female for ever, their Rights to the Monarchy of *Spain* and the *Indies*." "Treaty of Utrecht between Great Britain and France," Article 6.

[109] Ibid.

[110] The emergence of balance-of-power discourse is one of the most commonly noted features of the Peace of Utrecht. Rosenberg has recently challenge this emphasis, arguing that the balance of power was only a marginal aspect of the treaties, with the regulation of colonial trade constituting the real essence of the settlement. Rosenberg, *Empire of Civil Society*, 39–43. Although trading issues played an important part in the peace, Rosenberg's claims are overdrawn. As Holsti observes, if the British and French peace plans are considered, and the instructions to diplomats examined, "One gains the impression that most of the governments were seized by territorial and dynastic issues, not with trade." Holsti, *Peace and War*, 75–76.

[111] "Treaty of Utrecht between Great Britain and France," Article 6.

security. Delineating the geographical extension of sovereign rights is thus a necessary, though not sufficient, precondition for the emergence of balance of power discourse, and by circumscribing succession rights the Utrecht settlement achieved precisely this. It is not surprising, therefore, that this is the first time that the discourse appears; nor is it surprising that in the duke of Berry's renunciation the pursuit of "Equilibrium" and the consolidation of "political Boundarys" are paired.

On what legal foundation did this consolidation of territorial sovereignty rest? Were states obliged to accept the settlement and institute its provisions because the treaties expressed the will of God or because they had contracted with juridically equal sovereign states? As in the case of Westphalia, it was the former, vertical sense of legal obligation that undergirded the Peace of Utrecht. The treaties were indeed contracts between sovereigns, but fealty not mutuality gave them their sanctity. According to the preamble of the treaty between Great Britain and France, the ambassadors "invoked Divine Assistance" when negotiating the accords, and the signatories hoped "that God would be pleased to preserve this their Work intire and unviolated, and to prolong it to the latest Posterity."[112] Furthermore, the promises issued by the parties appealed to their abiding Christian faith and respect for the word of God. In concluding his renunciation, Philip declared that "I give again the pledge of my Faith and Royal Word, and I swear solemnly by the Gospels contained in this Missal, upon which I lay my Right Hand, that I will observe, maintain, and accomplish this Act and Instrument of Renunciation."[113] To the extent that a sense of mutual obligation undergirded the treaties, it was the mutuality of Christian brotherhood and sisterhood, not that of contractual reciprocity. References to "our most dear and most beloved" brother or sister punctuate the treaties, and the renewal of a "faithful Neighbourhood" is upheld as the goal of the peace.

The negotiations at Utrecht, like those at Osnabrück and Münster, bore virtually all of the hallmarks of old diplomacy. Some progress was made in managing the troublesome question of precedence: a round table was used to avoid squabbles over which representative would be seated at the head, and there was no final session for the signing of the treaties, circumventing a whole series of ceremonial problems.[114] These strategies, however, merely papered over an enduring reality of absolutist international society—sovereign inequality. There had been no fundamental transformation in the way sovereigns viewed one another, no shift from

---

[112] Ibid., Preamble.

[113] Ibid., Article 6.

[114] Anderson, *Rise of Modern Diplomacy*, 66; and Hamilton and Langhorne, *Practice of Diplomacy*, 80.

a hierarchical to an equalitarian social episteme. Like the negotiations at Westphalia, the proceedings at Utrecht assumed the status of a "congress," yet there was little more to this than the name. As Heeren records, the negotiations were largely bilateral and highly secretive: "The congress opened at Utrecht . . . at first between the plenipotentiaries of France, England, and Savoy only; those of the other allies arrived in February. The dissolution of the [Grand] alliance was already decided by the determination, that each of the confederates should submit his claims singly. The contests between the allies increased, while the negotiations were almost entirely in the hands of the English, and were carried on in secret directly between the cabinets of St. James and Versailles."[115] The structure of the congress, therefore, was by no means multilateral, and it is not surprising that it produced six separate treaties: Great Britain–France, Great Britain–Spain, France-Holland, France-Prussia, France-Savoy, and Savoy-Spain. The spirit of the negotiations was also far from multilateral. New norms of territoriality were certainly established in the collection of bilateral accords, but these emerged through the resolution of particularistic disputes in dyadic negotiations, not through legislation of the community of the states.

CONCLUSION

During the sixteenth and seventeenth centuries the European political landscape was fundamentally transformed, with a system of territorially demarcated sovereign states gradually replacing feudal heteronomy. For many this represents the dawn of the modern era, the birthplace of modern international society, the origin of the familiar. This chapter has advanced a different perspective. A system of sovereign states certainly emerged around the time of Westphalia, but it was a system based on decidedly premodern principles of political legitimacy, principles alien to the modern mind, not familiar. The moral purpose of the state was identified with the preservation of a divinely ordained, rigidly hierarchical social order. To this end, monarchs were endowed with supreme authority from God, a norm of authoritative procedural justice evolved, and law was defined as the command of a superior authority. These values not only provided the justificatory foundations for sovereignty, they shaped the basic institutional practices of absolutist international society, licensing the development of naturalist international law and old diplomacy over contractual international law and multilateralism. Contra Ruggie, it

---

[115] Heeren, *History of the Political System of Europe*, 181.

was the former not the latter that were implicated in the consolidation of territoriality that took place at Westphalia and Utrecht.

In a recent chapter on the post-Westphalian development of sovereign states, Krasner denies that a deep generative grammar shaped European state formation, arguing that material forces were determining. "In the effort to construct sovereignty," he writes, "ideas have been used to codify existing practices rather than to initiate new forms of order. Ideas have not made possible alternatives that did not previously exist; they legitimated political practices that were already facts on the ground."[116] From the perspective advanced in this chapter, such claims are problematic. Only by recognizing that ideas can be more than mere rationalizations, more than epiphenomenal reflections of material forces and incentives, can we explain why one set of basic institutional practices emerged in absolutist international society and not another. Only by understanding that the ideology of divine-right absolutism contained its own institutional logic, that it spawned a distinctive form of institutional rationality, can we explain why naturalist international law and old diplomacy reached high points at this time. Applying counterfactual logic, we have little reason to believe that in the absence of these constitutive metavalues such institutional practices would have predominated in absolutist international society. This does not mean, of course, that material factors were irrelevant in the development of absolutist international society; rather, it is to argue, in Marshall Sahlins's words, that "material effects depend on their cultural encompassment."[117]

---

[116] Krasner, "Westphalia and All That," 238.
[117] Sahlins, *Culture and Practical Reason*, 194.

CHAPTER SIX

Modern International Society

Diplomacy is no longer merely an art in which
personal ability plays an exclusive part; its tendency is to become a science which shall have
fixed rules for settling disputes. . . . It cannot be
disputed that great progress will have been made
if diplomacy succeeds in establishing in this Conference some of the rules of which I have spoken.
—His Excellency Mr. Staal, president of the
    Hague Conference, 1899

CONTRARY to the claims of Bodin and others, absolutism was neither perpetual nor immutable. In the latter half of the eighteenth century revolutionary changes in thought and practice undermined the ideological and
material foundations of dynastic rule. Echoing shifts in scientific thought,
political and economic theorists abandoned holistic conceptions of society, championing new ideas of political and economic individualism. The
impact of these ideas was profound, with political individualism fueling
the American and French Revolutions and economic individualism providing the ideological resources for the Industrial Revolution. In the ensuing fifty years European politics was riven by a protracted conflict over
the terms of legitimate rule, compounded by the economically induced
dislocation of traditional patterns of social organization and affiliation.
The ancien régime won a temporary reprieve at the end of the Napoleonic
Wars, reasserting the constitutional metavalues of the old order. By the
middle of the nineteenth century, however, the tide had changed. Justifying state power and authority in terms of the preservation of a divinely
ordained social order became more and more untenable; legitimate statehood and rightful state action were henceforth increasingly tied to the
augmentation of individuals' purposes and potentialities. As a consequence, the authoritative norm of procedural justice was supplanted by
a new principle that prescribed the legislative codification of formal, reciprocally binding rules of conduct. The ascendence of these new constitutional values marks the birth of modern international society, and the rise
of this new "standard of civilization" provided the crucial catalyst for the

development of the fundamental institutions of contractual international law and multilateralism.

This chapter traces this epochal transformation, applying the theoretical framework advanced in previous chapters to explain the unique institutional architecture of modern international society. The discussion is divided into three main parts. After detailing the shift from holistic to individualistic modes of thought in part 1, part 2 outlines the constitutional structure of the modern society of states, explaining the new rationale for sovereign authority and its impact on notions of procedural justice. Part 3 examines how these values shaped institutional design and action, leading states to favor one set of institutional solutions over others. The analysis focuses on the years between 1815 and 1945, as this was the crucial period of institutional innovation, the period in which states laid the foundations and began constructing the institutional edifice of contemporary international society. I have identified four developmental moments in this period: the Congress of Vienna (1814–15), when the constitutional values of absolutist international society were reaffirmed; the Hague Conferences of 1899 and 1907, when states first endorsed the basic institutional practices of multilateralism and contractual international law; the Versailles Peace Conference of 1919, when the institutional architecture of modern international society was first erected; and the San Francisco Conference of 1945, when the United States initiated a massive wave of institutional renovation and mass construction.

FROM HOLISM TO INDIVIDUALISM

The constitutional structure of modern international society is founded on a radically different social ontology from that of the absolutist society of states. Like those of ancient Greece and Renaissance Italy, the meta-values structuring the absolutist system were based on a holistic social ontology. That is, in each of these three cases the moral purpose of the state was linked to the preservation or cultivation of a particular type of collective life: for the ancient Greeks it was the cultivation of *bios politikos*, for the Renaissance Italians it was the pursuit of civic glory, and for the Europeans of the absolutist period it was the maintenance of a divinely ordained social order. In contrast, the metavalues that define legitimate statehood and rightful state action in modern international society are based on an individualist social ontology. The moral purpose of the modern state lies in the augmentation of individuals' purposes and potentialities, in the cultivation of a social, economic and political order that enables individuals to engage in the self-directed pursuit of their "interests."

As the eighteenth century progressed, holistic modes of thought were subjected to sustained attack. Scientific, economic, and political theorists all abandoned holistic ways of conceiving the natural and social world, calling for the dissolution of natural and social entities into their primary components. The nature and purpose of larger combinations—be they of atoms or humans—was no longer assumed. Only experience could reveal connections between elements. For scientists this involved controlled experimentation to demonstrate causal relations. For economists it entailed the creative division of labor and the test of efficiency. And for political theorists it meant reimagining the polity as a notionally equal, contractually based collectivity of free individuals.

David Hume's *A Treatise of Human Nature*, published in 1739, is one of the earliest and most significant statements of the new philosophy of science. Hume begins by distinguishing between simple and complex ideas, the latter being combinations of the former. The first stage in scientific thought is to break down complex ideas into their most simple components. Rejecting the doctrine of infinite divisibility, he argues that the "capacity of the mind is not infinite; consequently no idea of extension or duration consists of an infinite number of parts or inferior ideas, but of a finite number, and these [are] simple and indivisible."[1] Simple ideas are always based on sensory impressions, which means that knowledge is necessarily based on experience. "We cannot form to ourselves a just idea of the taste of pine-apple," he writes, "without having actually tasted it."[2] This is also true of the relation between simple impressions and ideas. The way that basic units are united into complex forms, Hume concludes, can only be determined by observing their "constant conjunction"; that is, by studying patterns of "resemblance," "contiguity," and "cause and effect."[3] Hume considers the last the most important: "The idea of cause and effect is deriv'd from *experience*, which informs us, that such particular objects, in all past instances, have been constantly conjoin'd with each other."[4]

Following their scientific counterparts, Adam Smith and other economic theorists engaged in a two-step process of disaggregation. They reduced society to its most fundamental elements—atomistic, autonomous individuals—and divided production processes into their most basic stages—the division of labor. Individuals' social roles, they argued, were not determined by convention or the will of God, nor were their relationships with others. Humans were portrayed as restless, acquisitive, and competitive, pursuing social positions commensurate with their ambi-

[1] Hume, *A Treatise of Human Nature*, 39.
[2] Ibid., 5.
[3] Ibid., 11.
[4] Ibid., 90.

tions and capacities, and forming social relationships for the sake of efficiency and productivity. In the pursuit of self-interest, individuals construct a division of labor (Smith's pin factory), which increases the productivity of each and the wealth of all (Smith's invisible hand).[5] Social positions and relationships are thus subject to constant processes of revision and reconstruction as the coordination of individual economic interests changes and the optimal division of labor is reestablished.

While this shift in economic thought was underway, political theorists were engaged in a radical reconceptualization of political community. The old image of the polity as a divinely ordained social organism—the family writ-large—was abandoned, replaced by a new idea of a contractual community of free individuals. Contractarian accounts of politics had a long lineage, first receiving expression in Hobbes's justification for absolutist sovereignty. For Hobbes, however, the social contract took place between individuals and the sovereign, not among the individuals themselves; it was an act of power transmission, not a moment of communal constitution. Locke, in contrast, imagined a social contract between individuals, an agreement among "free, equal and independent" men to make "*one Community*" and "*one Body Politick*."[6] These ideas were before their time, though, and they did not gain wide currency until the middle of the eighteenth century, when they provided ideological fuel for the American Revolution. By this time, however, Rousseau had advanced a more definitive statement of the new conception of political community. Before a people can agree on a form of government, he argues, they must agree to form a polity; legitimate rule must be based on agreement, and the process by which a people elect a king or government must be preceded by "the act by which a people becomes a people, for, since this act is necessarily prior to the other, it is the true foundation of society."[7]

By the end of the eighteenth century, the new preoccupation with the individual extended well beyond the confines of economic and political thought.[8] At the most popular levels, humans were increasingly seen as kernels of possibility, each with their own desires, aptitudes, and capacities. Understanding and cultivating these inner qualities became a paramount concern, with the self appearing as an object of contemplation and development in a way that had never been seen before.[9] As Charles Taylor observes, the modern sense of self is characterized by a profound sense of

---

[5] Smith, *Wealth of Nations*, 8, 477.

[6] Locke, *Two Treatises of Civil Government*, VIII:95, 165.

[7] Rousseau, "On Social Contract," 91.

[8] On this new concern with the individual, see Taylor, *Sources of the Self*; Lyons, *Invention of the Self*; Gerson, *Concept of the Self*; Berman, *Politics of Authenticity*; Weintraub, *Value of the Individual*; Hirschman, *Passions and the Interests*; and Yardley and Honness, *Self and Identity*.

[9] Logan, "Historical Change in Prevailing Sense of Self," 20–22.

inwardness: "We think of our thoughts, ideas, or feelings as being 'within' us, while the objects in the world which these mental states bear on are 'without.'"[10] The urge to explore, reveal, express, and even celebrate this interior self is a distinctly modern preoccupation, essentially foreign to the ancient Greeks, Renaissance Italians, and Europeans of the absolutist era. One of its earliest manifestations was the genre of autobiographical writing, of which Rousseau's *Confessions* is a prime example.[11] In earlier periods, life stories focussed on individual's public personas, on their cultivation of social virtues, on the great deeds they performed, and on the glory they brought their community.[12] After the late eighteenth century the focus turned inward, the aim being to unveil the real self, with all its strengths and vulnerabilities. This was part and parcel of what Marshall Berman calls the modern quest for "authenticity," the "persistent and intense concern with *being oneself.*"[13] The first step in this quest is "knowing oneself," to which the act of autobiography and the periodic visit to the psychoanalyst are but two approaches. The second step—that of "becoming oneself" though the cultivation and realization of inner purposes and potentialities—makes the quest for authenticity a social and political issue without precedent.

The ideology of modernity holds that individual purposes and potentialities are the product of personal choice alone, not the constructs of prevailing social values and functional requirements. "The modern individual," as David Kolb observes, "is stripped down to a unified core, a perceiving, choosing being potentially free to maximize whatever is desired."[14] Ideology, however, is never what it seems, and certain primary and substantive interests—principally economic maximization and technological progress—were smuggled into the new accounts of human nature. For instance, the individuals described in Smith's *Wealth of Nations* are driven by a specific set of interests and motivations. The division of labor is not the product of conscious human design but the inevitable result of the human "propensity to truck, barter, and exchange one thing for another."[15] To paraphrase Louis Dumont, the rise of modern individualism involved the transformation of *homo hierarchicus* to *homo economicus.*[16] Society was in turn understood as system of exchange relations. "Every man thus lives by exchanging," Smith argues, "or becomes in

---

[10] Taylor, *Sources of the Self*, 111.

[11] Rousseau, *Confessions.*

[12] Weintraub, *Value of the Individual*, xi–xvii.

[13] Berman, *Politics of Authenticity*, xv–xxiv.

[14] Kolb, *Critique of Pure Modernity*, 6.

[15] Smith, *Wealth of Nations*, 17.

[16] Dumont, *From Mandeville to Marx*, chapter 1.

some measure a merchant, and society itself grows to what is properly called a commercial society."[17]

THE CONSTITUTIONAL STRUCTURE OF MODERN INTERNATIONAL SOCIETY

The advent of this new individualist social ontology served to undermine the legitimacy of the absolutist state. Its raison d'être was predicated upon the image of society as a social organism, the preservation of which was dictated by God and delegated to European monarchs. This organic metaphor was now supplanted by the contrary image of society as a multitude of self-directing individuals, who formed relationships and allegiances according to their own desires and purposes. The crucial blow to absolutism, however, came from the resonance and articulation of these ideological developments with the concrete social and material transformations sweeping late-eighteenth-century Europe. The economic dislocations and upheavals of the industrial revolution uprooted the rigid, hierarchical social order that supported the absolutist state and provided its very rationale. The growing emphasis on industry over agriculture, the consequent migration to the cities, and the associated emergence of new economic and social classes undercut long-standing patterns of social organization and affiliation, freeing individuals from their traditional moorings. Far from being a temporary process of adjustment, this upheaval, mobility, and dislocation came to define modern society, resulting in what Ernest Gellner aptly calls "the society of perpetual growth."[18] These mutually reinforcing ideological, material, and social transformations left the hollow structures of expansive territorial states without a viable justificatory framework capable of supporting them on the new social and economic terrain. The problem of legitimacy was this: if autonomous, self-directing individuals only form social relationships and allegiances to further their particular interests, then why should a large-scale centralized state and not some other political entity or arrangement be the primary object of their political loyalties?

The Moral Purpose of the Modern State

In the period between the American Revolution in 1776 and the revolutionary turmoil of 1848 a new rationale for the state emerged to replace the principles of monarchical patriarchy and divine right. Legitimate

[17] Smith, *Wealth of Nations*, 26.
[18] Gellner, *Nations and Nationalism*, 23.

states came to be seen as those that expressed and furthered the interests of their citizens, understood not as subjects but as sovereign agents. Nowhere was the state's new raison d'être expressed more clearly than in the 1776 United States Declaration of Independence: "We hold these truths to be self-evident, that all men are created equal; that they are endowed by their Creator with certain inalienable rights; that among these are life, liberty, and the pursuit of happiness. *That, to secure these rights, governments are instituted among men, deriving their just powers from the consent of the governed* [my emphasis]."[19] Thirteen years later the French Declaration of the Rights of Man and Citizen upheld the same principle of legitimate statehood: "The aim of every political association," it declared, "is the preservation of the natural and inalienable rights of man; these rights are liberty, property, and resistance to oppression."[20] From this perspective, individuals are morally and practically prior to the state; their rights constitute the baseline, the state is but a human artifact instituted to protect their liberties. In fulfilling this role, the state provides the institutional climate necessary for human flowering; with their liberties protected, individuals can freely pursue their interests and maximize their potentials; with their rights guaranteed, they can fully develop their "individuality," the key to a flourishing society. John Stuart Mill explains that "[i]t is not by wearing down into uniformity all that is individual in themselves, but by cultivating it and calling it forth, within the limits imposed by the rights and interests of others, that human beings become a noble and beautiful object of contemplation; and . . . by the same process human life also becomes rich, diversified, and animating, furnishing more abundant aliment to high thoughts and elevating feelings, and strengthening the tie which binds every individual to the race, by making the race infinitely better worth belonging to."[21]

Under this new rationale, the state no longer ruled society according to God's will, it served the "people" according to their "common will," the "nation" according to the "national interest." As noted earlier, political community had been fundamentally reconceived. Instead of being treated as a natural component of the divine order, it was considered a human artifact, the creation of its members. For some it was the outcome of a social contract, for others the product of history, sentiment, and experience, but in both cases the existence of the "people" or the "nation" was attributed to human, not divine, will. The idea of the people or the nation was crucially important in the new account of state authority, as it was these earthly collectivities that endowed the state with sovereignty. Where

---

[19] "United States Declaration of Independence," 107.
[20] "French Declaration of the Rights of Man and Citizen," 118.
[21] Mill, *On Liberty*, 60.

sovereignty had once been bestowed by God, now it was invested by the body politic. As the French Declaration of the Rights of Man and Citizen declares, the "source of all sovereignty resides essentially in the nation; no group, no individual may exercise authority not emanating expressly therefrom."[22] Once this move had occurred, the absolutist dictum that the monarch should rule according to natural and divine law made even less sense than before, as sovereignty was no longer God's bequest. From now on the state was bound to observe the general will and to further the national interest. In the end, "God's will" and the "general will" proved equally amorphous and manipulable sources of government policy, but this shift in the source of legitimate state authority had profound implications for notions of procedural justice and, in turn, the institutional structures of both national and international governance.

The Legislative Norm of Procedural Justice

Once the state's raison d'être had been tied to the augmentation of individuals' purposes and potentialities, and the source of sovereignty had been located in the people, authoritative principles of procedural justice lost all credibility. If the people invested the institutions and representatives of the state with sovereign authority, and if the inalienable rights of individuals placed limits on the exercise of that authority, how could the command of a monarch standing above both the people and the law legitimately define rules of social, economic, and political conduct? The moral purpose of the modern state thus entailed a new principle of procedural justice—legislative justice. This principle prescribes two precepts of rule determination: first, that only those subject to the rules have the right to define them and, second, that the rules of society must apply equally to all citizens, in all like cases. Both precepts were enshrined in the French Declaration of the Rights of Man and Citizen, which states that "[l]aw is the expression of the general will; all citizens have the right to concur personally, or through their representatives, in its formation; it must be the same for all, whether it protects or punishes."[23]

These precepts are clearly expressed in Rousseau's political writings. Setting his sights on both Bodin's and Hobbes's defenses of absolutism, Rousseau denies that either paternal right or contractual agreement justify the unlimited power and authority of the monarch. The rule of the father (and hence the monarch) is far from natural, deriving its force from social institutions alone, and individuals cannot contract away their liber-

---

[22] "French Declaration of the Rights of Man and Citizen," 119.
[23] Ibid.

ties, for the social compact's only rationale is the protection of such rights. With Hobbes's thesis clearly in mind, he argues that "an agreement that stipulates absolute authority on the one hand and unlimited obedience on the other is vain and contradictory."[24] Free, equal, and reciprocal "agreements," he writes, "remain the basis of all legitimate authority among men."[25] The most famous of Rousseau's agreements is the social contract that binds individuals together into a "body politic" or "republic." In forming such a political society, each member agrees to submit entirely to the general will of the collectivity. The legitimacy of this initial accord stems from its universality and its reciprocity: "Each person, in giving himself to all, gives himself to no one, and as there are no associates over whom he does not acquire the same right as he concedes to them over himself, he gains the equivalent of all he loses and more to preserve what he has."[26]

Law, Rousseau argues, gives the body politic "movement and will." Yet law is no longer defined as the command of the superior, legal obligation does not rest on the sanctity of superordinate/subordinate relations, and legitimate law is neither arbitrary nor discriminating against individuals. Binding law can only result from agreements, and those agreements must be reciprocal. Rousseau places little store in natural law or the will of God. "No doubt there is a universal justice emanating from reason alone," he writes, "but in order to be admitted among us, this kind of justice must be reciprocal."[27] This emphasis on mutually binding agreements as the source of law means that only those subject to the law have the right to legislate. "Legislative power belongs to the people," he argues, "and can belong to it alone."[28] It follows that participation in the formulation of the law is the sole basis of legal obligation, and Rousseau considers such participation to be the mark of true freedom: "Obedience to the law one has prescribed for oneself is liberty."[29] Because all individuals possess the same rights, Rousseau holds that the laws legislated by the people or their representatives must apply equally to all citizens in all like cases. "Every authentic act of the general will," he writes, "favors all citizens equally, so that the sovereign, knows only the body of the nation and makes no distinctions between any of those who compose it."[30] Hence the law must be "general," it must treat "the subjects as a body

---

[24] Rousseau, "On Social Contract," 89.
[25] Ibid., 88.
[26] Ibid., 93.
[27] Ibid., 105.
[28] Ibid., 118.
[29] Ibid., 96.
[30] Ibid., 103.

and actions in the abstract, never one man as an individual, or a particular action."[31]

THE FUNDAMENTAL INSTITUTIONS OF MODERN
INTERNATIONAL SOCIETY

Modern constitutional metavalues took root slowly, gradually transforming the institutions and practices of national governance through the nineteenth century and into the twentieth. In some cases this process was relatively peaceful, as in Britain where the major reform bills of 1832, 1867, and 1884 progressively expanded the electorate from one-fifth to two-thirds of the adult male population.[32] Elsewhere it took a more violent turn. Holsti estimates that the "principles of liberalism and nationalism were the major causes of both civil and international wars between 1815 and 1914."[33] By the second half of the nineteenth century, the state's new raison d'être and associated legislative norm of procedural justice had become the prevailing measure of political legitimacy and rightful state action. This is not to say that institutional practices changed as quickly as ideology, but the progressive move toward constitutional and representative forms of governance remains one of the more remarkable features of the late nineteenth century. One by one, the European states embraced constitutionalism and rule of law, with even Russia adopting reforms in 1905. As David Thomson observes, "In almost the whole of western and central Europe, parliamentary institutions developed between 1871 and 1914," and during the same period we see the gradual movement toward universal suffrage.[34] By World War I, David Kaiser argues, "Every European government had to maintain a working majority within an elected parliament in order to carry on the essential business of the state."[35]

From the middle of the nineteenth century the norm of legislative procedural justice informed the paired evolution of the two principal fundamental institutions of contemporary international society: contractual international law, and multilateralism. The infiltration of the idea of law as reciprocal accord into the international society spurred not only the broadening and deepening of international law as an institution firmly grounded in the practices of states but also the development of multilateralism. Under the legislative principle, the development of modern interna-

---

[31] Ibid., 106.
[32] Cook and Stevenson, *Handbook of Modern British History*, 62.
[33] Holsti, *Peace and War*, 145.
[34] Thomson, *Europe Since Napoleon*, 323.
[35] Kaiser, *Politics and War*, 275–276.

tional law involves participation, negotiation, and dialogue aimed at achieving mutually binding agreements, and multilateralism represents precisely such a process. As Ruggie argues, multilateralism is an institutional practice that "coordinates behavior among three or more states on the basis of generalized principles of conduct: that is, principles which specify appropriate conduct for a class of actions, without regard to the particularistic interests of the parties or the strategic exigencies that may exist in any specific occurrence."[36] It is not surprising, therefore, that states have seen the development of international law and multilateralism as inextricably linked.

The legislative ideal of procedural justice first filtered into international legal thought in the late eighteenth century, finding expression in the writings of early "positivist" legal theorists. Vattel's *The Law of Nations*, published in 1773, represents an important bridge between the naturalism of the absolutist era and the positivism of the modern. Vattel begins by reasserting the sanctity of natural law as the basic legal framework obligating states, a framework that he calls "necessary law": "We call that the *Necessary law of Nations* which consists in the application of the law of nature to *Nations*. It is *Necessary* because nations are *absolutely* bound to observe it."[37] Yet despite these assertions, the logic of Vattel's treatise rests on the assumption that international law must depart significantly from the dictates of natural law. This is because states possess a natural right to liberty that would be violated under certain circumstances if the law of nature were rigorously applied in the form it takes between individuals: "It is therefore necessary, on many occasions, that nations should suffer certain things to be done, though in their own nature unjust and condemnable; because they cannot oppose them by open force, without violating the liberty of some particular state, and destroying the foundations of their natural society."[38] Viable international law is thus a compromise between the dictates of natural law and the liberty of states, the result of which is the "positive law of nations," a law grounded in the will of states and expressed through conventions, treaties and customs.[39]

It was not long before scholars of international law denied any role at all for the canons of natural law, placing all their emphasis on contractual, codified legal doctrine. In 1795 Robert Ward published *An Enquiry into*

---

[36] Ruggie, "Multilateralism," 14. This qualitative definition is the starting point for most theoretical and historical discussions of multilateralism, employed by scholars of divergent theoretical perspectives. See Martin, "Rational State Choice"; Caporaso, "International Relations Theory"; and Burley, "Regulating the World." The case for a contrasting "nominal" definition is made by Keohane in "Multilateralism: An Agenda for Research."

[37] de Vattel, *Law of Nations*, 1viii.

[38] Ibid., 1xiv.

[39] Ibid., 1xiv–1xv.

the Foundation and History of the Law of Nations, which typifies this new paradigm. Humanity's religious and cultural heterogeneity, Ward argues, prevents any consensus regarding the content of natural law. This is not to "reject the Law of Nature as forming *part* of the foundation of the Law of Nations; but simply to point out that while men have been known to entertain such discordant opinions concerning the *ramifications* of that law, it cannot lead us to that certainty concerning virtue, which would oblige *all mankind* to think of it exactly in the same manner."[40] Consequently, there needs to be "something more fixed and definite as the foundation of the Law of Nations."[41] Ward finds such certainty in treaties, conventions, and international customs, all of which are founded on the collective will of states.[42] Echoing Rousseau's remarks on the relationship between the general will and legal obligation, G. F. von Martens, one of Ward's peers, argues that states are obliged to respect these concrete accords not because they reflect the will of God but because they represent the "mutual *will* of the nations concerned."[43] In contrast to the work of classical international lawyers such as Grotius, both Ward and von Martens base their treatises on the historical development of international legal doctrine between European states—on "the facts," as Ward declares.

The revolutionary governments of France and the United States challenged the institutional practices of absolutist international society, calling for a new diplomatic and legal order based on the principle of legislative justice.[44] It was not was not until the middle of the nineteenth century, however, that this principle began structuring the actual practices of states, establishing over time a distinctly modern international institutional architecture. The precept that social rules should be authored by those subject to them came to license multilateral forms of rule determination, while the precept that rules should be equally applicable to all subjects, in all like cases, warranted the formal codification of contractual international law. The net result was a marked increase during the nineteenth century in the number of multilateral conferences, institutions, and organization.[45] Christopher Hill describes the quantum leap in multilat-

---

[40] Ward, *Foundations and History of the Law of Nations*, xxxii.

[41] Ibid., xxxvi.

[42] Ibid., 160–161.

[43] von Martens, *Law of Nations*, 47–48.

[44] Gilbert, "New 'Diplomacy' of the Eighteenth Century."

[45] On the proliferation of multilateral treaties, see Mosteky, *Index of Multilateral Treaties*. According to this source, between 1648 and 1814 the European states concluded only 127 multilateral treaties, less than one per year. In the period between 1814 and 1914, the figure jumped to 817. On the increase in the number of multilateral conferences and organizations, see Murphy, *International Organization and International Change*.

eral activity after the Congress of Vienna as "the most striking line of evolution in diplomacy."[46]

To illustrate how the metavalues of the new constitutional structure shaped the fundamental institutions of modern international society, the remainder of this chapter traces two key institutional developments of the late nineteenth and early twentieth centuries. The first is the growing commitment during this period to regular, then permanent, universal conferences of states. Once it was accepted that the rules governing international society should be authored by those subject to them and equally binding on all, some means had to be found to enable the collective legislation of international law. From 1850 onward, peacetime conferences of states emerged to fulfil this role. The second is the creation of the Permanent Court of Arbitration, which later became the International Court of Justice. Initiated at the first Hague Conference of 1899, the court's evolution provides a revealing window on the normative ascendancy of contractual international law and its acceptance as a basic institutional practice of international society. The importance of this conception of law in the court's constitution also highlights the radical difference between the modern and ancient Greek practices of arbitration.

The historical analysis focuses on a number of major crises and wars in the international system and the subsequent attempts by states to reestablish order. Such upheavals are instructive because in the process of constructing a new international order states are forced to address two questions: What constitutes a legitimate state? And what fundamental institutions are suited to maintain peace and security in a system of composed of such states? They thus represent useful sites in which to examine prevailing conceptions of the moral purpose of the state and procedural justice as well as the impact of these values on institutional design and action. In the period between 1814 and 1945, four moments in the development of modern institutions stand out: the Congress of Vienna (1814–15), the Hague Conferences of 1899 and 1907, the Versailles Peace Conference of 1918, and the San Francisco Conference of 1945. These are usefully characterized as moments of negation, foundation, construction, and renovation.

Negation: The Congress of Vienna

In the first half of the nineteenth century, modern conceptions of the moral purpose of the state and procedural justice influenced the international order only in a negative sense—they were reacted against, not acted upon.

---

[46] Hill, "Diplomacy and the Modern State," 90.

Napoleon's violent and audacious military campaign to establish French dominance over the European continent posed two challenges to the established order. It tore asunder the existing distribution of power and division of territory, and it denied the principle of legitimacy on which the authority of the absolutist states rested—the divine right of kings. After the eventual victory of the allied powers (Britain, Russia, Austria, and Prussia) a new international order was constructed at the Congress of Vienna (1814–15), an order that shaped relations between European states for years to come.[47] The conventional account of this settlement emphasizes the importance that the principle of equilibrium or balance of power played in negotiations.[48] This perspective credits Lord Castlereagh, the British foreign minister, with negotiating a stable balance of forces, and his Austrian counterpart, Prince Metternich, with sanctifying the new order with the principle of equilibrium.[49]

This interpretation captures an important dimension of the post-Napoleonic settlement, but it tells only half the story. An analysis of the Viennese negotiations reveals a second structuring principle, that of legitimacy. Here the crucial role was played by the French representative, Prince Talleyrand, who upheld the moral purpose of the absolutist state as the sole basis of legitimate political authority, rejecting the ideas of democracy and nationalism that fueled the French Revolution. Brandishing the divine right of kings, Talleyrand successfully reinstated France among the pantheon of Great Powers, later cultivating an alliance with Castlereagh and Metternich—the architects of equilibrium—that would determine the core territorial decisions of the settlement. By defining which political units constituted legitimate states, therefore, the principal of monarchical right laid the foundations for a settlement based on the balance of power. In a situation where old territorial boundaries had been obscured and overrun by years of warfare, and where a myriad of sovereign claims competed for recognition, the principles of legitimacy and equilibrium jointly structured the new international order.

The negotiations at Vienna were shaped by two prior factors. The first of these was the ambiguity of the Treaty of Paris, which ended the Napoleonic Wars in May 1814. The Parties pledged to convene in Vienna in two months time "for the purposes of regulating, in General Congress; the

---

[47] The classic accounts of the Congress of Vienna are: Nicholson, *Congress of Vienna*; Webster, *Congress of Vienna*; Kissinger, *World Restored*; Gulick, *Europe's Classical Balance of Power*.

[48] For statements of this position, see Kissinger, *World Restored*; and Gulick, *Europe's Classical Balance of Power*.

[49] Kissinger, *World Restored*, 5.

arrangements . . . to complete the provisions of the present Treaty."[50] It was distinctly unclear, however, who would have decision-making power at the congress. The Treaty of Paris had been signed by eight states (Britain, Russia, Austria, Prussia, France, Sweden, Spain, and Portugal), but Article 32 invited "[a]ll the powers engaged on either side in the present War" to participate in the congress.[51] To further complicate matters, the Great Powers (Britain, Russia, Austria, and Prussia) had signed a secret article expressing their determination to control all decisions of importance.[52] All of this resulted in three distinct groups of states with decision-making expectations: the full congress of European states, the eight signatories of the Treaty of Paris, and the four Great Powers. The impact of this confusion was greatly magnified by a second factor—the failure of the Great Powers to resolve their outstanding differences over territorial questions and the future distribution of power before arriving at the congress.

Before proceeding it is important to consider the objectives and strategies that Talleyrand sought to pursue at Vienna. His aims were threefold. First, he planned to reinstate France as one of the Great Powers of Europe. In a letter to Louis XVIII, the restored Bourbon monarch, he wrote that France should "resume the rank and consideration in the eyes of the nations of Europe, which, since the return of your Majesty, are ours of right."[53] Second, he wanted to override all of the decisions made by the Great Powers prior to the congress, "to annul all that had been done without France."[54] Finally, he hoped to have Poland reestablished as an independent state, and to ensure the restoration of the dethroned monarchs of Saxony and Naples.[55]

Talleyrand's strategy for achieving these goals was simple yet ingenious. The war against Napoleon was not just a defence of territory but also a defence of monarchical right as the legitimate basis of state power. By turning this principle against the victorious powers, Talleyrand saw that he could prevent the establishment of a purely mechanical balance of power and, in turn, realize French objectives. This strategy is clearly apparent in a letter he wrote to Metternich, the ideologue of equilibrium,

---

[50] "The First Peace of Paris, 30 May 1814," Article 32, in Israel, *Major Peace Treaties*, 513.

[51] Ibid.

[52] Secret Article 1 reads: "The disposal of the Territories given by His Most Christian Majesty . . . and the relations from whence a system of real and permanent balance of power in Europe is to be derived, shall be regulated at the Congress upon the principles determined upon the Allied Powers among themselves." Ibid., 514.

[53] Talleyrand to Louis XVII, 9 October 1814, in Pallain, *Correspondence*, 30–31.

[54] Talleyrand, *Memoirs*, 200.

[55] Louis XVIII insisted on these restorations in a letter to Talleyrand. Louis XVIII to Talleyrand, 13 October 1814, in Pallain, *Correspondence*, 44–45.

on 12 December 1814. The Treaty of Paris, he wrote, "proposed that the ultimate result of the operations of the Congress should be a real and durable equilibrium, it did not mean to sacrifice to the establishment of that equilibrium the rights which it should guarantee. It did not mean to confound, in one and the same mass, all territories and people, to divide them again according to certain proportions; it wished that every legitimate right should be respected, and that vacant territories, that is to say without a sovereign, should be distributed conformably to principles of political equilibrium, or, which is the same thing, to principles of the rights of every one, and the repose of all."[56] Talleyrand, therefore, not only upheld the moral foundations of the monarchical state but also asserted the need to moderate the principle of equilibrium with the principle of legitimacy, a strategy he pursued throughout the congress.

The Great Powers arrived in Vienna determined that all outstanding matters would be decided by them alone. Not only were the small powers to be excluded from key negotiations, so was France. Castlereagh, who was at least willing to entertain French views, wrote to the British prime minister that "the three Continental Courts seem to feel equal jealousy of admitting France either to arbitrate between them or to assume any leading influence in the arrangements consequent upon the peace."[57] Talleyrand's opportunity to break this clique came on 30 September when he was invited "to assist" at a conference of the four great powers. Upon arrival he was handed a protocol overviewing the decisions already reached by the allied powers. He responded by arguing that the Quadruple Alliance was no longer a legitimate decision-making body: "I declared that *allied powers*, and a *congress* in which powers that were not allied were to be found, were in my eyes very little able to arrange affairs loyally together. I repeated with some astonishment and even warmth, the word *allied powers* . . . 'allied.' I said, 'and against whom? It is no longer against France; for peace has been made. . . . It is surely not against the King of France; he is a guarantee of the duration of that peace. Gentlemen, let us speak frankly; if there are still *allied powers*, I am one too many here.'"[58] Talleyrand then argued that France had all the qualities of a Great Power, and that the principle of monarchical legitimacy on which the war had been fought would be fundamentally violated if France was not admitted as a full partner in negotiations: "The presence of a minister of Louis XVIII consecrates here the principle upon which all social order rests. The first need of Europe is to banish forever the opinion that right can be acquired by conquest alone, and to cause the revival of that sacred princi-

---

[56] Talleyrand to Metternich, 12 December 1814, in Metternich, *Memoirs*, 594–595.
[57] Castlereagh to Liverpool, 24 September 1814, in Webster, *British Diplomacy*, 195.
[58] Talleyrand, *Memoirs*, 203.

ple of legitimacy from which all order and stability spring. To show today that France troubles your deliberations, would be to say that true principles are no longer the only ones that guide you, and that you are unwilling to be just.[59] The representatives of the four Great Powers had no response to such arguments, choosing instead to withdraw the offending protocol. Friedrich von Gentz, who was the meeting's secretary, recorded that Talleyrand "hopelessly upset our plans. It was a scene I shall never forget."[60]

Over the following weeks the French foreign minister moved to further weaken the authority of the Great Powers by exploiting the ambiguities of the Treaty of Paris. While leading the calls by smaller powers to have the full congress convened, he simultaneously argued that if there were to be a small coordinating body it could legitimately consist only of the eight Paris signatories who had called the congress in the first place.[61] The Great Powers had no choice but to accept the creation of such a committee, and Talleyrand only ceased calling for a meeting of the full congress when Britain, Russia, Austria, and Prussia agreed to include France in any closed discussions. As Nicolson notes, before any of the key decisions were reached, "the Council of Four became the Council of Five."[62]

Talleyrand's artful use of the absolutist principle of legitimacy to gain a seat at the bargaining table had a decisive impact on subsequent territorial wranglings, the most important and divisive of which concerned Poland. After Napoleon's defeat, Russia occupied the bulk of Polish territory, with smaller areas falling under Prussian and Austrian control. Despite several previous agreements, the four Great Powers arrived in Vienna unable to agree on the country's future.[63] While their positions fluctuated during the course of the negotiations, they were essentially divided between those who wanted to use their Polish holdings to extend their spheres of influence and those who saw Poland as a crucial element in the construction of a stable balance of power. In the first camp, Tsar Alexander wanted a united Poland under Russian control, and Prussia would only relinquish its holdings if it received Saxony in compensation. In the other camp, Austria was prepared to give up its territory so long as both Prussia and Russia were denied control of Poland or Saxony, and Britain wanted Poland reestablished as an independent state free from either Russian or

---

[59] Ibid.

[60] Quote in Nicolson, *Congress of Vienna*, 142.

[61] This latter argument was set down in an "official note" that Talleyrand sent to the great powers following the meeting of 30 September. Talleyrand to Louis XVIII, 4 October 1814, in Pallain, *Correspondence*, 20.

[62] Nicolson, *Congress of Vienna*, 147.

[63] The previous agreements were The Convention of Kalisch (28 February 1813), The Treaty of Reichenbach (June 1813), and the Treaty of Teplitz (9 September 1813).

Prussian control. By December 1814 these differences had brought the Great Powers to the brink of war.[64]

It was at this point that Talleyrand intervened. Throughout the negotiations he had remained committed to the positions on Poland and Saxony that he first specified in his objectives before leaving Paris. In his view the principle of legitimacy demanded the reinstatement of the King of Saxony and the reestablishment of an independent Polish kingdom.[65] Having long advocated a European settlement in which legitimacy tempered the crude mathematics of equilibrium, Talleyrand saw in the Polish schism an opportunity to pursue both principles through a concrete political alliance. After enraging both the tsar and the Prussian representatives by accusing them of violating the principle of monarchical right, Talleyrand convinced Castlereagh and Metternich to conclude a defensive treaty with France to deter attempts by Russia and Prussia to impose their designs by force. Castlereagh wrote to the British prime minister that given "these circumstances I have felt it an act of imperative duty to concert with the French and Austrian Plenipotentiaries a Treaty of Defensive Alliance, confined within the strict necessity of this most extraordinary case. Without such a bond, I feel that our deliberations here are at an end."[66] The signing of the treaty on 3 January 1815 quickly brought results. The belligerent powers adopted more accommodating positions, resulting in the restoration of the King of Saxony, albeit with reduced territory, and the creation of a formally independent Polish state, minus the Duchy of Warsaw (which Russia retained). As far as Talleyrand was concerned, he had achieved his main objectives: France had once again assumed the status and influence of a Great Power, and the territorial settlements, however piecemeal, broadly reflected the absolutist principle of legitimacy.[67]

The international order created at Vienna was archaic. In a reaction against the revolutionary maxims which fermented twenty-five years of war and social upheaval, the Great Powers, including Britain, reasserted monarchical right as the basis of legitimate state power and authority. Not surprisingly, the modern principle of legislative procedural justice had little impact on either the negotiations or the resulting international

---

[64] The best account of these differences and the escalating tensions they generated is presented in Nicolson, *Congress of Vienna*, 148–181.

[65] The guidelines he drafted in Paris are recorded in Duff Cooper's classic biography *Talleyrand*, 240–243.

[66] Castlereagh to Liverpool, 1 January 1815, in Webster, *British Diplomacy*, 278.

[67] In a letter to Louis XVIII he wrote: "Not only does France no longer stand alone in Europe, but . . . France is in concert with two of the greatest of Powers, and three states of a second order, and will soon be in concert with all the States which are guided by other than revolutionary principles and maxims." Talleyrand to Louis XVIII, 4 January 1815, in Pallain, *Correspondence*, 242.

order. This is clearly apparent in the understandings of international law and diplomacy that prevailed at the congress. Talleyrand frequently declared that the conference's procedures and settlements had to reflect the principles of "public law," but he was not embracing the modern conception of law as reciprocal accord. Law meant the divine right of kings, the command of God. In an early dispatch to the French minister of foreign affairs in Paris, Talleyrand wrote that French policy is ruled by "the principle of public law which is recognized by all Europe, and from which springs, almost of necessity, the re-establishment of King Ferdinand IV on the throne of Naples, as well as the succession of the Carignan branch to the house of Saxony."[68] The nonparticipatory implications of this conception of law gave little impetus to genuine multilateral diplomacy at the congress. To begin with, none of the key negotiators, even Talleyrand, believed that the congress as a whole could, or should, legislate the final settlement. As Castlereagh explained to the British prime minister, the "Congress never could exist as a deliberative assembly, with a power of decision by a plurality of votes."[69] Furthermore, the negotiations between the Great Powers themselves were, in the end, largely bilateral, a fact reflected in the final Treaty of Vienna, which merely amalgamated a multitude of specific territorial agreements.[70]

Foundation: The Hague Conferences

Diplomatic historians usually identify efforts to apply the modern principle of legislative procedural justice to international relations with the Versailles Peace Conference of 1919 and the creation of the League of Nations. Critics blame the Versailles negotiators for the tragic reign of interwar idealism, chastising them for naively believing that liberal institutional ideals could be applied to relations between states.[71] For Morgenthau, this moment heralded the birth of "political" international law, a legal form fundamentally at odds with the realities of international politics.[72] For Nicolson, it marked the origin of "new diplomacy," a form of interstate interaction that "omits many of the merits of several [previous] systems . . . and exaggerates many of their faults."[73] Responsibility for these developments is almost always laid at the feet of the United States,

---

[68] Kings Ambassadors to Monsieur Le Comte, 27 September 1814, in Talleyrand, *Memoirs*, 221–222.

[69] Castlereagh to Liverpool, 9 October 1814, in Webster, *British Diplomacy*, 203.

[70] "Treaty of Vienna, 9 June 1815," in Israel, *Major Peace Treaties*, 519–575.

[71] The classic statement of this view is Carr, *Twenty Years' Crisis*.

[72] Morgenthau, "Positivism, Functionalism, and International Law," 278.

[73] Nicolson, *Evolution of Diplomatic Method*, 91.

and more particularly the American president, Woodrow Wilson. His "Fourteen Points" are said to epitomize Washington's mistaken assumption that the domestic political values of the United States could structure a new, fundamentally different international order.

Whether these developments were good or bad, it is wrong to assume that the modern international institutions of contractual international law and multilateralism originated at Versailles, as these practices were first endorsed and enacted by European states in the second half of the nineteenth century. It is impossible to identify the precise moment of this acceptance, especially since the corpus of international agreements and incidence of multilateral diplomacy grew steadily after 1850, but the first Hague Peace Conference of 1899 was undoubtedly a crucial watershed in the development of modern fundamental institutions. It was there, and at the second Hague Conference of 1907, that states first collectively embraced the legislative norm of procedural justice, championing both the idea of contractual international law and multilateralism. The Concert of Europe had institutionalized regular meetings of the Great Powers, but these gatherings lacked the universalist and legislative ideals that inspired the Hague conferences. Together, these conferences laid the foundations for the institutional construction that continued at Versailles, and the subsequent institutional developments of the twentieth century have largely been elaborations on basic architectural themes established during this early period of institutional innovation.

After 1815 the Great Powers entered a period of relative peace, but as the nineteenth century progressed they engaged in a costly and eventually disastrous arms race.[74] The Russian tsar proposed the Hague Conference of 1899 to arrest this economically debilitating and militarily destabilizing competition. In the circular note inviting other states to attend the conference, Count Mouravieff, the Russian foreign minister, wrote: "Economic crises, due in great part to the system of amassing armaments to the point of exhaustion, and the continual danger which lies in this accumulation of war material, are transforming the armed peace of our days into a crushing burden which the peoples have more and more difficulty bearing. It appears evident, then, that if this state of affairs be prolonged, it will inevitably lead to the very cataclysm which it is desired to avert, and the impending horrors of which are fearful to every human being."[75] In contrast to the Congress of Vienna, where the Great Powers explicitly rejected the idea that the community of states could, or should, legislate general rules of international conduct, the first Hague Conference was

[74] See Taylor, *Struggle for Mastery in Europe*.
[75] "Russian Circular Note Proposing First Peace Conference," in Scott, *Hague Conventions*, xiv.

organized precisely for such a purpose. In opening the first working session on 20 May the president of the conference stated: "Let me say that, following a general law, diplomacy is no longer merely an art in which personal ability plays an exclusive part; its tendency is to become a science which shall have fixed rules for settling disputes. Such at the present time is the ideal which it should have before its eyes, and it cannot be disputed that great progress will have been made if diplomacy succeeds in establishing in this Conference some of the rules of which I have just spoken."[76] Following this rule-making agenda, the twenty-seven participating states engaged in two projects: they formulated a new body of codified laws governing the conduct of war and the nature and use of armaments, and they established the Permanent Court of Arbitration to interpret and adjudicate these and other international laws.[77]

The conference's work was divided between three commissions, the Third Commission being responsible for "The Pacific Settlement of International Disputes." Although the commission discussed and endorsed various methods of conflict resolution—particularly third-party mediation—it devoted most of its attention to the creation of a system of international arbitration. From the outset, however, the deliberating states employed a fundamentally different conception of arbitration from that of the ancient Greeks. Reflecting modern ideals of procedural justice, arbitration was defined as the judicial interpretation of law, which was understood as codified reciprocal accord. By this time the rule of law was considered a defining characteristic of a civilized polity, and thus a desirable feature of a society of civilized states. As the commission's final report to the conference states: "Humanity, in its constant evolution, daily tends in increasing measure to place respect for the law as the foundation of its existence. *The society of civilized nations recognizes the existence of legal principles and rules set to a common standard—international law* [my emphasis]."[78] The report goes on to argue that the "further law progresses, and the more it enters into the society of nations, the more clearly arbitration appears woven into the structure of that society."[79]

---

[76] "Address of his Excellency Mr Staal, President of the Conference, 20 May 1899," in Scott, *Reports to the Hague Conferences*, 9.

[77] The new laws regulating warfare and armaments were contained in the Convention Respecting the Laws and Customs of War on Land, the Convention on the Adaptation to Maritime Warfare of the Principles of the Geneva Convention of 22 August 1864, the Declaration to Prohibit the Launching of Projectiles and Explosives from Balloons or by other Similar Methods, the Declaration to Prohibit the Use of Bullets which Expand and Flatten Easily in the Human Body, and the Declaration to Prohibit the Use of Projectiles, the Only Object of which is the Diffusion of Asphyxiating and Deleterious Gases.

[78] "Report to the Conference from the Third Commission on Pacific Settlement of International Disputes," in Scott, *Reports to the Hague Conferences*, 55.

[79] Ibid.

On 29 June 1899 the conference delegates signed the Convention for the Pacific Settlement of International Disputes, which established the Permanent Court of Arbitration, an institution then consisting of little more than a list of nominated arbitrators from which disputing parties could select a tribunal to settle their differences. Reflecting the jurisdictional canons applied to domestic courts, the new institution's role was explicitly restricted to the interpretation of questions of law. This was partly because arbitration was considered ideally suited for such purposes. Article 16 of the convention states that in "questions of a legal nature, and especially in the interpretation or application of international conventions, arbitration is recognized by the signatory Powers as the most effective, and at the same time the most equitable, means of settling disputes which diplomacy has failed to settle."[80] More importantly, though, the convention's signatories did not believe that a judicial body—national or international—could, or should, deal with nonlegal questions. As the Third Commission's report explains: "Article 16 determines the nature of controversies which are within the proper jurisdiction of arbitration. These are questions of a legal nature and principally questions of the interpretation or application of treaties. . . . Differences where the opposing claims of the parties cannot be stated as legal propositions are thus . . . outside the jurisdiction of an institution called upon to 'speak the law.' "[81] To confine arbitration within such bounds would have been unintelligible to the ancient Greeks, whose system relied not on codified law but on a judge's sense of justice—the ability to arrive at an equitable and fair decision in the absence of a body of codified interstate law. As Bozeman remarks, "Modern arbitration, when compared to Greek arbitration, assumes the character of litigation."[82]

These attempts to apply the modern principle of legislative procedural justice to international relations were given further impetus by the second Hague Conference of 1907. One of the conference's primary objectives was to develop a more effective judicial institution than the Permanent Court of Arbitration. Although the delegates agreed that the court had made an important contribution to international dispute settlement, they saw two important weaknesses in its operation as a legal institution. First, because the tribunals were selected by particular disputing parties to hear specific cases, the court did not exist as a coherent body operating in continuous session. This not only weakened the court's prestige, but it undermined its ability to generate new international law. As Joseph

[80] "Hague Convention of 1899 for the Pacific Settlement of International Disputes," in Scott, *Hague Conventions*, 55.

[81] Report to the Conference from the Third Commission on Pacific Settlement of International Disputes," in Scott, *Reports to the Hague Conferences*, 55.

[82] Bozeman, *Politics and Culture*, 84.

Choate, the chief American representative, submitted: "The fact that there was nothing permanent, or continuous, or connected in the sessions of the Court, or in the adjudication of the cases submitted to it, has been an obvious source of weakness and want of prestige in the tribunal. Each trial it had before it has been wholly independent of every other, and its occasional utterances, widely distant in point of time and disconnected in subject-matter, have not gone far towards constituting a consistent body of international law or of valuable contributions to international law, which ought to emanate from an international tribunal representing the power and might of all the nations."[83] With forty-four states from diverse regions of the world attending the second conference, it is not surprising that the second of the court's perceived weaknesses was its unrepresentative nature. As the First Commission's report to the conference observed: "It is not alone sufficient that it be permanent, although permanency is indeed a first requisite. If the Court is to develop an international, not a national system of law, it seems to need no argument that the various systems of law should find representation within the Court and upon the bench."[84] In attempting to overcome these two weaknesses, the delegates formulated a draft convention establishing a new Judicial Arbitration Court, to be "composed of judges representing the various juridical systems of the world, and capable of insuring continuity in jurisprudence of arbitration."[85] Unfortunately, disagreements over the selection of judges deferred the court's institution until after World War I.[86]

In addition to these attempts to refine and strengthen the judicial apparatus for interpreting international law, the Hague negotiators were more explicit about the role of multilateral diplomacy in the legislation of reciprocal international accords. While endorsing smaller multilateral initiatives, their desire to establish a regime of universally binding international laws led them to place particular emphasis on large-scale, preferably universal, conferences of states. In his opening address, the Dutch minister of foreign affairs argued that such conferences were "convoked to discuss rules of international law and to give them precision."[87] Although the creation of a permanent conference of states was not taken up until

[83] "Report to the Conference from the First Commission Recommending the Creation of a Court of Arbitral Justice," in Scott, *Reports to the Hague Conferences*, 234.

[84] Ibid., 242.

[85] "Draft Convention Relative to the Creation of a Judicial Arbitration Court," in Scott, *Hague Conventions*, 31.

[86] The best account of this dispute is found in Choate's memoirs, *Two Hague Conferences*, 81.

[87] "Opening Address of his Excellency Jonkheer Van Tets Van Gourdriaan, Minister of Foreign Affairs of the Netherlands, 15 June 1907," in Scott, *Reports to the Hague Conferences*, 195.

the Versailles Peace Conference in 1919, the organization of regular meetings was already firmly on the agenda. In submitting the Hague Convention of 1907 to the United States Senate, the secretary of state, Elihu Root, argued that the "achievements of the two Conferences justify the belief that the world has entered upon an orderly process through which, step by step, in successive Conferences . . . there may be continual progress toward making the practice of civilized nations conform to their peaceful professions."[88] Such optimism was poorly rewarded, though, and the intervention of World War I prevented an anticipated third Hague Conference.

Construction: The Versailles Peace Conference

In 1919, after four years of unprecedented violence and suffering, the world's leaders convened at the Palace of Versailles to construct a new, more peaceful international order. Two stories are told about this meeting, both stories of disaster. The first emphasizes the meeting's inequity, focusing on the domination of the great over the small, the victorious over the defeated, the unjust over the just. The second stresses its naivety, the substitution of prudence and sober power politics for an unwarranted faith in the rule of law and multilateralism. There is an element of truth in both of these accounts. The ambitions of the Great Powers indeed had an impact on the international order created at Versailles, but so too did the principle of legislative procedural justice and the resulting practices of contractual international law and multilateralism. In the settlement reached at the Congress of Vienna the prevailing rationale for the authority of the state—monarchical right—defined the terms and conditions within which the Great Powers could construct an equilibrium of power. At Versailles a similar phenomenon occurred. The ideals of law as reciprocal accord and participatory decision-making—which had already been endorsed at the international level by the Hague Conferences—left an important mark on the international order created by the Great Powers.

Before proceeding, two observations should be made about the Versailles negotiations.[89] First, the basic institutional framework that the delegates built into the Covenant of the League of Nations was largely a consolidation of the earlier Hague initiatives, not a new invention. Sec-

[88]   United States Senate Document no. 444, 60th Congress, 62.

[89]   The classic works on the Versailles Conference, often written by key participants, are: Miller, *Drafting the Covenant*; Marburg, *Development of the League of Nations Idea*; Baker, *Woodrow Wilson and World Settlement*; Lloyd George, *Truth About the Peace Treaties*; House and Seymour, *What Really Happened at Paris*; Nicolson, *Peacemaking*; Duggan, *League of Nations*; Schwarzenberger, *League of Nations*.

ond, this process of consolidation reflected a considerable consensus on basic institutional principles among the three main allies—Britain, France, and the United States—not the hegemony of a single power. Both of these facts will be apparent as the analysis unfolds.

The Hague Conferences left many significant legacies, especially in the areas of arms control and the laws of warfare, but one of their most important contributions was the enunciation, if not the realization, of two architectural principles for the construction of an international order: that there should be a universal conference of states based on the principle of multilateralism, and that there should be an international judicial body to interpret codified legal doctrine. As indicated above, both of these principles came to structure the international order created at Versailles. The drafting of the Covenant of the League of Nations was essentially a joint British and American project, with, if anything, London, not Washington, assuming a slightly more prominent role. The earliest drafts of the covenant—Britain's Phillimore Report of March 1918 and the July 1918 draft by the American diplomat Colonel Edward House[90]—envisaged a general conference of states and an international court, the same structure later advocated by the French at Versailles.[91] This basic institutional framework, which gave form to the institutional principles upheld at the Hague, was eventually augmented by the addition of an executive council of Great Powers. First advocated in a December 1918 draft by General Jan Smuts,[92] a member of the British League of Nations Commission, the structure of a conference, a council, and a judicial system found expression in all subsequent British and American drafts. These drafts differed, however, over the nature of the judicial institution to be created, with the British favoring a permanent court and Wilson proposing a looser system of tribunals, much like that established at the first Hague Conference.[93] Immediately prior to the opening of the Versailles Conference, the British and American delegates forged a single draft covenant—the Hurst-Miller draft—which incorporated London's vision of a permanent judicial court and from then on provided the basis for negotiations.[94]

The assumption that international law consists of reciprocal accords between states was clearly apparent in the way that Versailles delegates followed their Hague predecessors in confining the proposed court's

[90] House was one of Woodrow Wilson's closest friends and advisors. For an insightful analysis of their relationship see George and George, *Woodrow Wilson and Colonel House.*

[91] The texts of the Phillimore, the House, and the French draft covenants, along with the others, are reprinted in Baker, *Woodrow Wilson and World Settlement,* 67–88, 152–162.

[92] Ibid., 94–99.

[93] See the differences between the British draft covenant of 20 January 1919 and Wilson's draft of the same date. Ibid., 117–143.

[94] Ibid., 144–151.

jurisdiction to the interpretation of codified legal doctrine. In terms similar to those employed in the final covenant, Britain's Phillimore Report set the tone for all subsequent statements on the court's legitimate sphere of operation: "If a dispute should hereafter arise between any of the Allied States as to the interpretation of a treaty, as to any question of international law, as to the existence of any fact which if established would constitute a breach of any international obligation, or as to the nature and extent of the reparation to be made for any breach, if such a dispute cannot be settled by negotiation, arbitration is recognized by the Allied States as the most effective and at the same time the most equitable means of settling the dispute."[95] Using virtually the same words, Wilson's third draft covenant expressed a similarly circumscribed view of an arbitrator's jurisdiction: "The Powers signatory to this covenant undertake and agree that whenever any dispute or difficulty shall arise between or among them with regard to any question of the law of nations, with regard to the interpretation of a treaty, as to any fact which would, if established, constitute a breach of international obligation, or as to any alleged damage and the nature and measure of the reparation to be made therefore, if such a dispute or difficulty cannot be satisfactorily settled by ordinary processes or negotiation, to submit the whole subject matter to arbitration and to carry out in good faith any award or decision that may be rendered."[96] Although the French draft covenant devoted more attention to the sanctions to be inflicted on unlawful states, it also adopted the general position that the court's role was to "decide and pronounce upon questions of law at issue between states, on the basis of custom or of international conventions, as well as of theory and jurisprudence."[97]

Given this consensus among the three dominant states, it is not surprising that the final covenant defined the court's sphere of operation in precisely the same way: "Disputes as to the interpretation of a treaty, as to any question of international law, as to the existence of any fact which if established would constitute a breach of any international obligation, as to the extent and nature of the reparation to be made for any such breach, are to be among those which are generally suitable for submission to arbitration."[98] Finally, the court's role in interpreting international law was made abundantly clear in its Statute, which directed judges to apply international conventions, international custom "as evidence of a general practice accepted as law," "general principles of law recognized by civilized nations," and the "judicial decisions and the teachings of the most highly

[95] Ibid., 75.
[96] Ibid., 120.
[97] Ibid., 154.
[98] Ibid., 180.

qualified publicists of the various nations, as a subsidiary means for the determination of rules of law."[99] Each of these sources was thought to provide evidence of reciprocal accords between states, the essence of modern international law.

The international order constructed at Versailles also enshrined the architectural principle of multilateralism in two ways. To begin with, instead of the principle of equilibrium used at Vienna, the League of Nations was bound together by a reciprocal security guarantee in which each state agreed to assist in the protection of the others. Reflecting the intent of almost all previous drafts, the covenant states that the "Members of the League undertake to respect and preserve as against external aggression the territorial integrity and existing political independence of all Members of the League."[100] The importance of this quintessential multilateral accord cannot be understated. By defining the League's principal reason for existence, it circumscribed the realm of legitimate action open to members of the organization, both great and small. This was true in both a positive and a negative sense. It could oblige states to act in circumstances where they otherwise might not, which, as Ruggie observes, was one of the main reasons for the covenant's rejection by the United States Senate.[101] But it could also prevent strong and weak states alike from acting outside the accord's specific security agenda. Even the League's Council, which could be criticized for placing too much authority in the hands of the Great Powers, could only deal with issues "within the sphere of action of the League or affecting the peace of the world" (Article 4). More specifically, this meant it could consider peace threatening disputes not dealt with by the court (Article 15), and "advise upon the means" by which the collective security obligation could be fulfilled in cases of aggression against its members (Articles 10 and 16).[102] In the end, however, the unanimity rule governing voting in the Council and the Assembly effectively paralyzed the organization, preventing either collective action or Great Power adventurism.

The second way in which the principle of multilateralism structured the League was the Assembly's proposed role as a forum for negotiating new, universally binding principles of international conduct. It is important to recognize, however, that this role was severely circumscribed by the League's covenant, leaving the Assembly far from the "International

---

[99] "Statute of the Permanent Court of International Justice," Article 38, in Wheeler-Bennett and Fanshawe, *Information on the World Court*, 53.

[100] Baker, *Woodrow Wilson and the World Settlement*, 179.

[101] Ruggie, "Multilateralism," 10.

[102] "The Covenant of the League of Nations," in Baker, *Woodrow Wilson and the World Settlement*, 175–188.

Parliament" envisaged by Colonel House.[103] The Assembly's decision-making role was largely reactive, in most cases requiring the Great Power–dominated Council to refer to it matters for consideration (Article 15). The only avenue for the Assembly to initiate debate lay in Article 19, which allowed it to "advise the reconsideration by Members of the League of treaties which have become inapplicable and the consideration of international conditions whose continuance might endanger the peace of the world."[104] Yet despite these limitations, the fact that Assembly resolutions had to be unanimous indicates that the League's architects assumed that such decrees would carry weight. Furthermore, the Permanent Court's right to ascertain law from international custom and general principles recognized by states meant that the Assembly's resolutions could well achieve the status of international law, even if this was not the intent of the Paris negotiators. With hindsight, we see that the resolutions of the United Nations General Assembly have in fact assumed such a mantel.

If the post-Napoleonic settlement was archaic, then the international order constructed at Versailles was decidedly modern. The institutional implications of the moral purpose of the modern state that increasingly structured the domestic legitimacy and political life of the leading European states during the nineteenth century had begun to shape the fundamental institutions of international society at the Hague Conferences. By the time the Paris negotiators came to draft the Treaty of Versailles, the paired ideals of law as reciprocal accord and multilateralism effectively defined the horizons of their institutional imagination and expectation. As the preamble to House's draft covenant states, "International civilization having proved a failure because there has not been constructed a fabric of law to which nations have yielded with the same obedience and deference as the individuals submit to intra-national laws . . . it is the purpose of the States signatory to the Convention to form a League of Nations having for its purpose the maintenance throughout the world of peace, security, progress and orderly government."[105] Although the international order created at Versailles proved fragile and short-lived, the idea that a society of civilized states should be governed by fundamental institutions of reciprocally binding laws and multilateral diplomacy survived well beyond the traumas of the Second World War.

---

[103] House wrote in the letter to Wilson attached to his draft covenant of July 1918, "To all intents and purposes the representatives of the contracting powers become automatically an International Parliament, and I am sure it will be necessary for them to be in almost continuous session." Ibid., 80.

[104] Ibid., 183.

[105] Ibid., 82.

Renovation: The San Francisco Conference

Despite claims that an idealistic faith in international law and multilateralism contributed to the outbreak of the Second World War, the architects of the post-1945 international order did not abandon these institutional commitments. Instead, the new order reaffirmed the moral purpose of the modern state and the norm of legislative procedural justice. It was again constructed around the basic and by now familiar architectural principles laid down at the Hague: that there should be a universal conference of states based on the principle of multilateralism, and that there should be an international judicial body to interpret the reciprocal accords between states. Upheld by the Atlantic Charter, the Dumbarton Oaks Conference, and the Yalta Agreements, these principles were given new life through a substantial process of renovation, not revolution.

In 1949 the International Law Commission approved a "Draft Declaration on Rights and Duties of States," which declared that the "[s]tates of the world form a community governed by international law," that "the progressive development of international law requires effective organization of the community of states," and that "a primary purpose of the United Nations is to maintain international peace and security, and the reign of law and justice is essential to the realization of this purpose."[106] This declaration, which was meant to supplement the statement of guiding principles in the UN Charter, highlights the extent to which international law had become one of the fundamental institutions governing relations between states. Its reference to the relationship between legal doctrine and international organization, however, indicates that this was not the international law of Grotius and Pufendorf, but rather the positivist notion of law as reciprocal accord, a conception which, as we have seen, places a premium on multilateralism.

The competence of the judicial body created under the new international order once again provides a useful indicator of the prevailing conception of international law. Although the San Francisco delegates decided to replace the League's court with the International Court of Justice, the new institution's statute was little more than a revision of its predecessor's.[107] Not surprisingly, it too limits the court's jurisdiction to

---

[106] "Draft Declaration on Rights and Duties of States," in Sohn, *Basic Documents of the United Nations*, 26.

[107] The Committee of Jurists set up after the Dumbarton Oaks Conference in April 1945 to draft the new court's statute made a conscious decision to modify the statute of the Permanent Court of Justice rather than draft a new one. See "Report on Draft of Statute of an International Court of Justice Referred to in Chapter VII of the Dumbarton Oaks Proposals," in *Documents of the United Nations Conference*, 821–854.

the adjudication of narrowly defined legal disputes involving "the interpretation of a treaty," "any question of international law," "the existence of any fact which, if established, would constitute a breach of an international obligation," and "the nature or extent of the reparation to be made for the breach of an international obligation."[108] In ruling on such disputes, judges are expected to base their decisions solely on the terms of relevant agreements or on evidence of reciprocally binding norms and principles embraced by the community of states. The statute instructs them to apply "international conventions, whether general or particular, establishing rules expressly recognized by the contesting states," "international custom, as evidence of a general practice accepted as law," "the general principles of law recognized by civilized nations," and "judicial decisions and the teachings of the most highly qualified publicists of the various nations, as subsidiary means for determination of rules of law."[109] Since the idea of law as reciprocal accord was by this time fundamental to the domestic legitimacy of the leading states, and was already institutionalized at the international level by the Hague and Versailles Conferences, it was unlikely that the new court's jurisdiction would depart very far from past practices.

The San Francisco negotiators did, however, substantially strengthen the universal conference of states—the principal multilateral forum of the international system—a move explicitly designed to facilitate and encourage peace through international law. In comparison to the largely reactive role of the League's Assembly, the United Nation's Charter grants the General Assembly a quasi-legislative role. In fulfilling the organization's primary purpose of solving international disputes "in conformity with the principles of justice and international law" (Article 1), the General Assembly is authorized to "initiate studies and make recommendations for the purposes of . . . promoting international cooperation in the political field and encouraging the progressive development of international law and its codification" (Article 13).[110] To understand this role—which still leaves the General Assembly well short of an "international parliament"—it is useful to employ Rosalyn Higgins's distinction between "contractual" and "general" international law, the latter being the same as customary international law. Higgins correctly argues that the General Assembly's quasi-legislative role is largely restricted to the development of general international law, that is, to the generation of reciprocally binding

---

[108] "Statute of the International Court of Justice," Article 36, in Brownlie, *Basic Documents of International Law*, 396.

[109] Article 38, Ibid., 397.

[110] "The Charter of the United Nations," in Brownlie, *Basic Documents in International Law*, 2, 5.

norms, rules, and principles of international behavior.[111] According to Nagendra Singh, a former president of the International Court of Justice, the General Assembly does this by adopting general legal conventions, by convening international conferences which then produce such conventions, or by formulating Assembly resolutions.[112] The last of these, Higgins argues, are not necessarily binding, but when they embody the principle of reciprocity in the form of general rules of conduct they become an important source of customary international law.[113]

This should not suggest that the General Assembly has no role in the development of more clearly defined contractual international law. To the contrary, in 1947 it established the International Law Commission, the aim of which is to facilitate "the progressive development of international law and its codification."[114] In the first instance this entails a process of legal innovation, that is, "the preparation of draft conventions on subjects which have not yet been regulated by international law or in regard to which the law has not yet been sufficiently developed." It also involves a process of legal consolidation, whereby customary international law is translated into a contractual form. This means "the more precise formulation and systematization of international law in fields where there already has been extensive state practice, precedent and doctrine."[115] Whether innovating or consolidating, the commission has no independent decision-making power, its recommendations requiring approval by the General Assembly before becoming reciprocally binding international accords.

Post-1945 initiatives thus reasserted and reconstructed institutional principles and practices that were first endorsed and initiated by the international community in the late nineteenth century. The proliferation of these basic institutional practices, and their application to an ever widening realm of interstate relations, was, of course, greatly accelerated by American hegemony and leadership. In the history of modern international society, however, this seems less a period of architectural innovation than one of mass construction.

CONCLUSION

Historians have long characterized the period between 1776 and 1848 as an "Age of Revolutions." For Eric Hobsbawm, this period witnessed "the

---

[111] Higgins, *Development of International Law*, 1–10.
[112] Singh, "The UN and the Development of International Law," 392–393.
[113] Higgins, *Development of International Law*, 5.
[114] "Statute of the International Law Commission," Article 1, in Sohn, *Basic Documents of the United Nations*, 32.
[115] Article 15, Ibid., 33.

greatest transformation in human history since the remote times when men invented agriculture and metallurgy, writing, the city and the state."[116] The revolutionary significance of this period has been largely overlooked by international relations scholars, though. When seeking inspiration from history, they generally turn to 1648 and the Peace of Westphalia. It was then that the great shift from heteronomy to sovereignty occurred, the moment when modern international society is thought to have begun its long and often tortured evolution. The Age of Revolutions was, however, more than a domestic affair, more than a ripple below the surface of international society. As we have seen, mutually reinforcing revolutions in scientific, economic, and political thought and practice undermined the foundations of absolutist rule, spawning a new rationale for state sovereignty and a new conception of procedural justice. The effects of this change were felt well beyond state boundaries. As the terms and institutions of domestic governance transformed, states began to champion a new set of constitutional metavalues at the international level. A liberal-constitutionalist standard of civilization emerged as the dominant measure of legitimate statehood, and a legislative norm of procedural justice shaped international institutional design and action, licensing the basic institutional practices of contractual international law and multilateralism. This shift is clearly apparent in the differences between the Viennese settlement of 1814–15 and the ordering principles and initiatives states embraced and pursued from the Hague Conferences onward.

This argument has important implications for a thesis on sovereignty recently advanced by Samuel Barkin and Bruce Cronin. Adopting a similar stance to my own, they argue that we cannot understand how the international system functions unless we explore the changing terms in which sovereignty has been defined. "Thus an institutional, as opposed to a purely legal, understanding of sovereignty must address the legitimization of the nation-state system as well its formal legal definition."[117] They go on to distinguish between two different ways in which sovereignty has been interpreted: "state sovereignty, which stresses the link between sovereign authority and a defined territory, and national sovereignty, which emphasizes a link between sovereign authority and a defined population."[118] While I share the spirit of their enterprise, their "ideal types" of state sovereignty and national sovereignty obscure more than they reveal. For instance, because the sovereign rights of nations were rejected at both the Congress of Vienna and at the end of the Second World War—the former asserting the rights of monarchs, the latter the rights of political communities (collectivities of rights bearing individu-

---

[116] Hobsbawm, *Age of Revolutions*, 1.
[117] Barkin and Cronin, "State and the Nation," 107–108.
[118] Ibid., 108.

als)—Barkin and Cronin assume that in both cases sovereignty was justified in statist, not cultural, terms. As we have seen, though, the principles of legitimacy that prevailed in each of these contexts were radically different, despite both being "statist." At Vienna the absolutist divine right of kings determined the state's legitimacy, whereas after 1945 it rested on the civil-political values of the moral purpose of the modern state. By painting over these crucial differences between the terms of legitimacy structuring the post-Napoleonic and post-1945 international orders, Barkin and Cronin obscure the very factors that generated the contrasting fundamental institutions of the absolutist and modern societies of states.

By attributing the development of modern fundamental institutions to an ideological revolution that began in the late eighteenth century and transformed the terms of legitimate rule in the nineteenth, this chapter also challenges recent arguments that attribute the rise of multilateralism to American hegemony. As we saw in chapter 1, both rationalists and constructivists have assigned Washington almost sole responsibility for the design and construction of our present institutional framework. Rationalists portray such initiatives as the rational actions of a hegemon under conditions of bipolarity: the "U.S. preference for multilateral over discriminatory bilateral solutions," Martin contends, "can be seen as a result of structural conditions."[119] Constructivists, on the other hand, see these acts of institutional construction as an effort by American policymakers to transplant the New Deal regulatory state into the international arena. "The formal characteristics of multilateralism," Burley claims, "are the byproduct of a distinctly American effort to regulate the world."[120] Nothing in this chapter denies that the United States played a prominent role in the long construction of modern fundamental institutions or that Washington greatly accelerated their development after 1945. Nevertheless, the historical analysis presented above suggests that both multilateralism and contractual international law significantly predate *Pax Americana* and that images of the United States as a lone institutional architect and reformer are greatly overdrawn. Would we have the present variety and density of international legal and multilateral institutions without the efforts of the United States? No. Did the United States introduce new architectural principles into international society and create novel institutional forms from scratch? No. As we have seen, the United States was part of a coalition of states that began instituting contemporary fundamental institutions in the late nineteenth century, and after 1945 American policymakers reasserted architectural principles first endorsed by the community of states at least fifty years before and built on institutional foundations already in place.

---

[119] Martin, "Rational State Choice," 113.

[120] See Burley, "Regulating the World," 126; see also Martin, "Rational State Choice"; Ruggie, "Multilateralism"; and Ruggie, *Winning the Peace.*

CHAPTER SEVEN

Conclusion

In 1337 Ambrogio Lorenzetti was commissioned to decorate the Council Chamber of the Palazzo Publico in Siena, the meeting place of the city-state's governors. He painted two murals—the "Allegory of Good Government" and the "Allegory of Bad Government"—which celebrate Sienese civil and political values. The former is dominated by two figures. To the right sits a magisterial knight dressed in Siena's colors who represents the authority of the city-state; to the left sits the female embodiment of justice, her hands holding the scales of justice in balance. A long rope runs from the scales to the knight's left hand, passing on its way through the hands of another woman, this time Concordia. Before reaching the knight, the rope is also held by twenty-four leading citizens, all of identical height. The knight is flanked by embodiments of six additional civic virtues. To his right sit Magnanimity, Temperance, and again Justice; to his left Peace, Fortitude, and Prudence. Above fly the angelic figures of Faith, Hope, and Charity. Continuing the mural on the adjacent wall, Lorenzetti portrays Siena ruled by these civic ideals. Within the city's walls women dance, artisans labor, merchants trade, and harmony abounds. In the surrounding countryside peasants harvest bountiful crops, hunters chase game, traders go to and fro, and peace reigns. At the base of the mural, Lorenzetti translates his symbolism into a maxim of good government: "The holy Virtue [Justice], wherever she rules, induces to unity the many souls [of citizens], and they, gathered together for such a purpose, make the Common Good their Lord; and he, in order to govern his state, chooses never to turn his eyes from the resplendent faces of the Virtues who sit around him. Therefore to him in triumph are offered taxes, tributes, and lordship of towns; therefore, without war, every civic result duly follows—useful, necessary, and pleasurable."[1]

Lorenzetti's allegory captures in artistic form an enduring political reality: the inextricable connection between moral values, the identity of the state, and rightful state action. To argue that such a relationship shapes political life within the state is uncontroversial. Most scholars would acknowledge that visions of ideal political orders play important roles in

[1] The translation of the inscription quoted here comes from Starn, *Ambrogio Lorenzetti*, 53. For other detailed analyses of Lorenzetti murals see: Burckhardt, *Siena*; Hook, *Siena*; Gardner, *Siena and San Gimignano*; and Skinner, "Ambrogio Lorenzetti."

defining the nature and powers of national political institutions. Claiming that such values structure political life between states, however, contradicts the canons of traditional international relations thought. International politics is generally presented as the antithesis of domestic politics, a world of self-interest and power where moral values hold little sway.[2] To repeat Wight's oft-quoted dictum, domestic politics is the realm of the good life, international politics is the realm of survival.[3] Even those who emphasize the social dimensions of international politics stress that international society is "a practical association," bound together by minimal rules of conduct and functional cooperation, not moral purposes and conceptions of justice.

By asserting the importance of culturally and historically contingent values in shaping institutional practices between states, therefore, this book runs against the grain of traditional international relations scholarship. Instead of invoking the interests of dominant states or the functional utility of particular institutional solutions, I have argued that international institutional action is shaped by deep constitutive values. Societies of states are communities of mutual recognition; they are bound together by intersubjective meanings that define what constitutes a legitimate state and what counts as appropriate state conduct. These meanings are fruitfully conceived as constitutional structures: value-complexes that incorporate a hegemonic conception of the moral purpose of the state, an organizing principle of sovereignty, and a norm of pure procedural justice. Together, these values give societies of states their distinctive characters, not the least by shaping their institutional profiles. In different cultural and historical contexts, different ideals of the "civilized" state have prevailed, and these ideals have generated different notions of procedural justice. It is these latter values that have determined the basic institutional practices adopted by states, and that explain why institutional forms have varied from one society of states to another. By informing the institutional imaginations of international institutional architects and by structuring the moral discourse surrounding institutional production and reproduction, prevailing norms of procedural justice have licensed some practices over others, making some appear mandatory for "civilized" states and others beyond the pale.

The heuristic value of this theoretical framework lies in its capacity to explain both the generic nature of fundamental institutions and institutional variations across societies of sovereign states. As chapter 1 demonstrates, existing perspectives that emphasize spontaneous evolution,

---

[2] The best discussion of this dichotomous characterization of domestic and international politics is Walker, *Inside/Outside*.

[3] Wight, "Why Is There No International Theory?" 17–34.

hegemonic construction, rational institutional selection, or the sovereign identity of the state struggle to explain these characteristics. The first begs more questions than it answers, the second and third are indeterminate, and the fourth is under-specified. Only by understanding how context-specific ideas about the moral purpose of the state inform procedural mores can we explain the divergent institutional practices of societies of states. Believing that the moral purpose of the city-state lay in the cultivation of *bios politikos*, the ancient Greeks embraced a discursive norm of procedural justice, enacting this in their interstate relations through the practice of third-party arbitration. Linking the city-state to the pursuit of civic glory, the Renaissance Italians upheld a ritual norm of procedural justice, performing oratorical diplomacy between states. Casting the state as the protector of a divinely ordained social order, Europeans of the absolutist era assumed an authoritative conception of procedural justice, constructing the international institutions of naturalist international law and old diplomacy. Tying the moral purpose of the modern state to the augmentation of individuals' purposes and potentialities, modern institutional architects have championed a legislative norm of procedural justice, endorsing the paired institutions of contractual international law and multilateralism. In all of these cases, it would be extremely difficult to explain the institutional preferences pursued without reference to the social epistemes defining legitimate statehood and appropriate modes of interaction and rule determination.

In this concluding chapter, I consider some of the theoretical, conceptual, and analytical implications of my argument and historical analysis. The discussion is divided into five parts, dealing in turn with the nature of sovereignty, ontological versus deontological conceptions of institutional rationality, the question of international systems change, holistic versus systemic forms of constructivism, and the relationship between critical theory and constructivism.

THE NATURE OF SOVEREIGNTY

State sovereignty is generally understood in highly categorical and invariant terms. Realists assume that sovereignty is an empirical characteristic of the state, that the state "decides for itself how it will cope with its internal and external problems."[4] More socially inclined theorists treat sovereignty as the foundational organizing principle of international society, the principle by which certain political units are identified and licensed as legitimate actors on the international stage. In both cases sov-

---

[4] Waltz, *Theory of International Politics*, 96.

ereignty is assumed to have a fixed meaning. Whether in practice or principle, sovereignty is taken to mean the absolute authority of the state within
its borders and the absence of any higher authority outside those borders.
In Alan James words, "Sovereignty may be seen as a moat, cutting the
state off from constitutional subordination to other states and thus expressing the fact of its own constitutional independence."[5] Most authors
admit that the practice of sovereignty never matches the purity of this
conception, but they maintain that it remains a theoretically powerful
assumption, the necessary point of departure for understanding the politics of anarchy. "The starting point of international relations," Bull
writes, "is the existence of *states*, or independent political communities,
each of which possesses a government and asserts sovereignty in relation
to a particular portion of the earth's surface and a particular segment of
the human population."[6]

   A recent wave of constructivist scholarship has challenged this categorical understanding of sovereignty. Instead of treating sovereignty as an
unambiguous quality of statehood or a definitive principle of international society, constructivists argue that sovereignty "is a variable, social,
and practically constituted regime."[7] Where the traditional approach has
been to acknowledge and then bracket variations in the practice of sovereignty—to assume practical uniformity and conceptual consistency for
the sake of theory building—constructivists insist that our understanding
of international politics will be handicapped until we recognize that "sovereignty is a practical category whose empirical contents are not fixed but
evolve in a way reflecting the active practical consensus among coreflective statesmen."[8] Giving flesh to this insight, a wealth of studies have
appeared that explore the socially constructed, historically contingent nature of sovereignty. These range from Ruggie's investigations into the
world historical transition from heteronomous to sovereign systems of
rule, through Jackson's, Barkin and Cronin's, and Thomson's analyses
of significant shifts in the meaning of sovereignty in the modern era, to
Bartelson's genealogical history of the conceptual discourse of sovereignty.[9] In a variety of ways, all of these studies are concerned with "the
constitutive relationship between state and sovereignty; the ways
the meaning of sovereignty is negotiated out of interactions within intersubjectively identifiable communities; and the variety of ways in which

   [5] James, *Sovereign Statehood*, 39.
   [6] Bull, *Anarchical Society*, 8.
   [7] Thomson, *Mercenaries, Pirates, and Sovereigns*, 13.
   [8] Ashley, "Poverty of Neorealism," 272–273.
   [9] Ruggie, "Continuity and Transformation" and "Territoriality and Beyond"; Jackson,
Quasi-States; Barkin and Cronin, "State and the Nation"; Thomson, *Mercenaries, Pirates,
and Sovereigns*; and Bartelson, *Genealogy of Sovereignty*.

practices construct, reproduce, reconstruct, and deconstruct both state and sovereignty."[10]

This book contributes to the emerging constructivist perspective on sovereignty, but does so in a unique way. Despite emphasizing the varied meaning of sovereignty—its contingent nature as an historically grounded practical discourse—constructivists have continued to treat sovereignty as the basic structuring principle of international society. By employing the idea of constitutional structures to conceptualize the normative foundations of international society, I have not only embedded the principle of sovereignty within a wider complex of constitutive metavalues, I have assigned it a secondary, dependent value. This is not to deny that sovereignty is the basic organizing principle of our present society of states, or that it was any less important in structuring the ancient Greek, Renaissance Italian, or absolutist systems. Rather, it is to acknowledge precisely what sovereignty is—an organizing principle, no more or no less. It is a principle that specifies *how* power and authority will be organized, a principle that mandates territorially demarcated, autonomous centers of political authority. There is nothing in the principle of sovereignty, though, that specifies *why* power and authority should be organized in such a fashion; the only way to justify this form of political organization is by appealing to a set of higher-order values that sovereign states are thought to realize. In other words, the legitimacy of the sovereign state rests on values other than the principle of sovereignty. I have employed the concept of the moral purpose of the state to conceptualize these justificatory values, and have suggested that different hegemonic ideas about the moral purpose of the state have given sovereignty different meanings in different historical contexts. This conceptual move is intended to facilitate a more sophisticated and systematic understanding of the normative foundations of international societies, and to enable us to comprehend their divergent qualities as well as their similarities.

THE ONTOLOGY OF INSTITUTIONAL RATIONALITY

Most theories of institutional selection employ a *deontological* conception of institutional rationality. That is, they bracket the social conditions shaping the identities and interests of institutional agents, adopting a purely strategic model of cognition and choice. The culturally contingent intersubjective values that inform actors' senses of self, shape their preferences, and license some modes of goal attainment over others are largely ignored, and institutional rationality is defined as the efficient pursuit of

[10] Biersteker and Weber, "Social Construction," 11.

exogenously determined interests within the constraints of available information, the interests and strategies of other actors, and the distribution of power.

This deontological conception of institutional rationality is apparent in two aspects of neoliberal regime theory: its bracketing of preference formation, and its socially barren conception of international context. In adopting a "constraint-choice" approach to institutional analysis, neoliberals assume rather than explain state interests.[11] The constitutive social forces that shape the substantive and procedural preferences of states are treated as exogenous, and they focus instead on the logic and process of goal attainment. Neoliberals are at pains to stress the importance of the international context in which states seek to pursue their interests and construct institutions, but their understanding of that context is strategic, not social. The shadow of the future, multilevel games, and the distribution of power are all factored in, but beyond the existing array of international regimes, the assumed context of interstate interaction is devoid of cultural and intersubjective content. Of course, Keohane and others acknowledge the importance of constitutive social forces in shaping state interests,[12] and recognize that "interaction takes place within the context of norms that are shared,"[13] but these are ad hoc observations that have had little effect on their underlying conception of institutional rationality.

The argument and analysis presented in previous chapters highlight the limitations of this deontological conception of institutional rationality, and advance an *ontological* conception instead. Abstract models of institutional rationality that imagine timeless, context-free rational actors, unfettered and unconstituted by cultural values and historical experience, cannot explain why the ancient Greeks chose arbitration to solve their cooperation problems, why the Renaissance Italians chose oratorical diplomacy, why Europeans of the absolutist period chose naturalist international law and old diplomacy, or why modern states have chosen contractual international law and multilateralism. Nor can this explanatory weakness be overcome by appealing to the material and strategic context in which institutional selection takes place.[14] Contrary to Martin's expectations, institutional practices have transcended shifts in the balance of power, and states have engaged in different practices under similar structural conditions. When it comes to explaining why states privilege one set

---

[11] See Axelrod and Keohane, "Achieving Cooperation"; Keohane, *Afer Hegemony*; Keohane, "Demand for International Regimes"; Oye, "Explaining Cooperation"; Snidal, "Game *Theory* of International Politics"; and Stein, *Why Nations Cooperate.*

[12] Keohane, *After Hegemony*, 75.

[13] Axelrod and Keohane, "Achieving Cooperation," 238.

[14] Martin, "Rational State Choice."

of institutional practices over others, therefore, deontological conceptions of institutional rationality are simply indeterminate.

Only by treating institutional rationality as a culturally and historically contingent form of consciousness—a way of thinking that is as normative as it is calculating, as value-laden as it is logical—can we explain the contrasting institutional practices of different societies of states. As the preceding case studies testify, the imaginations of institutional architects and the discursive strategies surrounding institutional production and reproduction have been informed and structured by deep-seated cultural values concerning how "civilized" states *ought* to conduct their affairs. It has mattered less whether, in an abstract rational sense, arbitration, oratorical diplomacy, or multilateralism constitute the most *efficient* response to particular coordination and collaboration problems than that at particular historical moments states have deemed these to be the *right* responses. This is not to say, of course, that states will always employ their favored institutional practices to resolve their cooperation problems, or that such practices are always effective; rather, it is to argue that when states do seek institutional solutions, culturally and historically specific beliefs about procedural justice will inform their institutional choices.

The ontological conception of institutional rationality proposed here might also be termed *embedded* rationality, for it grounds the cognitive processes of institutional selection within deep-seated cultural mentalities that are conditioned by intersubjective values. Keohane implies such a conception of institutional rationality when he writes that "fundamental practices seem to reflect historically distinctive combinations of material circumstances, *social patterns of thought*, and individual initiative [my emphasis]."[15] Yet an ontological or embedded conception of rationality that can accommodate "social patterns of thought" must, of necessity, have an intersubjective dimension, a dimension that is missing from Keohane's own conceptual moves away from classical, deontological rationality. The idea of "bounded rationality" recognizes the psychological and organizational limitations that constrain the choices that individuals and collectivities make, but these are subjective, not intersubjective, limitations; they are constraints internal to the mental processes or decision-making procedures of actors. Likewise, the notion of "empathetic rationality" acknowledges that actors are not always egoistic, that their interests are often other-regarding. But altruistic interests remain subjective; while they might be based on intersubjective beliefs about justice and morality, they constitute an attitude toward the other, not a value that we necessarily *share* with the other. An ontological or embedded conception of institutional rationality seeks to capture the intersubjective forces that

[15] Keohane, "International Institutions," 171.

shape cognition and choice; it refers to the social foundations of collective action, to the metavalues that condition the institutional texture of international society.

THE DIMENSIONS OF INTERNATIONAL SYSTEMS CHANGE

All but the most blinkered scholars now struggle with two contradictory intuitions about the present international order. First, there is the sense that we are witnessing a fundamental transformation in the nature of international politics. This is countered, though, by the equally powerful intuition that the system of sovereign states exhibits a remarkable degree of resilience and adaptability. For every example of eroding state power and authority, one also finds the state extending its rule into a new field of social life. And for every agenda-setting initiative by an international or nongovernmental organization, one is reminded that the state remains the principal agency of implementation. Any plausible account of the nature and trajectory of contemporary international politics needs to accommodate, if not reconcile, these contradictory intuitions.

The debate about international continuity and change has so far revolved around whether or not the principle of sovereignty continues to structure international life. The argument for continuity is most forcefully presented by realist scholars, whose ability to stand fast against the winds of change is at times truly titanic.[16] Krasner's "institutional perspective" on the persistence of sovereignty is one of the more sophisticated of these arguments. Unlike traditional realists, he claims that the persistence of sovereign states cannot be explained in terms of their material capabilities or their ability to fulfil their various functional roles. "It is not longer obvious," he writes, "that the state system is the optimal way to organize political life."[17] Nevertheless, he contends that the principle of sovereignty—understood as a set of rules about how authority is organized in the modern world—remains an institution of considerable depth and breadth. It not only constitutes individuals' identities as citizens (which he takes to be primary), it is extensively linked to other social institutions and practices. "The historical legacy of the development of the state system," he concludes, "has left a powerful institutional structure, one that will not be dislodged easily, regardless of changed circumstances in the material environment."[18]

[16] On the realist attitude toward international change, see Lebow, "Long Peace"; Koslowski and Kratochwil, "Understanding Change"; Kratochwil, "Embarrassment of Changes"; Reus-Smit, "Realist and Resistance Utopias"; and Walker, "Realism."

[17] Krasner, "Sovereignty," 67.

[18] Ibid., 90.

Critiques of the realist preoccupation with stasis are legion, but attempts to move beyond criticism to develop systematic accounts of fundamental international change are comparatively rare. Ruggie's ambitious attempt to develop a constructivist perspective on epochal transformation of international society is a notable exception. Fundamental change, he argues, occurs when there is a redefinition of the principle on which political units are separated—the "mode of differentiation." The shift from the medieval order to the modern represented just such a transformation, with the principle of sovereignty gradually supplanting the old heteronomous mode of differentiation.[19] Changes in "material environments," "strategic behavior," and "social epistemes" spurred this revolution, he argues, and further changes in these underlying dynamics are likely to be important indicators of yet another fundamental transformation in the mode of differentiation and, in turn, the nature of the international system. Although guarded in his predictions, Ruggie identifies changes of this nature in the construction of "multiperspectival institutional forms" and in the rise of a new social episteme around global environmental protection. Both entail the "unbundling of territoriality" and may signal the decline of sovereignty and the advent of a "postmodern" system of rule.[20]

Understanding international continuity and change in terms of the persistence or demise of sovereignty is intuitively attractive but ultimately problematic, for it leaves considerable historical variation and change unexplained. To begin with, this approach obscures the significant differences between historical systems of sovereign states. As we have seen, the ancient Greek, Renaissance Italian, absolutist European, and modern systems have all been organized on the principle of sovereignty, yet their institutional practices have differed greatly. This brings us to a second, more telling, analytical weakness of sovereignty-based conceptions of international systems change. That is, they obscure and leave unexplained the last great epochal international transformation—the decline of the absolutist order and the rise of the modern. This transition did not involve the rise or decline of a sovereignty regime, but rather the transition from one sovereignty regime to another. Marked by a deep-seated change in the moral purpose of the sovereign state, this transformation fundamentally altered the nature of the international system, redefining the terms of legitimate statehood and rightful state action, and spawning an entirely new set of basic institutional practices. Focusing on the rise and decline of sovereignty contributes little to our understanding of this momentous change.

---

[19] Ruggie, "Continuity and Transformation," 279.
[20] Ruggie, "Territoriality and Beyond," 168–174.

The theoretical and analytical framework presented in this book suggests an alternative way of conceiving international systems change. If constitutional structures define and shape the nature of international systems of rule, as previous chapters contend, then changes in the metavalues that comprise those structures must be a primary determinant of systems change. It follows that both our conceptualization of systems change and our analyses of historical patterns and future trajectories of change ought to focus on changes in those structures, in particular on changes in prevailing ideas of the moral purpose of the state, that have given historical meaning to the principle of sovereignty and informed norms of procedural justice. By embracing a more complex understanding of the normative foundations of systems of rule, this perspective frees us from the prevailing conceptual and analytical framework of extremes, which conceives systems change only in terms of the existence or absence of the organizing principle of sovereignty. More specifically, it enables us to distinguish between two different forms of systems change: *purposive* change, and *configurative* change. Purposive change involves a redefinition of the moral purpose of the state, leading to shifts in the meaning of sovereignty and procedural justice. The transition from the absolutist to the modern systems was just such a systems change. Configurative change entails not only a shift in the moral purpose undergirding a system of rule but also a change in the organizing principle that governs the distribution of authority. The shift from feudalism to absolutism was this type of systems change.

Conceiving international systems change in this manner prompts a series of questions about continuity and change in contemporary world politics. Sovereignty-based conceptions of change ask only whether the principle and practice of sovereignty is robust or in decline. In contrast, the perspective outlined above encourages us to ask: Is the constitutional structure of modern international society robust or in a process of transition? If it is in transition, are we witnessing a purposive change or a configurative change; does it entail a redefinition of the moral purpose of the state, with a resulting shift in the meaning of sovereignty and the realm of legitimate state action, or does it involve a deeper shift in the organizing principle that apportions legitimate political authority? In either case, how will these purposive or configurative changes alter norms of procedural justice and in turn shape the institutional practices employed to resolve cooperation problems between individuals and collectivities? Exploring these questions further is beyond the purpose and scope of this book,[21] but any attempt to answer them should investigate the impact

---

[21] For a preliminary exploration of some of these questions, see Reus-Smit, "Normative Structure."

of several ideational and organizational aspects of contemporary world politics. On the ideational front, these are the development of international human rights norms, the resurgence of nationalism, the discourse of global environmental protection, the global renaissance of neoclassical ideology, and tensions between Western and non-Western cultural discourses; on the organizational front, they are the density and relative autonomy of international institutions, the growing web of connections between nongovernmental organizations and international organizations, the growing trend toward regionalism, and the evolution of multiperspectival institutional forms, most notably in Europe. The long-term effect of these factors is unclear, as some reflect and reinforce the present constitutional structure of international society, some push toward a redefinition of the hegemonic conception of the moral purpose of the state, and some anticipate a nonsovereign system of rule.[22]

THE RICHNESS OF HOLISTIC CONSTRUCTIVISM

Constructivism in the study of international relations is a broad church, encompassing a range of conceptual, analytical, and methodological approaches. Constructivists are united, though, by a common orientation toward the nature of social and political life, an orientation characterized by three ontological propositions: they emphasize the importance of normative and ideational structures in defining actors' social identities and in shaping how actors interpret their material environment; they stress the way in which actors' social identities affect their interests and the strategies they employ to realize those interests; and they highlight the mutually constitutive relationship between the knowledgeable practices of actors and social structures. Informed by these propositions, two broad forms of constructivism in international relations have emerged: *systemic* constructivism, and *holistic* constructivism.

The former adopts a third-image perspective, focusing solely on systemic interactions between unitary states. This approach is most clearly elaborated in Wendt's theoretical writings.[23] Like other constructivists, Wendt believes that the identity of the state informs its interests and, in turn, its actions. His commitment to systemic theorizing, however, com-

---

[22] For a discussion of the contradictory implications of some of these aspects of contemporary world politics and their implications for patterns of global governance, see Reus-Smit, "Changing Patterns."

[23] In fact, Wendt seems to think of constructivism only in systemic terms, claiming that constructivism, like realism, has "a commitment to states as the units of analysis, and to the importance of systemic or 'third image' theorizing." Wendt, "Constructing International Politics," 72.

pels him to distinguish between the state's corporate identity and its social identity. The first of these refers to its internal human, material, and ideological characteristics, to "the intrinsic, self-organizing qualities that constitute actor individuality." The second refers to "sets of meanings that an actor attributes to itself while taking the perspective of others," to the "cognitive schemas that enable an actor to determine 'who I am/we are' in a . . . social role structure of shared understandings and expectations."[24] In his quest for a purely third-image theory, Wendt brackets the corporate sources of state identity and interest, and concentrates entirely on the constitutive role of international social interaction, exploring how structural contexts, systemic processes, and strategic practice produce and reproduce egoistic or collective state identities.[25] The result is a strictly interactive form of constructivism—a social billiard ball theory.

Wendt's writings have been immensely important in the development of constructivist international theory, exposing the limitations of rationalist and materialist perspectives and advancing a rich conceptual apparatus and instructive theoretical schema. Unfortunately, systemic constructivism has significant analytical limitations, especially when it comes to explaining the rise and decline of international societies. In bracketing the domestic sources of state identity, Wendt confines the constitutive processes that shape international societies within a very narrow and exclusive realm; the identities of states are thought to be constituted by the normative structures of international society, and those structures are seen as the product of state practice. Within this schema, social interaction is the only constitutive dynamic. This concentration on systemic processes is sufficient so long as we are not trying to explain systems change, either purposive or configurative. Social interaction is clearly important in the reproduction of hegemonic conceptions of state identity, but how do these conceptions change? Without introducing nonsystemic sources of state identity at some point in the structuration process—sources that first percolate either in the social order that precedes the rise of a system of states or in the domestic or transnational realms of an existing international system—systemic constructivism cannot account for shifts from nonsovereign to sovereign orders, or from one sovereign order to another. In sum, third-image constructivism accommodates the reproduction of social and political forms, but not their production or transformation.

Given this limitation, constructivists who wish to explain forms of international change have adopted a more encompassing, holistic perspective on the constitutive processes that have affected the rise, development, and transformation of international societies. To accommodate the full

---

[24] Wendt, "Collective Identity Formation," 385.
[25] Ibid., 388–391.

spectrum of conditioning factors, they forgo the parsimonious elegance of systemic theorizing, and bring the "corporate" and "social" together into a unified analytical perspective, treating "domestic" and "international" structures and processes as two faces of a single social and political order. They set out to show how these structures and processes generate systemic and systems change, how culture, norms, and ideas inform the practices of social agents, in turn shaping systems of rule and patterns of governance. Their approach is more concrete and explicitly historical than systemic constructivism, and their goal is historically informed conceptual and theoretical insights into the nature and evolution of international societies, not abstract general theory. This is reflected in two distinct, yet complementary, expressions of holistic constructivism: one focusing on grand shifts between international systems, the other on changes within the modern society of states. The former is exemplified by Ruggie's work on the transition from the medieval system of rule to the modern, the latter by Kratochwil's work on the end of the Cold War.[26] Both authors focus on how domestic and international social phenomena interact to condition the norms and rules that structure international orders, employing a holistic perspective to explain systems and systemic change respectively.

The argument and analysis presented in this book contribute to the development of a holistic constructivist perspective on international relations. The constitutive processes discussed in previous chapters are incomprehensible from a systemic standpoint; ideas about the moral purpose of the state, the meaning of sovereignty, and procedural justice are rooted in the cultural and ideological terrain of everyday life, whether that be within heteronomous, suzerain, or sovereign systems of rule. As the transition from the absolutist to the modern era demonstrates, new constitutional values grow out of deep-seated ontological changes in human consciousness, changes that reinforce, and are reinforced by, changes in material conditions. In time they come to define the terms of legitimate governance in core states, which then transmit them to the international arena, enshrining them as dominant standards of legitimate sovereignty and rightful state conduct. Through the repeated discursive practices of the community of states, these metavalues become structural features of international society, undergirding the prevailing system of rule and shaping the production and reproduction of the fundamental institutions that states create to solve cooperation problems and facilitate coexistence. Systemic constructivism is blind to such processes. In bracketing the "corpo-

---

[26] For other holistic constructivist explanations of aspects of international change, see Klotz, *Norms in International Relations*; Price, *Chemical Weapons Taboo*; Ruggie, *Multilateralism Matters*; and Thomson, *Mercenaries, Pirates, and Sovereigns*.

rate" realm, it occludes the original sources of state identity, even if it comprehends the social interactive reproduction of that identity. Holistic constructivism loses much in the way of parsimony, but this is more than compensated by its enhanced heuristic power, a power that is demonstrated by the preceding explanation of the divergent institutional practices that characterize different societies of states.

THE CONTRIBUTION TO CRITICAL INTERNATIONAL THEORY

Like much holistic constructivist research, this book is intended to contribute to the development of a broadly defined critical theory of international relations.[27] Andrew Linklater argues that the development of such a theory involves three tasks. The first involves critical philosophical inquiry into the moral foundations of the present system of sovereign states, with particular emphasis on the ethics of inclusion and exclusion that license the partitioning of the world into particularistic moral and political communities.[28] The second task entails sociological inquiry into the origins of modern international society and "the constraints upon, and prospects for, the appearance of post-sovereign international relations."[29] In Cox's words, a critical theory "does not take institutions and social and power relations for granted but calls them into question by concerning itself with their origins and how and whether they might be in the process of changing."[30] The third task involves praxeological inquiry into how state and nonstate actors can exploit promising dynamics of change to promote emancipatory transformations in the nature of social and political community.[31]

This book contributes to the second of these tasks. It does so in three ways. First, it explains and illustrates the complexity and historical contingency of the normative foundations that undergird societies of sovereign states. The concept of constitutional structures, of which the principle of sovereignty is but a part, permits a richer understanding of those foundations; it enables us to speak more accurately and systematically about the values, principles, and norms that give territorial statehood its legitimacy, and about the very real differences between the complexes of metavalues that have underpinned and defined different societies of sovereign states. Second, it shows how hegemonic ideas about the moral

[27] Friedrich Kratochwil, John Ruggie, Janice Thomson, and Alexander Wendt, to name a few, have all linked constructivism to critical international theory.

[28] Linklater, "Question of the Next Stage," 92–93.

[29] Ibid., 94–96.

[30] Cox, "Social Forces," 208.

[31] Linklater, "Question of the Next Stage," 96–97.

purpose of the state and systemic norms of procedural justice inform the institutional rationality of international institutional architects, leading them to construct distinctive types of fundamental institutions. This not only explains the contrasting institutional profiles of different societies of sovereign states, it suggests that there are significant cognitive and discursive limits to the forms of institutional cooperation that are possible in particular cultural and historical settings. As we saw in the absolutist case, procedural mentalities license some forms of institutional action, but they also impede the development of others. Third, it expands our understanding of international change. As explained above, the idea of constitutional structures enables us to distinguish between systemic change, purposive systems change, and configurative systems change. Together, the insights contained in this book make an important, though necessarily incomplete, contribution to the historical sociology of international societies.

The precepts of critical international theory were first elaborated in the "Third Debate" of the 1980s.[32] To carve out space for new questions and novel theoretical and methodological approaches, critical theorists of the Third Debate tended to work at a metatheoretical level, concentrating on the critique of dominant rationalist and materialist perspectives, and on the anticipation, if not the articulation, of alternative modes of understanding. With the exception of instructive works by Cox, Der Derian, and others, there was little critical international sociology conducted during that period. We are now blessed with a wealth of constructivist research in this area, to which this book is a further contribution. If the task is to understand the rise, development, and potential demise of the modern international society, or to comprehend changing patterns of moral inclusion and exclusion in contemporary global politics, then the recent wave of constructivist scholarship has much to offer. Curiously, though, there has been little dialogue between theorists of the Third Debate and constructivists. Despite Linklater's claim that critical theory must encompass normative, sociological, and praxeological forms of inquiry, he works solely in the first of these areas, with little recognition of the sociological work of constructivists. For their part, many constructivists have assumed the mantel of critical theory, but have lost sight of the normative ethos inherent in such a theory. This lack of engagement is a serious impediment to the development of critical international theory, for unless

---

[32] For a representative sample of critical theoretic writings of the Third Debate, see Ashley, "Political Realism" and "Poverty of Neorealism"; Cox, "Social Forces"; Linklater, *Beyond Realism and Marxism* and "Realism"; Hoffman, "Critical Theory"; and Lapid, "Third Debate."

the normative and the sociological are brought together, no progress can be made on the praxeological front.[33]

A FINAL WORD ON ARISTOTLE

International relations scholars have long harked back to the writings of great political thinkers, appealing to the wisdom of Thucydides, Machiavelli, Hobbes, Locke, Rousseau, or Kant to lend their arguments authority. Echoing through contemporary debates we hear that "the strong do what they have the power to do and the weak accept what they must," that when "men live without a common power to keep them in awe, they are in that condition which is called war, as is of every man, against every man," and that "the Republican Constitution, in addition to the purity of its origin . . . includes the prospect of realizing the desired object: Perpetual Peace among Nations." There is wisdom in each of these refrains, resonating at different levels with the many confusing and contradictory aspects of international relations. If I were to seek intellectual ancestry for the argument advanced in this book, though, I would return to the writings of Aristotle, a classical thinker who never appears on the standard list of canonical sources. In the opening paragraph of *The Politics*, he writes: "Observation tells us that every state is an association, and that every association is formed with a view to some good purpose. I say good because in all their actions all men do in fact aim at what they think good."[34] Aristotle had little to say about relations between states, but these opening words provide the crucial insight that solves the mystery of fundamental institutions. Intersubjective beliefs about the moral purpose of the state provide the justificatory basis for sovereign rights, they inform notions of international procedural justice, and these notions constitute and constrain institutional design and action, leading states to embrace different institutional practices in different historical contexts.

---

[33] For a more detailed explanation of the relationship between critical theory and constructivism, see Price and Reus-Smit, "Dangerous Liaisons."

[34] Aristotle, *Politics*, Book 1.I, 54.

Bibliography

Adas, Michael. *Machines as the Measure of Men: Science, Technology, and Ideologies of Western Dominance*. Ithaca: Cornell University Press, 1989.

Adcock, Frank, and D. J. Mosley, *Diplomacy in Ancient Greece*. London: Thames and Hudson, 1975.

Adkins, Arthur. *Merit and Responsibility: A Study of Greek Values*. Oxford: Clarendon, 1960.

Albrecht-Carrie, Rene. *A Diplomatic History of Europe Since the Congress of Vienna*. New York: Harper and Row, 1958.

Alsop, Susan Mary. *The Congress Dances*. London: Weidenfeld and Nicolson, 1984.

Anderson, Benedict. *Imagined Communities: Reflections on the Origin and Spread of Nationalism*. 2d ed. London: Verso, 1991.

Anderson, Matthew. *Rise of Modern Diplomacy: 1450–1919*. London: Longman, 1993.

Anderson, Perry. *Lineages of the Absolutist State*. London: Verso, 1974.

———. *Passages from Antiquity to Feudalism*. London: Verso, 1978.

Andrews, A. "The Government of Classical Sparta." In *Ancient Society and Institutions: Studies Presented to Victor Ehrenberg*, edited by E. Badian, 1–20. Oxford: Basil Blackwell, 1966.

Andrews, Bruce. "Social Rules and the State as a Social Actor." *World Politics* 27, no. 4 (1975): 521–540.

Arendt, Hannah. *The Human Condition*. Chicago: University of Chicago Press, 1958.

Aristotle. *Nichomachean Ethics*. New York: Bobbs-Merrill, 1962.

———. *The Politics*. Harmondsworth: Penguin, 1981.

———. *The Art of Rhetoric*. Harmondsworth: Penguin, 1991.

Ashcraft, Richard. *Revolutionary Politics and Locke's Two Treatises of Government*. Princeton: Princeton University Press, 1986.

Ashley, Maurice. *The Age of Absolutism 1648–1775*. London: Weidenfeld and Nicolson, 1974.

Ashley, Richard K. "Political Realism and Human Interests." *International Studies Quarterly* 25, no. 3 (1981): 204–236.

———. "The Poverty of Neorealism." *International Organization* 38, no. 2 (1984): 225–261.

———. "Untying the Sovereign State: A Double Reading of the Anarchy Problematic." *Millennium: Journal of International Studies* 17, no. 2 (1988): 227–262.

Axelrod, Robert, and Robert O. Keohane. "Achieving Cooperation under Anarchy: Strategies and Institutions." In *Cooperation under Anarchy*, edited by Kenneth A. Oye, 226–254. Princeton: Princeton University Press, 1986.

Baker, Ray Stannard. *Woodrow Wilson and World Settlement*. 3 vols. London: Heinemann, 1923.

Barkin, Samuel J., and Bruce Cronin. "The State and the Nation: Changing Norms and the Rules of Sovereignty in International Relations." *International Organization* 48, no. 1 (1994): 107–130.

Baron, Hans. *Crisis of the Early Italian Renaissance*. 2 vols. Princeton: Princeton University Press, 1955.

Bartelson, Jens. *A Genealogy of Sovereignty*. Cambridge: Cambridge University Press, 1995.

Bassett Moore, John. *History and Digest of the International Institutions to Which the United States Has Been a Party*. Vol. 5. Washington: Government Printing Office, 1892.

Bauslaugh, Robert A. *The Concept of Neutrality in Classical Greece*. Berkeley: University of California Press, 1989.

Bayley, C. C. *War and Society in Renaissance Florence*. Toronto: Toronto University Press, 1961.

Becker, Marvin. "Individualism in the Early Italian Renaissance: Burden or Blessing." *Studies in the Renaissance* 19, (1972): 273–297.

Beitz, Charles. *Political Theory and International Relations*. Princeton: Princeton University Press, 1979.

Beloff, Max. *The Age of Absolutism: 1660–1815*. London: Hutchinson's University Library, 1954.

Berman, Marshall. *The Politics of Authenticity: Radical Individualism and the Emergence of Modern Society*. New York: Atheneum, 1970.

Biagioli, Mario. *Galileo Courtier: The Practice of Science in the Culture of Absolutism*. Chicago: University of Chicago Press, 1993.

Biersteker, Thomas J. and Cynthia Weber. "The Social Construction of State Sovereignty." In *State Sovereignty as a Social Construct*, edited by Thomas J. Biersteker and Cynthia Weber, 1–21. Cambridge: Cambridge University Press, 1996.

———. *State Sovereignty as a Social Construct*. Cambridge: Cambridge University Press, 1996.

Bodin, Jean. *Six Books of the Commonwealth*. Oxford: Basil Blackwell, 1967.

Bohman, James F., David R. Hiley, and Richard Shusterman. *The Interpretive Turn: Philosophy, Science, Culture*. Ithaca: Cornell University Press, 1991.

Boissevain, J. "Patronage in Sicily." *Man*, n.s., 1 (1966): 18–33.

Bonadella, Peter, and Mark Musa, eds. *The Portable Machiavelli*. Harmondsworth: Penguin, 1979.

Bonney, Richard. *The European Dynastic States 1494–1660*. New York: Oxford University Press, 1991.

Bozeman, Adda. *Politics and Culture in International History*. Princeton: Princeton University Press, 1960.

———. *The Future of Law in a Multicultural World*. Princeton: Princeton University Press, 1971.

Briggs, Robin. *Early Modern France 1560–1715*. Oxford: Oxford University Press, 1977.

Brilmayer, Lea. *Justifying International Acts*. Ithaca: Cornell University Press, 1989.

Browlie, Ian, ed. *Basic Documents in International Law.* Oxford: Clarendon, 1983.

Brucker, Gene A. "The Uniqueness of Florence's Experience." *Medieval and Renaissance Studies* (summer 1976): 3–23.

———. *The Civic World of Early Renaissance Florence.* Princeton: Princeton University Press, 1977.

———. *Renaissance Florence: Society, Culture, and Religion.* Goldbach: Keip Verbig, 1994.

Bull, Hedley. "International Theory: The Case for a Classical Approach." In *Contending Approaches to International Relations*, edited by Klauss Knorr and James N. Rosenau, 20–38. Princeton: Princeton University Press, 1969.

———. *The Anarchical Society: A Study of Order in World Politics.* New York: Columbia University Press, 1977.

Bull, Hedley, and Adam Watson, eds. *The Expansion of International Society.* Oxford: Clarendon Press, 1984.

Bull, Hedley, Benedict Kingsbury, and Adam Roberts, eds. *Hugo Grotius and International Relations.* Oxford: Clarendon, 1984.

Bullard, Melissa Meriam. "Lorenzo de'Medici: Anxiety, Image Making, and Political Reality in the Renaissance." In *Lorenzo de' Medici Studi*, edited by Gian Carlo Garfagnini, 3–40. Florence: Leo S. Olschki, 1992.

———. "The Language of Diplomacy in the Renaissance." In *Lorenzo de' Medici: New Perspectives*, edited by B. Toscani, 263–278. New York: Peter Lang Publishing, 1993.

———. *Lorenzo il Manifico: Image and Anxiety, Politics and Finance.* Florence: Leo S. Olschki, 1994.

Burckhardt, Jacob. *The Civilization of the Renaissance in Italy.* Harmondsworth: Penguin, 1990.

Burckhardt, Titus. *Siena: The City of the Virgin.* London: Oxford University Press, 1960.

Burgess, Glenn. "Divine Right of Kings Reconsidered." *English Historical Review* 107, no. 425 (1992): 837–861.

Burke, Peter. *Culture and Society in Renaissance Italy 1420–1540.* London: B. T. Batsford, 1972.

Burley, Anne-Marie. "Regulating the World: Multilateralism, International Law, and the Projection of the New Deal Regulatory State." In *Multilateralism Matters: The Theory and Praxis of an Institutional Form*, edited by John Gerard Ruggie, 125–156. New York: Columbia University Press, 1993.

Burns, J. H. "The Idea of Absolutism." In *Absolutism in Seventeenth Century Europe*, edited by John Miller, 21–42. New York: St. Martin's Press, 1990.

Burton, J. W. *Systems, States, Diplomacy and Rules.* Cambridge: Cambridge University Press, 1968.

Butterfield, Herbert. "The Balance of Power." In *Diplomatic Investigations*, edited by Herbert Butterfield and Martin Wight, 149–175. London: Allen and Unwin, 1966.

Butterfield, Herbert, and Martin Wight, eds. *Diplomatic Investigations.* London: Allen and Unwin, 1966.

Buzan, Barry. "From International System to International Society: Structural Realism and Regime Theory Meet the English School." *International Organization* 47, no. 3 (1993): 327–352.

Caldwell, Wallace E. *Hellenic Conceptions of Peace.* New York: Columbia University Press, 1919.

Camilleri, Joseph A., and Jim Falk. *The End of Sovereignty?* London: Edward Elgar, 1992.

Caporaso, James A. "International Relations Theory and Multilateralism: The Search for Foundations." In *Multilateralism Matters: Theory and Praxis of an Institutional Form,* edited by John Gerard Ruggie, 51–90. New York: Columbia University Press, 1993.

Carr, Edward Hallett. *The Twenty Years' Crisis: 1919–1939.* New York: Harper and Row, 1964.

Castiglione, Baldesar. *The Book of the Courtier.* Harmondsworth: Penguin, 1976.

Castlereagh, Viscount. *Correspondence, Despatches, and Other Papers of Viscount Castlereagh.* 12 vols. London: William Shobert, 1982.

"Charter of the United Nations." In *Basic Documents in International Law,* edited by Ian Brownlie, 1–34. Oxford: Clarendon Press, 1983.

Choate, Joseph. *The Two Hague Conferences.* Princeton: Princeton University Press, 1913.

Church, William F., ed. *Impact of Absolutism in France: National Experience under Richelieu, Mazarin, and Louis XIV.* New York: John Wiley and Sons, 1969.

Cicero. *De Officiis.* Cambridge: Harvard University Press, 1990.

Cohen, David. "Justice, Interest, and Political Deliberation in Thucydides." *Quaderni Urbanati Di Cultura Classica* 16, no. 1 (1984): 35–60.

Collins, Stephen L. *From Divine Cosmos to Sovereign State: An Intellectual History of Consciousness and the Idea of Order in Renaissance England.* Oxford: Oxford University Press, 1989.

Connolly, William E. *The Terms of Political Discourse.* 3d ed. Princeton: Princeton University Press, 1993.

Connor, William. *Thucydides.* Princeton: Princeton University Press, 1984.

Connor, W. R. "Polarization in Thucydides." In *Hegemonic Rivalry from Thucydides to the Nuclear Age,* edited by Richard Ned Lebow and Barry S. Strauss, 53–69. Boulder, Co.: Westview, 1991.

Cook, Chris, and John Stevenson. *The Longman Handbook of Modern British History: 1714–1980.* London: Longman, 1983.

Cooper, Duff. *Talleyrand.* London: Jonathan Cape, 1938.

Corrigan, Philip, and Derek Sayer. *The Great Arch: English State Formation as Cultural Revolution.* Oxford: Basil Blackwell, 1985.

Cox, Robert. "Social Forces, States and World Orders: Beyond International Relations Theory." In *Neorealism and Its Critics,* edited by Robert O. Keohane, 204–254. New York: Columbia University Press, 1986.

———. *Production, Power and World Order: Social Forces in the Making of History.* New York: Columbia University Press, 1987.

Creed, J. L. "Moral Values in the Age of Thucydides." *Classical Quarterly* 23, no. 2 (1973): 213–231.

Cronin, Vincent. *The Florentine Renaissance*. London: Pimlico, 1992.

———. *The Flowering of the Renaissance*. London: Pimlico, 1992.

Czempiel, Ernst-Otto, and James N. Rosenau, eds. *Global Changes and Theoretical Challenges: Approaches to World Politics for the 1990s*. Lexington, Mass.: Lexington Books, 1989.

———. *Governance Without Government: Order and Change in World Politics*. Cambridge: Cambridge University Press, 1992.

de Callières, Francois. *The Art of Diplomacy*. New York: Holmes and Meier, 1983.

de Vattel, E. *The Law Of Nations or Principles of the Law of Nature Applied to the Conduct and Affairs of Nations and Sovereigns*. London: Stevens and Sons, 1834.

Der Derian, James. *On Diplomacy*. Oxford: Basil Blackwell, 1987.

DiMaggio, Paul J., and Walter W. Powell. *The New Institutionalism in Organizational Analysis*. Chicago: University of Chicago Press, 1991.

Documents of the United Nations Conference on International Organization, San Francisco, 1945. 12 vols. New York: United Nations Information Organization, 1945.

Domat, Jean. "Le Droit Public." In *The Impact of Absolutism in France*, edited by William F. Church, 76–80. New York: John Wiley and Sons, 1969.

Donnelly, Jack. *Universal Human Rights in Theory and Practice*. Ithaca: Cornell University Press, 1989.

Dover, K. J. *Greek Popular Morality in the Time of Plato and Aristotle*. Berkeley: University of California Press, 1974.

Doyle, Michael. "Thucydidean Realism." *Review of International Studies* 16, no. 3 (1990): 223–237.

Doyle, William. *The Old European Order: 1660–1800*. Oxford: Oxford University Press, 1978.

Duggan, Stephen Pierce, ed. *The League of Nations: The Principle and the Practice*. London: Allen and Unwin, 1919.

Dumont, Louis. *From Mandeville to Marx: The Genesis and Triumph of Economic Ideology*. Chicago: University of Chicago Press, 1977.

Elliot, John H. *Imperial Spain: 1469–1716*. Harmondsworth: Penguin, 1963.

Evangelista, Matthew. "Democracies, Authoritarian States, and International Conflict." In *Hegemonic Rivalry from Thucydides to the Nuclear Age*, edited by Richard Ned Lebow and Barry S. Strauss, 213–234. Boulder, Co.: Westview, 1991.

Filmer, Robert. *Patriarcha and Other Political Works*. Oxford: Blackwell, 1949.

Finnemore, Martha. *National Interests in International Society*. Ithaca: Cornell University Press, 1996.

Fliess, Peter. *Thucydides and the Politics of Bipolarity*. Nashville: Louisiana State University Press, 1966.

Forcacs, David. *An Antonio Gramsci Reader: Selected Writings 1916–1935*. New York: Schocken Books, 1988.

Forde, Stephen. "Thucydides on the Causes of Athenian Imperialism." *American Political Science Review* 80, no. 2 (1986): 433–448.

Foucault, Michel. "Disciplinary Power and Subjection." In *Power*, edited by Stephen Lukes, 227–231. New York: New York University Press, 1986.

"French Declaration of the Rights of Man and Citizen." In *The Human Rights Reader*, edited by Walter Laqueur and Barry Rubin, 118–119. New York: Penguin, 1979.

Fubini, Ricardo. "The Italian League and the Policy of the Balance of Power at the Accession of Lorenzo de' Medici." *The Journal of Modern History* 67, supplement (1995): s166–s199.

Gardner, Edmund G. *The Story of Siena and San Gimignano*. London: J. M. Dent, 1902.

Garner, Richard. *Law and Society in Classical Athens*. London: Croom Helm, 1987.

Garst, Daniel. "Wallerstein and his Critics." *Theory and Society* 14, no. 4 (1985): 469–497.

———. "Thucydides and Neorealism." *International Studies Quarterly* 33, no. 1 (1989): 3–27.

Gellner, Ernest. "Patrons and Clients." In *Patrons and Clients in Mediterranean Societies*, edited by Ernest Gellner and John Waterbury, 1–6. London: Gerald Duckworth and Co., 1977.

———. *Nations and Nationalism*. Oxford: Blackwell, 1983.

George, Alexander L., and Juliette L. George. *Woodrow Wilson and Colonel House: A Personality Study*. New York: Dover, 1956.

Gerson, Kenneth J. *The Concept of the Self*. New York: Holt, Rinehart and Winston, 1971.

Giddens, Anthony. *Central Problems in Social Theory*. Berkeley: University of California Press, 1979.

———. *The Constitution of Society*. Berkeley: University of California Press, 1984.

———. *The Nation-State and Violence*. Cambridge: Polity, 1985.

———. *The Consequences of Modernity*. Stanford: Stanford University Press, 1990.

Gilbert, Felix. "The New Diplomacy of the Eighteenth Century." *World Politics* 4, no. 1 (1951): 1–38.

Gilpin, Robert. *War and Change in World Politics*. Cambridge: Cambridge University Press, 1981.

———. "The Richness of the Tradition of Political Realism." *International Organization* 38, no. 2 (1984): 287–304.

———. "The Theory of Hegemonic War." *Journal of Interdisciplinary History* 18, no. 4 (1988): 591–613.

———. "Peloponnesian War and Cold War." In *Hegemonic Rivalry from Thucydides to the Nuclear Age*, edited by Richard Ned Lebow and Barry S. Strauss, 31–49. Boulder, Co.: Westview, 1991.

Goldstein, Judith. "Creating the GATT Rules." In *Multilateralism Matters: The Theory and Praxis of an Institutional Form*, edited by John Gerard Ruggie, 201–232. New York: Columbia University Press, 1993.

Goldstein, Judith, and Robert O. Keohane. "Ideas and Foreign Policy: An Analytical Framework." In *Ideas and Foreign Policy: Beliefs, Institutions and Political*

Change, edited by Judith Goldstein and Robert O. Keohane, 3–30. Ithaca: Cornell University Press, 1993.

———. eds. *Ideas and Foreign Policy: Beliefs, Institutions and Political Change*. Ithaca: Cornell University Press, 1993.

Gong, Gerrit W. *The 'Standard of Civilization' in International Society.* Oxford: Clarendon Press, 1984.

Greenfeld, Liah. *Nationalism: Five Roads to Modernity.* Cambridge: Harvard University Press, 1992.

Grendler, Paul F. *Schooling in Renaissance Italy: Literacy and Learning 1300–1600.* Baltimore: Johns Hopkins University Press, 1989.

Grieco, Joseph M. "Anarchy and the Limits of Cooperation: A Realist Critique of the Newest Liberal Institutionalism." *International Organization* 42, no. 3 (1988): 485–507.

———. *Cooperation among Nations: Europe, America, and Non-Tariff Barriers to Trade.* Ithaca: Cornell University Press, 1990.

———. "Understanding the Problem of International Cooperation: The Limits of Neoliberal Institutionalism and the Future of Realist Theory." In *Neorealism and Neoliberalism: The Contemporary Debate*, edited by David A. Baldwin, 301–338. New York: Columbia University Press, 1993.

Gross, Leo. "The Peace of Westphalia 1648–1948." *American Journal of International Law* 42, no. 1 (1948): 20–41.

Grotius, Hugo. *The Law of War and Peace: De Jure Belli ac Pacis Libri Trea.* New York: Bobbs-Merrill, 1925.

Guicciardini, Francesco. *The History of Italy.* Princeton: Princeton University Press, 1984.

Gulick, Edward Vose. *Europe's Classical Balance of Power.* Ithaca: Cornell University Press, 1955.

Gundersheimer, W. L. *Ferrara: The Style of Renaissance Despotism.* Princeton: Princeton University Press, 1973.

Gutmann, Myron P. "Origins of the Thirty Years War." *Journal of Interdisciplinary History* 18, no. 4 (1988): 749–770.

Haas, Ernst. *When Knowledge is Power: Three Models of Change in International Organizations.* Berkeley: University of California Press, 1990.

———. "Nationalism: An Instrumental Social Construction." *Millennium: Journal of International Studies* 22, no. 1 (1993): 505–546.

Haas, Peter M., Robert O. Keohane, and Marc A. Levy, eds. *Institutions for the Earth: Sources of Effective International Environmental Protection.* Cambridge: MIT Press, 1993.

Habermas, Jürgen. *Communication and the Evolution of Society.* Boston: Beacon Press, 1979.

———. *Theory of Communicative Action.* Boston: Beacon Press, 1984.

———. *Moral Consciousness and Communicative Action.* Cambridge: MIT Press, 1990.

Hagen, William W. "Seventeenth Century Crisis in Brandenburg: The Thirty Years' War, the Destabilisation of Serfdom, and the Rise of Absolutism." *American Historical Review* 94, no. 2 (1989): 302–335.

Hale, J. R. "International Relations in the West: Diplomacy and War." In *The New Cambridge Modern History*. Vol. 1, *The Renaissance: 1493–1520*, 259–291. Cambridge: Cambridge University Press, 1961.

———. *War and Society in Renaissance Europe: 1450–1620*. Baltimore: Johns Hopkins University Press, 1985.

Hamilton, Keith, and Langhorne, Richard. *The Practice of Diplomacy*. London: Routledge, 1995.

Hansen, Morgens H. "The Tradition of Athenian Democracy A.D. 1750–1990." *Greece and Rome*, 2d ser., 39, no. 1 (1992): 14–30.

Harris, Tim. "Tories and the Rule of Law in the Reign of Charles II." *Seventeenth Century* 8, no. 1 (1993): 9–27.

Hart, H. L. A. *The Concept of Law*. 2d ed. Oxford: Clarendon Press, 1994.

Heeren, A. H. L. *History of the Political System of Europe and Its Colonies: From the Discovery of America to the Independence of the American Continent*. Vol. 1. Boston: Butler and Sons, 1829.

Hegel, G. W. F. *Introduction to 'The Philosophy of History.'* Indianapolis: Hackett, 1988.

———. *Philosophy of Right*. Oxford: Oxford University Press, 1967.

Held, Virginia, Sidney Morgenbesser, and Thomas Nagel, eds. *Philosophy, Morality, and International Affairs*. New York: Oxford University Press, 1974.

Heller, Agnes. *Beyond Justice*. Oxford: Basil Blackwell, 1987.

Herlihy, David. *Medieval and Renaissance Pistoia*. New Haven: Yale University Press, 1967.

Herodotus. *The Histories*. Harmondsworth: Penguin, 1972.

Higgins, Rosalyn. *The Development of International Law through the Political Organs of the United Nations*. Oxford: Oxford University Press, 1963.

Hilderbrand, Robert C. *Dumbarton Oaks: The Origins of the United Nations and the Search for Postwar Security*. Chapel Hill: University of North Carolina Press, 1990.

Hiley, David R., James F. Bohman, and Richard Shusterman, eds. *The Interpretive Turn: Philosophy, Science and Culture*. Ithaca: Cornell University Press, 1974.

Hill, Christopher. *The World Turned Upside Down*. Harmondsworth: Penguin, 1975.

———. "Diplomacy in the Modern State." In *The Condition of States: A Study in International Theory*, edited by Cornelia Navari, 85–101. Milton Keynes, England: Open University Press, 1991.

Hill, David Jayne. *A History of Diplomacy in the International Development of Europe*. Vol. 3. New York: Longmans, Green, and Co., 1905.

Hinsley, F. H. *Power and the Pursuit of Peace: Theory and Practice in the History of Relations between States*. London: Cambridge University Press, 1967.

———. *Sovereignty*. Cambridge: Cambridge University Press, 1986.

Hirschman, Albert O. *The Passions and the Interests*. Princeton, Princeton University Press, 1977.

Hobbes, Thomas. *Leviathan*. London: Fontana, 1962.

Hobsbawm, Eric J. *The Age of Revolution: Europe from 1789–1848*. London: Weidenfeld and Nicolson, 1962.

———. *Industry and Empire*. Harmondsworth: Penguin, 1968.

————. *Nations and Nationalism Since 1780*. 2d ed. Cambridge: Cambridge University Press, 1992.

Hobson, John M. *Wealth of States: A Comparative Sociology of International Economic and Political Change*. Cambridge: Cambridge University Press, 1997.

Hoffman, Mark. "Critical Theory and the Inter-Paradigm Debate." *Millennium: Journal of International Studies* 16, no. 3 (1987), 231–49.

Holmes, George. *The Florentine Enlightenment: 1400–1450*. Oxford: Clarendon, 1969.

Holsti, Kalevi J. *Peace and War: Armed Conflicts and International Order 1648–1989*. Cambridge: Cambridge University Press, 1991.

Hook, Judith. *Siena: A City and its History*. London: Hamish Hamilton, 1979.

House, Edward Mandall, and Charles Seymour, eds. *What Really Happened at Paris*. London: Hodder and Stoughton, 1921.

Howard, Michael. *The Causes of War*. London: Unwin, 1983.

Howard-Ellis, C. *The Origin, Structure and Working of the League of Nations*. London: Allen and Unwin, 1928.

Hudson, Manley O. *The Permanent Court of International Justice*. New York: Macmillan, 1934.

Hume, David. *A Treatise on Human Nature*. Oxford: Clarendon Press, 1978.

Humphreys, Sally. "The Evolution of the Legal Process in Ancient Attica." In *Tria Corda: Scritti in Onore do Arnaldo Momigliano*, edited by E. Gabba, 229–256. Como: Edzioni New Press, 1983.

————. "Social Relations on Stage: Witnesses in Classical Athens." *History and Anthropology* 1, no. 4 (1985): 313–369.

————. "The Discourse of Law in Archaic and Classical Greece." *Law and History Review* 6, no. 2 (1988): 465–493.

Ilardi, Vincent. "The Italian League, Francesco Sforza, and Charles VII (1454–1461)." *Renaissance Studies* 11, (1959): 129–166.

Israel, Fred. *Major Peace Treaties of Modern History 1648–1967*. New York: McGraw Hill, 1967.

Jackson, Robert H. *Quasi-States: Sovereignty, International Relations, and the Third World*. Cambridge: Cambridge University Press, 1990.

Jaeger, Werner. *Paedeia: The Ideals of Greek Culture*. Vol. 1. New York: Oxford University Press, 1945.

James, Alan. "International Society." *British Journal of International Studies* 4, no. 2 (1978): 91–106.

————. *Sovereign Statehood: The Basis of International Society*. London: Allen and Unwin, 1986.

Jepperson, Ronald L. "Institutions, Institutional Effects, and Institutionalism." In *The New Institutionalism in Organizational Analysis*, edited by Walter W. Powell and Paul J. DiMaggio, 143–163. Chicago: University of Chicago Press, 1991.

Johnson, Laurie M. *Thucydides, Hobbes and the Interpretation of Realism*. DeKalb, Ill.: Northern Illinois University Press, 1993.

Jones, P. J. "Communes and Despots: The City-State in Late Medieval Italy." *Transactions of the Royal History Society*, no. 15 (1965): 71–96.

Kagan, Donald. *The Outbreak of the Peloponnesian War.* Ithaca: Cornell University Press, 1969.

Kaiser, David. *Politics and War: European Conflict from Philip II to Hitler.* Cambridge: Harvard University Press, 1990.

Kantotowicz, Ernst. *The King's Two Bodies: A Study in Medieval Political Theology.* Princeton: Princeton University Press, 1957.

Katzenstein, Peter J. and Nobuo Okawara. *Japan's National Security: Structure, Norms and Policy Responses in a Changing World.* Ithaca: Cornell East Asia Series, 1993.

———. "Japan's National Security: Structure, Norms and Policies." *International Security* 17, no. 4 (1993): 84–118.

Katzenstein, Peter J., ed. *The Culture of National Security: Norms and Identity in World Policies.* New York: Columbia University Press, 1996.

Kelson, Hans. *The Law of the United Nations.* London: Stevens and Sons, 1950.

Kent, Francis William. *Household and Lineage in Renaissance Florence: The Family Life of the Capponi, Cinori, and Ruccellai.* Princeton: Princeton University Press, 1977.

Kent, Francis William, Patricia Simons, and J. C. Eade, eds. *Patronage, Art, and Society in Renaissance Italy.* New York: Oxford University Press, 1987.

Keohane, Nannerl O. *Philosophy and the State in France: The Renaissance to the Enlightenment.* Princeton: Princeton University Press, 1980.

Keohane, Robert O. "The Demand for International Regimes." In *International Regimes*, edited by Stephen D. Krasner, 141–72. Ithaca: Cornell University Press, 1983.

———. *After Hegemony: Cooperation and Discord in the World Political Economy.* Princeton: Princeton University Press, 1984.

———. "International Institutions: Two Approaches." *International Studies Quarterly* 32, no. 4 (1988): 379–396.

———. *International Institutions and State Power: Essays in International Theory.* Boulder, Co.: Westview, 1989.

———. "Multilateralism: An Agenda for Research." *International Journal* 45, no. 4 (1990): 731–764.

Kimmel, Michael S. *Absolutism and its Discontents: State and Society in Seventeenth Century France and England.* New Brunswick: Transaction Books, 1988.

Kindleberger, Charles. *The World In Depression 1929–1939.* London: Penguin, 1973.

Kisser, Edgar. "The Formation of State Policy in Western European Absolutisms: A Comparison of England and France." *Politics and Society* 15, no. 3 (1986/7): 235–258.

Kissinger, Henry A. *A World Restored.* New York: Grosset and Dunlap, 1964.

Klotz, Audie. *Norms in International Relations.* Ithaca: Cornell University Press, 1995.

———. "Norms Reconstituting Interests: Global Racial Equality and U.S. Sanctions against South Africa." *International Organization* 49, no. 3 (1995): 451–478.

Knorr, Klauss, and James N. Rosenau. *Contending Approaches to International Relations*. Princeton: Princeton University Press, 1969.

Kohl, Benjamin G. "The Changing Concept of the Studia Humanitatas in the Early Renaissance." *Renaissance Studies* 6, no. 2 (1992): 185–209.

Kolb, David. *The Critique of Pure Modernity: Hegel, Heidegger, and After*. Chicago: University of Chicago Press, 1986.

Koslowski, Rey, and Friedrich Kratochwil. "Understanding Change in International Politics: The Soviet Empire's Demise and the International System." In *International Relations Theory and the End of the Cold War*, edited by Richard Ned Lebow and Thomas Risse Kappen, 127–166. New York: Columbia University Press, 1995.

Krasner, Stephen D. "State Power and the Structure of International Trade." *World Politics* 28, no. 3 (1976): 317–343.

———. *International Regimes*. Ithaca: Cornell University Press, 1983.

———. "Sovereignty: An Institutional Perspective." *Comparative Political Studies* 21, no. 1 (1988): 66–94.

———. "Westphalia and All That." In *Ideas and Foreign Policy: Beliefs, Institutions, and Political Change*, edited by Judith Goldstein and Robert O. Keohane, 235–264. Ithaca: Cornell University Press, 1993.

———. "Compromising Westphalia." *International Security* 20, no. 3 (1995/96): 115–51.

Kratochwil, Friedrich. "Regimes, Interpretation and the 'Science' of Politics: A Reappraisal." *Millennium: Journal of International Studies* 17, no. 2 (1988/89): 263–284.

———. *Rules, Norms, and Decisions: On the Conditions of Practical and Legal Reasoning in International Relations and Domestic Affairs*. Cambridge: Cambridge University Press, 1989.

———. "The Embarrassment of Changes: Neorealism as the Science of *Realpolitik* without Politics." *Review of International Studies*, 19, no. 1 (1993): 63–80.

Kratochwil, Friedrich, and John Gerard Ruggie. "International Organization: A State of the Art on an Art of the State." *International Organization* 40, no. 4 (1986): 753–775.

Kraut, Richard. *Aristotle on the Human Good*. Princeton: Princeton University Press, 1989.

Lapid, Yosef. "The Third Debate: On the Prospects of International Theory in a Post-Positivist Era." *International Studies Quarterly*, 33, no. 3 (1989): 235–254.

Laqueur, Walter, and Barry Rubin, eds. *The Human Rights Reader*. New York: Penguin, 1979.

Larus, Joel, ed. *Comparative World Politics: Readings in Western and Premodern Non-Western International Relations*. Belmont: Wadsworth Publishing, 1965.

Laven, Peter. *Renaissance Italy: 1464–1534*. London: Balsford, 1966.

Lebow, Richard Ned. "Thucydides, Power Transition Theory, and the Causes of War." In *Hegemonic Rivalry from Thucydides to the Nuclear Age*, edited by Richard Ned Lebow and Barry S. Strauss, 125–168. Boulder, Co.: Westview, 1991.

Lebow, Richard Ned. "The Long Peace, the End of the Cold War, and the Failure of Realism." In *International Relations Theory and the End of the Cold War*, edited by Richard Ned Lebow and Thomas Risse-Kappen, 23–56. New York: Columbia University Press, 1995.

Lebow, Richard Ned, and Barry S. Strauss, eds. *Hegemonic Rivalry from Thucydides to the Nuclear Age*. Boulder, Co.: Westview, 1991.

Lee, Stephen J. *The Thirty Years War*. London: Routledge, 1991.

Limm, Peter. *The Thirty Years War*. London: Longman, 1984.

Linklater, Andrew. *Beyond Realism and Marxism: Critical Theory and International Relations*. London: Macmillan, 1990.

———. "The Problem of Community in International Relations." *Alternatives* 15, no. 2 (1990): 135–154.

———. "The Question of the Next State in International Relations Theory: A Critical-Theoretical Point of View." *Millennium: Journal of International Studies* 21, no.1 (1992): 77–98.

Lloyd-George, David. *The Truth about the Peace Treaties*. London: Victor Gollanz, 1938.

Locke, John. *Two Treatises on Civil Government*. Cambridge: Cambridge University Press, 1988.

Logan, Richard D. "Historical Change in Prevailing Sense of Self." In *Self and Identity: Psychological Perspectives*, edited by K. Yardley and T. Honness, 13–26. New York: John Wiley, 1978.

Luard, Evan. *A History of the United Nations*. Vol 1. London: Macmillan, 1982.

Lumsdaine, David Halloran. *Moral Vision in International Politics: The Foreign Aid Regimes 1949–1989*. Princeton: Princeton University Press, 1993.

Lyons, John O. *The Invention of the Self: The Hinge of Consciousness in the Late Eighteenth Century*. Carbondale, Ill.: Southern Illinois University Press, 1978.

Machiavelli, Niccolo. *Florentine History*. New York: E. P. Dutton and Co., 1909.

———. "The Art of War." In *The Portable Machiavelli*, edited by Peter Bonadella and Mark Mussa, 480–517. Harmondsworth: Penguin, 1979.

———. "The Discourses." In *The Portable Machiavelli*, edited by Peter Bonadella and Mark Mussa, 167–418. Harmondsworth: Penguin, 1979.

———. "The Prince." In *The Portable Machiavelli*, edited by Peter Bonadella and Mark Mussa, 77–166. Harmondsworth: Penguin, 1979.

Maio, Dennis Peter. "*Politeia* and Adjudication in Fourth Century B.C. Athens." *American Journal of Jurisprudence* 28, no. 1 (1983): 16–45.

Major, J. Russell. *From Renaissance Monarchy to Absolute Monarchy: French Kings, Nobles, and Estates*. Baltimore: Johns Hopkins University Press, 1994.

Mallet, Michael. *Mercenaries and the Masters: Warfare in Renaissance Italy*. Totowa, N.J.: Rowman and Littlefield, 1976.

———. "Diplomacy and War in Later Fifteenth Century Italy." In *Lorenzo De' Medici Studi*, edited by Gian Carlo Garfagnini. Florence: Leo S. Olschki, 1992.

Marburg, Theodore. *Development of the League of Nations Idea*. 2 vols. New York: Macmillan, 1932.

Marston, F. S. *The Peace Conference of 1919: Organization and Procedure*. Oxford: Oxford University Press, 1944.

Martin, Lisa. "The Rational State Choice of Multilateralism." In *Multilateralism Matters: The Theory and Praxis of an Institutional Form*, edited by John Gerard Ruggie, 91–121. New York: Columbia University Press, 1993.

Martines, Lauro. *Social World of the Florentine Humanists 1390–1460*. London: Routledge and Kegan Paul, 1963.

———. *Lawyers and Statecraft in Renaissance Florence*. Princeton: Princeton University Press, 1968.

———. *Power and the Imagination: City-State in Renaissance Italy*. Baltimore: Johns Hopkins University Press, 1988.

Mattingly, Garrett. *Renaissance Diplomacy*. Cambridge: Houghton Mifflin, 1955.

McCall, George T., and J. L. Simmons. *Identities and Interactions*. New York: Free Press, 1966.

McElroy, Robert W. *Morality and American Foreign Policy: The Role of Ethics in International Affairs*. Princeton: Princeton University Press, 1992.

Mearsheimer, John. "The False Promise of International Institutions." *International Security* 19, no. 3 (1994/1995): 5–49.

Mettam, Roger. "France." In *Absolutism in Seventeenth Century Europe*, edited by John Miller, 43–67. New York: St. Martin's Press, 1990.

Metternich, Prince Richard, ed. *Memoirs of Prince Metternich 1773–1815*. Vol 2. London: Richard Bundle, 1880.

Meyer, John W. "The World Polity and the Authority of the Nation-State." In *Institutional Structure: Constituting State, Society, and the Individual*, edited by George M. Thomas, John W. Meyer, Francisco O. Ramirez, and John Boli, 41–70. London: Sage, 1987.

Meyer, John W., John Boli, and George M. Thomas. "Ontology and Rationalization." In *Institutional Structure: Constituting State, Society, and the Individual*, edited by George M. Thomas, John W. Meyer, Francisco O. Ramirez, and John Boli, 12–37. London: Sage, 1987.

Mill, John Stuart. *Three Essays: On Liberty, Representative Government, The Subjection of Women*. Oxford: Oxford University Press, 1975.

Miller, David Hunter. *The Drafting of the Covenant*. 2 vols. New York: Putnam, 1928.

Miller, John. "Britain." In *Absolutism in Seventeenth Century Europe*, edited by John Miller, 195–224. New York: St. Martin's Press, 1990.

———, ed. *Absolutism in Seventeenth Century Europe*. New York: St. Martin's Press, 1990.

Modelski, George. "The Long Cycle of Global Politics and the Nation-State." *Comparative Studies in Society and History* 20, no. 4 (1978): 214–235.

Mogami, Toshiki. "The United Nations as an Unfinished Revolution." *Alternatives* 15, no. 2 (1990): 177–198.

Morgenthau, Hans J. "Positivism, Functionalism, and International Law." *American Journal of International Law* 34, no. 2 (1940): 260–284.

———. "The Permanent Values in Old Diplomacy." In *Diplomacy in a Changing World*, edited by Stephen D. Kentesz and M. A. Fitzsimmons, 10–20. Notre Dame: University of Notre Dame Press, 1959.

Morgenthau, Hans J. *Politics Among Nations: The Struggle for Power and Peace.* 6th ed. New York: Alfred A. Knopf, 1985.

Morrow, James D. "Modelling the Forms of International Cooperation: Distribution versus Information." *International Organization* 48, no. 3 (1994): 387–424.

Mostecky, Vaclav. *Index of Multilateral Treaties: A Chronological List of Multi-Party International Agreements from the Sixteenth Century through 1963.* Cambridge: Harvard Law School Library, 1965.

Mousnier, Roland E. *Institutions of France Under Absolute Monarchy 1598–1789.* 2 vols. Translated by Arthur Goldhammer. Chicago: University of Chicago Press, 1979.

Murphy, Craig N. *International Organization and Industrial Change: Global Governance Since 1850.* Oxford: Oxford University Press, 1994.

Najemy, John M. "Guild Republicanism in Trecento Florence: The Successes and Ultimate Failure of Corporate Politics." *American Historical Review* 184, no. 1 (1979): 53–71.

Nardin, Terry. *Law, Morality, and Relations of States.* Princeton: Princeton University Press, 1983.

Navari, Cornelia, ed. *The Condition of States: A Study of International Political Theory.* Milton Keynes, England: Open University Press, 1991.

Neufeld, Mark. "Interpretation and the 'Science' of International Relations." *Review of International Studies* 19, no. 1 (1993): 39–62.

Neumann, Iver B., and Jennifer M. Welsh. "The Other in European Self-Definition: An Addendum to the Literature on International Society." *Review of International Studies* 17, no. 4 (1991): 327–348.

Nicolson, Harold. *Peacemaking 1919.* London: Constable, 1933.

———. *The Congress of Vienna: A Study in Allied Unity 1812–1822.* London: Readers Union, 1948.

———. *The Evolution of Diplomatic Method.* London: Constable, 1954.

Niebuhr Tod, Marcus. *International Arbitration amongst the Greeks.* Oxford: Clarendon, 1913.

North, Douglass, and Robert Thomas. *The Rise of the Western World: A New Economic History.* Cambridge: Cambridge University Press, 1973.

Nye, Joseph. *Bound to Lead: The Changing Nature of American Power.* New York: Basic Books, 1990.

Ober, Josiah. *Mass and Elite in Democratic Athens.* Princeton: Princeton University Press, 1989.

Onuf, Nicholas. *World of Our Making: Rules and Rule in Social Theory and International Relations.* Columbia: University of South Carolina Press, 1989.

———. "Sovereignty: Outline of a Conceptual History." *Alternatives* 16, no. 4 (1991): 425–446.

Orwin, Clifford. "The Just and the Advantageous in Thucydides: The Case of the Mytilenian Debate." *American Political Science Review* 78, (1984): 485–494.

Osborne, Robin. "Law in Action in Classical Athens." *Journal of Hellenic Studies* 105, (1985): 40–58.

Ostwald, Martin. *Law, Society, and Politics in Fifth Century Athens.* Berkeley: University of California Press, 1986.

Oye, Kenneth A. "Explaining Cooperation under Anarchy: Hypotheses and Strategies." In *Cooperation under Anarchy*, edited by Kenneth A. Oye, 1–24. Princeton: Princeton University Press, 1986.

Pallain, M. G., ed. *The Correspondence of Prince Talleyrand and King Louis XVIII during the Congress of Vienna*. New York: Charles Scribner, 1881.

Palston, Jackson H. *International Arbitration from Athens to Locarno*. Stanford: Stanford University Press, 1929.

Parker, David. "Sovereignty, Absolutism, and the Function of Law in Seventeenth Century France." *Past and Present*, no. 122 (1989): 36–74.

Parker, Geoffrey. *Thirty Years War*. London: Routledge, 1987.

Pearson, Lionel. *Popular Ethics in Ancient Greece*. Stanford: Stanford University Press, 1962.

Phillipson, Coleman. *The International Law and Custom of Ancient Greece and Rome*. 2 vols. London: Macmillan, 1911.

Physsenzides, Nearque. *L'Arbitrage International et L'Establissement D'un Empire Grec*. Brussels: J. Goemaere, 1897.

Pitkin, Hanna. *Fortune is a Woman: Gender and Politics in the Thought of Niccolo Machiavelli*. Berkeley: University of California Press, 1984.

Plato. *The Republic*. Harmondsworth: Penguin, 1955.

———. *The Laws*. Harmondsworth: Penguin, 1970.

Poggi, Gianfranco. *The Development of the Modern State: A Sociological Introduction*. Stanford: Stanford University Press, 1978.

Pollock, Frederick. *The League of Nations*. London: Stevens and Sons, 1920.

Price, Richard. "Interpretation and Disciplinary Orthodoxy in International Relations." *Review of International Studies* 20, no. 2 (1994): 201–204.

———. *The Chemical Weapons Taboo*. Ithaca: Cornell University Press, 1997.

Price, Richard, and Christian Reus-Smit. "Dangerous Liaisons? Critical International Theory and Constructivism. *European Journal of Internatonal Relations* 4, no. 3 (1998): 259-294.

Pufendorf, Samuel. *Two Books of the Elements of Universal Jurisprudence*. Oxford: Clarendon, 1931.

———. *On the Duty of Man and Citizen according to Natural Law*. Cambridge: Cambridge University Press, 1991.

Raeder, A. *L'Arbitrage International Chez les Hellenes*. New York: Putnam, 1912.

Ralston, Jackson H. *International Arbitration from Athens to Locarno*. Palo Alto: Stanford University Press, 1929.

Rawls, John. "Two Concepts of Rules." *The Philosophical Review* 64, no. 1 (1955): 3–32.

———. *A Theory of Justice*. Oxford: Oxford University Press, 1973.

Reich, Robert B., ed. *The Power of Public Ideas*. Cambridge: Harvard University Press, 1988.

Renan, Ernest. "What Is a Nation?" In *Readings in World Politics*, edited by Robert A. Goldwin, 401–410. New York: Oxford University Press, 1993.

Rengger, Nicholas J. "Culture, Society, and Order in World Politics." In *Dilemmas in World Politics*, edited by John Baylis and Nicholas J. Rengger, 85–103. Oxford: Clarendon, 1992.

Reus-Smit, Christian. "Realist and Resistance Utopias: Community, Security and Political Action in the New Europe." *Millennium: Journal of International Studies* 21, no. 1 (1992): 1–28.

———. "Beyond Foreign Policy: State Theory and the Changing Global Order." In *The State in Transition: Transformations of the Australiam State*, edited by Paul James, 161–195. St. Leonards: Allen and Unwin, 1996.

———. "The Normative Structure of International Society." In *Earthly Goods: Environmental Change and Social Justice*, edited by Fen Osler Hampson and Judith Reppy, 96–121. Ithaca: Cornell University Press, 1996.

———. "Changing Patterns of Governance: From Absolutism to Global Multilateralism." In *Between Sovereignty and Global Governance: The United Nations, the State, and Civil Society*, edited by Albert Paolini, Anthony Jarvis, and Christian Reus-Smit, 3–28. London: Macmillan, 1997.

———. "The Constitutional Structure of International Society and the Nature of Fundamental Institutions." *International Organization* 51, no. 4 (1997): 555–589.

Revon, Michel. *L'Arbitrage International: So–Passe, Son Present, Son Avenir.* Paris: New Library of War and Jurisprudence, 1892.

Ricoeur, Paul. *Hermeneutics and the Human Sciences.* Cambridge: Cambridge University Press, 1981.

Roberts, Adam, and Benedict Kingsbury, eds. *United Nations, Divided World: The UN's Role in International Relations.* Oxford: Clarendon, 1993.

Robertson, Roland. *Globalization: Social Theory and Global Culture.* London: Sage, 1992.

Rosenberg, Justin. "Secret Origins of the State: The Structural Basis of Raison d'Etat." *Review of International Studies* 18, no. 2 (1992): 131–159.

———. *The Empire of Civil Society.* London: Verso, 1994.

Rousseau, Jean-Jacques. *The Confessions of Jean-Jacques Rousseau.* Baltimore: Penguin, 1953.

———. "Discourse on the Origin of Inequality." In *Rousseau's Political Writings*, edited by Alan Ritter and Julia Conway Bonadella, 3–57. New York: Norton, 1988.

———. "On Social Contract or Principles of Political Right." In *Rousseau's Political Writings*, edited by Alan Ritter and Julia Conway Bonadella, 84–174. New York: Norton, 1988.

Rowen, Herbert H. *The King's State: Proprietary Dynasticism in Early Modern France.* New Brunswick: Rutgers University Press, 1980.

Rubinstein, Nicolai. "Lorenzo de' Medici: The Formation of His Statecraft." *Proceedings of the British Academy* 63 (1977): 71–94.

Ruggie, John Gerard. "Continuity and Transformation in the World Polity: Toward a Neorealist Synthesis." *World Politics* 35, no. 2 (1983): 261–285.

———. "International Regimes, Transactions, and Change: Embedded Liberalism in the Postwar Economic Order." In *International Regimes*, edited by Stephen D. Krasner, 195–232. Ithaca: Cornell University Press, 1983.

———. "International Structure and International Transformation: Space, Time, and Method." In *Global Changes and Theoretical Challenges*, edited by Ernst-

Otto Czempiel and James N. Rosenau, 21–36. Lexington, Mass.: Lexington Books, 1989.

———. "Multilateralism: The Anatomy of an Institution." In *Multilateralism Matters: The Theory and Praxis of an Institutional Form*, edited by John Gerard Ruggie, 3–50. New York: Columbia University Press, 1993.

———. "Territoriality and Beyond: Problematizing Modernity in International Relations." *International Organization* 47, no. 1 (1993): 139–174.

———. "The False Promise of Realism." *International Security* 20, no. 1 (1995): 62–70.

———. *Winning the Peace: America and World Order in the New Era.* New York: Columbia University Press, 1996.

———, ed. *Multilateralism Matters: The Theory and Praxis of an Institutional Form.* New York: Columbia University Press, 1993.

Russett, Bruce. *Grasping the Democratic Peace: Principles for a Post–Cold War World.* Princeton: Princeton University Press, 1993.

Sahlins, Marshall. *Culture and Practical Reason.* Chicago: University of Chicago Press, 1976.

Schwarzenberger, George. *The League of Nations and World Order.* London: Constable, 1936.

Scott, James. *Domination and the Arts of Resistance.* New Haven: Yale University Press, 1990.

Scott, James Brown. *The Proceedings of the Hague Peace Conferences: The Conference of 1907.* Vol 2. New York: Oxford University Press, 1921.

———, ed. *The Hague Conventions and Declarations of 1899 and 1907.* Oxford: Oxford University Press, 1915.

———, ed. *Reports to the Hague Conferences of 1899 and 1907.* Oxford: Clarendon Press, 1917.

Sealey, Raphael. *The History of the Greek City-States: 700–338 B.C.* Berkeley: University of California Press, 1976.

———. *The Athenian Republic: Democracy or the Rule of Law.* University Park, Pa.: Pennsylvania State University Press, 1987.

Shapiro, Michael. "Sovereignty and Exchange in the Orders of Modernity." *Alternatives* 16, no. 4 (1991): 447–478.

Shue, Henry. "Liberty and Self-Respect." *Ethics* 85, no. 3 (1975): 195–203.

Simons, Patricia. "Patronage in Tornaquinci Chapel, Santa Maria Novella, Florence." In *Patronage, Art, and Society in Renaissance Italy*, edited by F. W. Kent, Patricia Simons, and J. C. Eade, 221–250. New York: Oxford University Press, 1987.

Singh, Nagendra. "The U.N. and the Development of International Law." In *United Nations, Divided World: The UN's Role in International Relations*, edited by Adam Roberts and Benedict Kingsbury, 384–419. Oxford: Clarendon, 1993.

Skinner, Quentin. "Meaning and Understanding in the History of Ideas." *History and Theory* 17, no. 1 (1969): 3–53.

———. *The Foundations of Modern Political Thought.* Vol. 1, *The Renaissance.* Cambridge: Cambridge University Press, 1978.

Skinner, Quentin. "Ambrogio Lorenzetti: The Artist as Political Philosopher." *Proceedings of the British Academy* 72 (1986): 1–56.

———. "Machiavelli's Discorsi and the Pre-Humanist Origins of Republican Ideas." In *Machiavelli and Republicanism*, edited by Gisela Bock, Quentin Skinner, and Maurizo Viroli, 121–142. Cambridge: Cambridge University Press, 1993.

Skocpol, Theda. "Wallerstein's World Capitalist System: A Theoretical and Historical Critique." *American Journal of Sociology* 82, no. 5 (1977): 1075–1090.

Smith, Adam. *An Inquiry into the Nature and Causes of the Wealth of Nations.* Chicago: University of Chicago Press, 1976.

Smith, Anthony. *National Identity.* Reno: University of Nevada Press, 1991.

Snidal, Duncan. "The Game *Theory* of International Relations." In *Cooperation under Anarchy*, edited by Kenneth A. Oye, 25–57. Princeton: Princeton University Press, 1986.

Sohn, Louis B., ed. *Basic Documents on the United Nations.* London: Stevens and Sons, 1956.

Spruyt, Henrik. *The Sovereign State and Its Competitors.* Princeton: Princeton University Press, 1994.

Starn, Randolph. *Ambrogio Lorenzetti: The Palazzo Pubblico, Siena.* New York: George Braziller, 1994.

Stein, Arthur A. "Coordination and Collaboration: Regimes in an Anarchic World." In *International Regimes*, edited by Stephen D. Krasner, 115–140. Ithaca: Cornell University Press, 1983.

———. *Why Nations Cooperate: Circumstance and Choice in International Relations.* Ithaca: Cornell University Press, 1990.

Strang, David. "Contested Sovereignty: The Social Construction of Colonial Imperialism." In *State Sovereignty as a Social Construct*, edited by Thomas J. Biersteker and Cynthia Weber, 22–47. Cambridge: Cambridge University Press, 1996.

Strang, David, and Patricia Mei Yin Chang. "The International Labor Organization and the Welfare State: Institutional Effects on National Welfare Spending 1960–1980." *International Organization* 47, no. 2 (1993): 235–262.

Strang, David, and John W. Meyer. "Institutional Conditions for Diffusion." *Theory and Society* 22, no. 4 (1993): 487–511.

Strayer, Joseph R. *On the Medieval Origins of the Modern State.* Princeton: Princeton University Press, 1970.

Sutherland, N. M. "The Origins of the Thirty Years War and the Structure of European Politics." *English Historical Review* 107, no. 424 (1992): 587–625.

Swidler, Ann. "Culture in Action: Symbols and Strategies." *American Sociological Review* 51, no. 2 (1986): 273–286.

Takabatake, Sumio. "The Idea of Xenos in Classical Athens: Its Structure and Peculiarities." In *Forms of Control and Subordination in Antiquity*, edited by Toru Yuge and Masaoko Doi, 449–455. Leiden, Netherlands: E. J. Brill, 1988.

Talleyrand, Prince. *Memoirs of Prince De Talleyrand.* Vol 1. New York: Putnam, 1891.

Taylor, A. J. P. *The Struggle for Mastery In Europe: 1848–1918.* Oxford: Oxford University Press, 1971.

Taylor, Charles. "Interpretation and the Sciences of Man." In *Philosophy and the Human Sciences*, edited by Charles Taylor, 15–57. Cambridge: Cambridge University Press, 1985.

———. *Philosophy and the Human Sciences*. Cambridge: Cambridge University Press, 1985.

———. *Sources of the Self: The Making of the Modern Identity*. Cambridge: Harvard University Press, 1989.

———. *The Malaise of Modernity*. Concord: Anansi, 1991.

Thomas, George M., John W. Meyer, Francisco O. Ramirez, and John Boli, eds. *Institutional Structure: Constituting State, Society, and the Individual*. Newbury Park, England: Sage, 1987.

Thompson, John. *Studies in the Theory of Ideology*. Berkeley: University of California Press, 1984.

———. *Ideology and Modern Culture: Critical Social Theory in the Era of Mass Communication*. Stanford: Stanford University Press, 1990.

Thompson, William. "Uneven Economic Growth, Systemic Changes, and Global Critique." *International Studies Quarterly* 27, no. 3 (1983): 341–356.

Thomson, David. *Europe Since Napoleon*. London: Longmans, 1962.

Thomson, Janice E. *Mercenaries, Pirates, and Sovereigns*. Princeton: Princeton University Press, 1994.

Thucydides. *History of the Peloponnesian War*. Harmondsworth: Penguin, 1972.

Tilly, Charles. *Big Structures, Large Processes, Huge Comparisons*. New York: Russell Sage Foundation, 1984.

———. "War Making and State-Making as Organized Crime." In *Bringing the State Back In*, edited by Peter Evans, Dietrich Rueschemeyer, and Theda Skocpol, 169–191. Cambridge: Cambridge University Press, 1985.

———. *Coercion, Capital, and European States A.D. 990–1990*. Oxford: Blackwell, 1990.

Toulmin, Stephen. *Cosmopolis: The Hidden Agenda of Modernity*. Chicago: University of Chicago Press, 1990.

Toynbee, Arnold. *A Study of History*. London: Oxford University Press, 1935.

"Treaty of Munster." In *Consolidated Treaty Series*, edited by Clive Parry. Vol. 1, 319–356. New York: Dobbs Ferry, 1969.

"Treaty of Osnabruck." In *Consolidated Treaty Series*, edited by Clive Parry. Vol. 1, 198–269. New York: Dobbs Ferry, 1969.

"Treaty of Utrecht between Great Britain and France." In *Major Peace Treaties of Modern History: 1648–1967*, edited by Fred L. Israel. Vol. 1, 177–239. New York: McGraw Hill, 1967.

Trexler, Richard C. *Public Life in Renaissance Florence*. New York: Academic Press, 1980.

Ullmann, Walter. *The Medieval Idea of Law: A Study in Fourteenth Century Legal Scholarship*. New York: Barnes and Noble, 1946.

———. *A History of Political Thought in the Middle Ages*. Harmondsworth: Penguin, 1965.

———. *The Individual and Society in the Middle Ages*. London: Methuen, 1967.

"United States Declaration of Independence." In *The Human Rights Reader*, edited by Walter Laquer and Barry Rubin, 106–9. New York: Meridian, 1990.

United States Senate. *United States Senate Document no. 444*, 60th Cong., 1st sess., 1907.

von Martens, G. F. *Summary of the Law of Nations Founded on the Treaties and Customs of Modern Nations*. Philadelphia: Thomas Bradford, 1795.

Waley, David. *The Italian City-Republics*. 2d ed. New York: Longman, 1978.

Walker, R. B. J. "History and Structure in the Theory of International Relations." *Millennium: Journal of International Studies* 18, no. 2 (1989): 163–183.

———. *Inside/Outside: International Relations as Political Theory*. Cambridge: Cambridge University Press, 1993.

Walker, R. B. J., and Saul H. Mendlovitz, eds. *Contending Sovereignties: Redefining Political Community*. Boulder, Co.: Lynne Rienner Publishers, 1990.

Wallerstein, Immanuel. *The Capitalist World Economy*. Cambridge: Cambridge University Press, 1979.

Waltz, Kenneth. *Man, the State and War*. New York: Columbia University Press, 1954.

———. *Theory of International Politics*. New York: Random House, 1979.

Walzer, Michael. "On the Role of Symbolism in Political Thought." *Political Science Quarterly* 82, no. 2 (1967): 191–205.

———. *Spheres of Justice: A Defense of Pluralism and Equality*. New York: Basic Books, 1983.

Ward, A. W. "The Peace of Westphalia." In *The Cambridge Modern History*. Vol. 4, 400–432. Cambridge: Cambridge University Press, 1907.

Ward, Robert. *An Enquiry into the Foundations and History of the Law of Nations from the Time of the Greeks to the Age of Grotius*. Vol 1. London: Butterworth, 1795.

Watson, Adam. *The Evolution of International Society*. London: Routledge, 1992.

Weber, Cynthia. *Simulating Sovereignty: Intervention, the State, and Symbolic Exchange*. Cambridge: Cambridge University Press, 1995.

Weber, Max. "Politics as a Vocation." In *Max Weber*, edited by H. H. Gerth and C. Wright Mills, 75–83. New York: Oxford University Press, 1970.

Weber, Steven. "Shaping the Postwar Balance of Power: Mulitlateralism and NATO." In *Multilateralism Matters: The Theory and Praxis of an Institutional Form*, edited by John Gerard Ruggie, 233–292. New York: Columbia University Press, 1993.

Webster, Charles K. *The Congress of Vienna*. London: Thames and Hudson, 1963.

———, ed. *British Diplomacy 1813–1815: Selected Documents Dealing with the Reconstruction of Europe*. London: G. Bell, 1921.

Wedgwood, C. W. *The Thirty Years War*. London: Jonathan Cape, 1964.

Weingast, Barry R. "A Rational Choice Perspective on the Role of Ideas: Shared Belief Systems and State Sovereignty in International Cooperation." *Politics and Society* 23, no. 4 (1995): 449–464.

Weintraub, Karl Joachim. *The Value of the Individual: Self and Circumstance in Autobiography*. Chicago: University of Chicago Press, 1978.

Weissman, Ronald F. E. *Ritual Brotherhood in Renaissance Florence*. New York: Academic Press, 1982.

———. "Taking Patronage Seriously: Mediterranean Values and Renaissance Society." In *Patronage, Art, and Society in Renaissance Italy*, edited by F. W. Kent, Patricia Simons, and J. C. Eade, 25–45. Oxford: Clarendon Press, 1987.

Wendt, Alexander. "The Agent-Structure Problem in International Relations Theory." *International Organization* 41, no. 3 (1987): 335–370.

———. "Anarchy Is What States Make of It: The Social Construction of Power Politics." *International Organization* 46, no. 2 (1992): 391–426.

———. "Collective Identity Formation and the International State." *American Political Science Review* 88, no. 2 (1994): 384–395.

———. "Constructing International Politics." *International Security* 20, no.1 (1995): 71–81.

Wendt, Alexander, and Duvall, Raymond. "Institutions and International Order." In *Global Changes and Theoretical Challenges: Approaches to World Politics for the 1990's*, edited by Ernst-Otto Czempiel and James N. Rosenau, 51–74. Lexington, Mass.: Lexington Books, 1989.

Westermann, William. "Interstate Arbitration in Antiquity." *The Classical Journal* 2, no. 5 (1907): 197–211.

———. *The Slave Systems of Greek and Roman Antiquity*. Philadelphia: The American Philosophical Society, 1955.

Wheeler-Bennett, J. W., and Maurice Fanshawe. *Information on the World Court 1918–1928*. London: Allen and Unwin, 1929.

Wight, Martin. "Why Is There No International Theory?" In *Diplomatic Investigations*, edited by Herbert Butterfield and Martin Wight, 17–34. London: Allen and Unwin, 1966.

———. *Systems of States*. Leicester: Leicester University Press, 1977.

Yardley, K., and T. Honness, eds. *Self and Identity: Psychological Perspectives*. New York: John Wilet, 1978.

Yoder, Amos. *The Evolution of the United Nations System*. New York: Crane Russak, 1989.

Young, Oran R. "Regime Dynamics: The Rise and Fall of International Regimes." In *International Regimes*, edited by Stephen D. Krasner, 93–114. Ithaca: Cornell University Press, 1983.

———. "International Regimes: Toward a New Theory of Institutions." *World Politics* 39, no. 1 (1986): 104–122.

Yuge, Toru, and Masaoko Doi, eds. *Forms of Control and Subordination in Antiquity*. Leiden, Netherlands: E. J. Brill, 1988.

Zacher, Mark W. "The Decaying Pillars of the Westphalian Temple: Implications for International Order and Governance." In *Governance without Government: Order and Change in World Politics*, edited by James N. Rosenau and Ernst-Otto Czempiel, 58–101. Cambridge: Cambridge University Press, 1992.

Zampaglione, Gerardo. *The Idea of Peace in Antiquity*. Notre Dame: University of Notre Dame Press, 1973.

Zolberg, Aristide R. "Origins of the Modern World System: A Missing Link." *World Politics* 33, no. 2 (1981): 253–281.